WHAT READERS A
'SWIMMING W

'I thoroughly enjoyed reading Swimming with Stingrays. Les Clayden has led a very interesting and varied life and his experiences and adventures are both humorous, sad and exciting. He encapsulates the atmosphere of the East and West End of London in that era perfectly. I was disappointed when the story ended as I wanted to know what happened next.'

'It made me laugh and cry, it is such a fascinating autobiography to read it was very hard to put down, it would make a great movie.'

'A very readable book about Les, a character who made his way through post war London reflecting the times and how you can work your way through situations and take opportunities when presented to make your mark on life.

A very entertaining book and a really good read for all.'

SWIMMING WITH STINGRAYS

THE OTHER SIDE OF LIFE

LESLIE J CLAYDEN

First published in 2018 by: Britain's Next Bestseller
An imprint of Live It Ventures LTD
27 Old Gloucester Road
London,
WC1N 3AX
www.bnbsbooks.co.uk
Copyright © 2018 by Leslie J Clayden
The moral right of Leslie J Clayden to be identified as the author of this work has been asserted by him in accordance with the Copyright, Designs and Patents Act 1988.
All rights reserved.
Except as permitted under current legislation, no part of this work may be photocopied, stored in a retrieval system,
published, performed in public, adapted, broadcast, transmitted, recorded or reproduced in any form or by any means, without the prior permission of the copyright owners.
All enquiries should be addressed to Britain's Next Bestseller.
Cover design by Stephen Brian Leonard (Seven Crimson Designs)
ISBN 978-1-910565-26-1 (pb)
Printed in the U.K

FOR OLGA

ACKNOWLEDGMENTS

I would like to thank my son Leslie and daughter Natasha, for the many hours they spent in helping me research and edit this book.

Their dedication and love helped me to finish a project that started over twenty years ago.

Thank you to Stephen Brian Leonard (Seven Crimson Designs) for his inventive cover design.

I would also like to thank my two great friends, Frank and Dick for giving me the motivation to finish this autobiography.

Special thanks to Jeffrey Archer for telling me his story of experiencing eighteen rejections for his first novel, "Not a Penny More, Not a Penny Less, " which then went on to become an international best seller and told me to never give up in getting my autobiography published.

CONTENTS

1. The East End — 1
2. The Lyceum — 25
3. Bow Street — 37
4. Mecca — 53
5. Led Zeppelin — 65
6. The Café de Paris — 77
7. The Hammersmith Palais — 81
8. "The Cat's Whiskers" — 93
9. Miss World — 107
10. Security Express — 129
11. Moscow — 137
12. Crackers — 141
13. Southwark Police — 145
14. Second-hand cars — 151
15. Danka — 155
16. Punk — 163
17. The IRA — 171
18. Ronnie Biggs — 181
19. The Court — 187
20. The Freemasons — 197
21. Judo — 203
22. Arm Wrestling — 209
23. 24 hours — 227
24. Chiba City — 245
25. Channel 7 — 253
26. Eurovision International — 265
27. BBC World Teletext — 277
28. Swimming with Stingrays — 285
29. The British National Theatre Schools — 291
30. Olga — 303

About the Author — 339

ONE

THE EAST END

My life began on June 6th 1951.

Born in the Mile End Hospital, East London, made me a true Cockney. I could never understand how anyone born south of the River Thames could pretend to be Cockney, when you were supposed to be born within the sound of Bow Bells. They must have had Superman's hearing!

I lived in number 4 Cephas Avenue, Stepney in a large Edwardian house owned by Charringtons brewery with my mum, dad, nan, grandfather and mum's two sisters, Pamela and Barbara, along with their brother George.

It was a big house with a small garden, no bathroom and an outside loo. I lived with my parents in the basement of the house, which often got flooded when it rained very heavily. It was also infested with mice and was generally damp and cold in the winter.

The rest of the family lived on the remaining three floors. My uncle George, who left school at fifteen, had a small workshop in the attic where he loved to work on small electrical appliances. He'd built up a local round with a hand cart, knocking on doors to ask if anyone needed any of their electrical appliances repaired, whether it be electric fires or irons, although at that time most people in the East End used flat irons and mangles to rinse their washing.

Dad worked in a fruit and veg shop in East Ham, as did his father and grandfather. Mum worked as a machinist in a local factory which was known as the 'rag trade'. I never understood as a little boy why mum went to work every day to make rags! My two aunts, Pamela and Barbara, also worked as machinists in the rag trade.

Grandad worked in the docks of East London as a tally, which meant he used to check the cargos being unloaded from the ships. He would be given the inventory of the cargo and then check it as it was taken ashore, which was pretty amazing considering pocket calculators didn't exist back then and he'd left school at the age of eleven.

He was extremely good at his he job - so much so, that the other tellers on the docks would give him their work to do for a drink. This job in the docks gave him plenty of opportunity to fiddle the dockets and he would often come home with contraband booze and cigarettes which he either gave away to friends or sold.

He was a small wiry man with a violent temper and would often come home drunk and hit my grandmother for no reason. The rest of the family were terrified of him and apparently, when he'd been younger, he'd had quite a reputation as a prize fighter, winning most of his fights for money, bare knuckle. To me, his only grandson, he showed nothing but love and affection and I was the only baby whose nappy he'd ever changed.

This was the Vanner family of Stepney.

As I grew up, I could never say grandad and it would always come out sounding like Gandy, a name which stayed with him until he died, much to the amusement of the rest of the family. The family used to say that he even looked like a white version of Mahatma Gandhi, the famous Indian pacifist, who'd visited the East End of London and had loved its people. None of the family, of course, would ever dare let my grandad hear their laughter at this for fear of a clip round the ear!

My grandmother stayed at home to look after me and keep the house clean. England, in the early 1950's, still had food rationing from the Second World War and even with everyone in the house working, there was never much money to go around and for me, as the youngest, to even get two boiled eggs a week for breakfast was a luxury. However, my nan was a great cook and managed to make the most appetising food from nothing.

The street we lived in was like most other East End streets of the time; we had a pub on one corner, a church at the end of the street and a corner shop run by Victor and his mum, who were Polish Jews who'd come to England before the war. Victor's mum spoke hardly any English and sat in the corner of the shop, dressed all in black, holding a big wooden spoon which used to scare the shit out of me as small boy.

Victor was a gentle giant who was always friendly to me and the other kids in the street and would give us a sweet when we did the errands for our parents. He was, at the time, the only man in the street who owned a car - a big black Austin - and every Sunday, when the shop was closed, he would take a different kid from the street for a ride as a treat. That was the only time any of us had a chance to ride in a car and for me it was really exciting.

When I started to go to the local primary school, in Redmans Road, Stepney, money was still tight and I remember occasionally having to put cardboard inside my shoes to cover the holes. The thing I hated most was when I needed my hair cut and my mum would put a teacloth around my neck and a pudding basin on top of my head and cut the hair around it, leaving me looking like Friar Tuck from Robin Hood. Even though I was only four or five at the time, I had to be held down because I would scream in protest.

Bath-times consisted of an old tin bath placed in front of the fire in the front room which would be filled with boiling water from a kettle and because this procedure took so long, the bath water was used more than once by different people in the family. With me being the youngest, I was often left until last, so I was faced with grey, soapy water. When I was a bit older, the local council opened a public baths in the Mile End Road and my dad would take me there once a week. It was a real treat to sit in my own bath and have hot and cold water poured in as needed. Afterwards, the best bit of all was my dad buying me hot buttered toast for a snack.

While I growing up as a young child in Stepney, I was often ill and my mother would say I'd catch anything that was going around. I had whooping cough, the mumps, bronchitis and German measles. As a five year old I could never understand at the time what I'd done to the Germans for them to give me the measles - I didn't know any Germans! All I did know was that the Germans had bombed the crap out of the East End during the war.

There were still many 'bomb sites' scattered around the East End of London. These were patches of wasteland that had not yet been built upon and they made excellent adventure playgrounds for us kids during the summer holidays. They often had derelict buildings which had been boarded up to try and stop kids from getting inside because they could be very dangerous.

One such building was an abandoned printing press on wasteland around the corner from where I lived. At five years old I was the youngest member of our street gang who, with little money during the long hot summer holidays, had to devise our own entertainment. I'd been warned by my parents not to go inside the printing press building but at five years old you tend to have a short memory, so with the rest of the gang on one hot July day, we decided to investigate the mysteries of the abandoned building.

We found a way inside and I was disappointed not to find some magical world of mystery and so, after a few of the older boys had broken some of the few remaining windows, I was eager to get out of this dark and gloomy place so full of rubbish. Peter, who was about eight years old, decided before we left it will be fun to set light to some of the rubbish inside and pour some discarded ink jars on top! Needless to say within minutes the place was ablaze and full of smoke. I ran like hell back to my home with flames already engulfing the building behind me.

Within a short time, there were five fire engines surrounding the building putting the fire out. A little while later there was a knock on my door which my nan answered to a very large fire officer in full uniform, who asked her if Leslie lived here. I do not know who was more shocked, me or my nan! He told her that some boys had set fire to the disused printing press building and been told that I was responsible. I'd been grassed up by my mates for something I hadn't done.

My nan, who was a small woman, stood up to this six foot plus giant and told him in no uncertain terms that her grandson was a good boy and would never do anything like that. He was having none of it and suggested to her that I needed a good hiding to prevent me from doing it again in the future. My nan, who I'd never seen get angry before, pushed him away from the door and politely told him to get lost. My nan was always my hero!

I got my revenge on Peter who'd started the fire and had tried to blame it on me a year later. He was very big for his age and used to bully the rest of the kids in the street. He lived in a small block of council flats in our street which were only two storeys high. One day we were both on the first landing and he started arguing with me so I pushed him away and unfortunately he had his back to the stairs behind him. He lost his balance and fell down the stairs cutting his head, and that was the last problem I and any of the other kids had with his bullying.

The highlight of my week then used to be going to Saturday morning pictures. This was the ABC cinema in what was called "The Waste". I still don't know to this day why it was called that. My parents would give me the few pennies needed for the entrance fee and I would go with the rest of the gang from the street. The problem was I was officially too young to go inside, so the older boys would take my money buy their tickets and I would wait outside the emergency exit door at the back of the cinema for them to let me inside.

EACH SATURDAY MORNING I would be in the magical world of *Superman*, *The Lone Ranger*, *Zorro* and many others. The noise from the kids inside, screaming and booing every time a baddie came on screen, I will never forget. To this day I am still a big fan of what we now call the movies.

The ABC was like all cinemas at the time - one big screen with a downstairs and a balcony. A few years later Princess Margaret went there to see the premier of *Sparrows Can't Sing*, a film set in the East End, starring Barbara Windsor. Normally all film premiers in London are held in the West End, so this was something really special and they spent a lot of money doing the place up. For as long as I can remember there would always be a tea stall outside the cinema, which the powers-that-be thought was an eyesore for the princess, so they asked the owner if on the day of the premier, would he move his stall out of sight, behind a tree. He was having none of it and flatly refused. They came up with the idea that a fresh coat of green paint would camouflage the stall in between the trees where it stood. The owner was so pleased with the new look that he said he was quite willing to give Princess Margaret a free cup of tea and a sausage roll, but I don't remember whether she took him up on his offer.

When I was about six or seven, my parents bribed my aunt Pamela to take me to the ABC to see a Disney cartoon, because we wanted to go to the early evening show. I didn't have time for my tea, so I said I wouldn't go unless they made me a chip butty with salt and vinegar to take with me. By the time we got inside the cinema I was starving and asked aunty Pam for my sandwich, which she took from her bag. As she opened the sandwich which was still hot, the cinema filled with the aroma of freshly cooked chips covered in salt and vinegar. There were quite a few people inside who started to turn round to the direction of the smell and started to ask what was causing it! My poor aunt nearly died of embarrassment and told my parents she would never take me to the pictures ever again, especially with a chip butty.

EVERY YEAR from October the kids in the street would start collecting money for Guy Fawkes night. This normally involved dressing a dummy up in old clothes, finding an old pram to sit it in and finding a good pitch to stand and ask passers-by for a penny for the Guy. I used to go with some friends to the corner of Charringtons brewery and wait for the drivers and workers to come by at the end of their shift. Friday pay day was always the best and quite often I would get sixpence or a shilling especially if they'd been drinking. The gang would collect wood from all over the area to build a giant bonfire on the bomb site near where I lived.

This particular year I was about five years old, and they'd started to collect wood in September and the bonfire grew to the biggest I'd ever seen. I kept asking the older members of the gang when were they going to set it alight? They kept telling me November 5th, Guy Fawkes night, the problem was November 5th never seemed to come to a five year old and I became more and more impatient waiting for the day. I didn't understand what was so special about the 5th November anyway and decided to borrow a box of matches from my mum who was a heavy smoker and see what the bonfire looked like, when it was alight. So, when no one was around during the day I crept up to this massive pile of old furniture and timber that was a least twenty foot high and set fire to it! This was at least two weeks before November 5th. The fire took hold quickly and I ran away to the sounds of fire engines racing to the scene.

It didn't take long for the rest of the gang to find out that I was the culprit responsible for destroying all their hard work. I was too frightened to leave my house and my parents also found out that I was the kid responsible for spoiling the street's bonfire night. I not only got a good hiding from my parents but also from the gang as well and couldn't sit down for a good few days!

MY FAMILY, like most East End families, loved a party and a knees-up. Almost every Saturday night somebody in our street or nearby would have a party after the pubs closed. I used to find myself standing outside our local pub, with a bottle of ginger beer and a packet of crisps. This was the time when pubs did not let children inside.

Obviously I used to get very bored and find ways to amuse myself. One particular night when I was getting cold standing outside, I took my arm out of my jacket sleeve and tucked the empty sleeve into the outside pocket. As some of the customers were leaving the pub a little worse for drink, they stopped, looked at my missing arm and took pity on me thinking that I'd broken it and gave me some money. I soon discovered that this was an easy way of topping up my pocket money, so I would deliberately stand there with a sad and miserable face and when asked what I'd done, I would tell them that I had fallen over and broken my arm. On a good night I found I could earn over 10 shillings! Which for me then was a fortune.

I GOT into real trouble once with my mother who, as a heavy smoker, used to leave the ends of finished cigarettes in an ashtray which were known as dog-ends. I found some matches lying around and picked up a dog end from the ashtray and lit it, mimicking what I'd seen my mum do many times. I'd always wondered as a five year old what they'd taste like, thinking that if my mum got through fifty or sixty a day, that they must taste better than chocolate. But, before I'd had a chance to find out my mum caught me red-handed, expecting a good hiding I was surprised when she took out a cigarette lit it and forced me to smoke it until I was sick as a dog. It was the best lesson I could have had and I never touched a cigarette again for the rest of my life. The old saying 'you have to be cruel to be kind' is very true and even though these days you'd probably get locked up for treating your kids in such a way, it was the best medicine that she could have done for me, to stop me ever again from smoking.

ACCORDING TO MY FAMILY, I was a little sod who was always getting into trouble. I remember once walking to my auntie's who lived about fifteen minutes from my house and on the way I saw a man standing on top of a ladder cleaning windows. I thought it would be good fun to stand at the bottom and shake the ladder, the poor bloke was shitting himself and at first started to say "Be a good boy don't do that" and as I shook it more and more, he became more angry and started to swear at me.

Fortunately he didn't fall off and as he started to climb down I ran off to my aunt's with him chasing me. When my aunt opened the door she saw the look of terror on my face and asked what was wrong? I told her some strange man was chasing me, so when he suddenly appeared a moment later, she'd already armed herself with a broom ready to hit him! When he told her that I was trying to shake him off his ladder, she said "My little Leslie would never do such a thing" and threatened to call the police if he didn't clear off.

The local primary school was like most in the East End at that time, filled with mostly poor kids with holes in their shoes and tatty clothes. The only milk that most of them got to drink was the small free bottle given out by the school in the morning.

Unlike most other kids I didn't mind school and really enjoyed reading about the Romans and the Greeks and liked history in general. I was a bit of a loner at school and didn't have many friends, so I was not in any of the many gangs that existed then. If I got picked on I was left to defend myself or I'd try to make them laugh with a joke or impression of one of the teachers if there were too many of them. Fighting inside and outside of school was quite common and I learned to become a survivor.

Things at home were getting a bit better. Pamela was the next to marry a furniture maker, nice bloke named Kenny, of course, Gandy never liked any of them, including my dad!

My grandad "Gandy" with my mum on her wedding day

LIKE MANY STREETS in the East End, we had a local milkman who would deliver milk to the door step. Our milkman was a kind, elderly man. One day, I asked my parents if I could help him deliver the milk at weekends when I wasn't at school to earn some pocket money.

My parents said they would ask him and he agreed to give

me a try. So, the next morning at 4am, I got up, dressed and joined him on his electric float delivering milk around our local streets. It was tiring, getting up so early but still an adventure for me.

All went well until the next day when, during the middle of his round, he stopped in a quite street, got out and went to the back of his float.Being the noisy little sod that I was, I wondered what he was doing, so I got out to take a look. I then saw him taking a piss in one of his empty milk bottles!

I don't know, who was more shocked, him or me.

He then told me to swear not to tell anyone. Being eight years old, a secret like that is hard to keep and I soon told my nan, who told my mum and dad. The news spread like wildfire down the rest of the street and soon, most of the neighbours cancelled their milk delivery from him.

He came and told my parents, in no uncertain terms, that I was sacked.

This ended my short career as a milkman.

I never even got paid!

BY THE TIME I was eleven years old, I'd read every book in the school library on the Romans and Greeks and was determined to join the army when I was older. My dad had now left the shop where he'd worked in East Ham and now worked on a veg stall owned by his brother Ernie that was in a prime position outside Whitechapel tube station. The only trouble was my dad's brother was a gambler and he'd lost it to someone he owed money to. That really pissed my dad off and they didn't speak for quite a while.

Dad then managed to get two stalls in Whitechapel market, rented from the council but not in such a good position as the first one had been. Mum had been promoted in the sweat shop where she worked to a forelady, which meant she had to make the first dress or suit which was then copied by all the other machinists, so obviously they had to be perfect. She worked for a Jew called Grunberg who owned a Rolls-Royce and later bought a hotel in Israel, not bad work if you could get it I used to go to the factory sometimes during the school holidays and he would always give me some pocket money because he liked the good work that my mum did.

I used to help my dad serving on the stall after school and on Saturdays for pocket money. I got used to lifting heavy weights which helped me to become quite strong for my age. Around this time Charringtons brewery, who owned our house and the ones next to it, decided they wanted to demolish those five or six houses and poor old Victor's shop to build a new car park for their lorries.

The brewery offered my grandparents another house around the corner in Edwin Street. This one had a proper bathroom and a nice garden, but there were only two bedrooms, not enough room for me and my mum and dad. So they offered my mum and dad one of their flats in Lewisham, South London, where all the pretend bloody Cockneys lived! It was a small flat, two bedrooms, above a shop in Station Approach, which was a road leading to Lewisham station. It was also next door to a pub called the Mid-Kent Tavern and my parents liking a drink as they did, took the flat immediately.

My problem was that although I'd just failed my 11-plus, one of my favourite teachers told me he could still get me into the local grammar school even with my bad spelling, (It wasn't until many years later that I was to discover that I was dyslexic.)

Also the few friends I had still lived in the East End so if I was to move to Lewisham with my parents, it would mean I'd come home to an empty flat because they still worked in the East End and wouldn't get home before 7pm. I decided to live with my grandparents Monday to Friday, and go to school there and see my parents at weekends.

I went to look at the local grammar school which was housed in a dark old Victorian building that looked like something straight out of a Charles Dickens novel. I didn't like the look of it at all. At the same time I'd heard of a brand new school that had just been built in Stepney Green which was London's first comprehensive school. It was eight storeys high with two lifts and a technical block plus a separate gym. This I liked the look of.

So I joined this school and Harold Wilson (who was later to become Prime Minister) officially opened it, because this was around the time of a very successful film called *To Sir With Love* starring Sidney Poitier and Lulu, and told the story of a black American teacher who comes to a tough East End school to teach and also because it was London's first comprehensive it attracted some very good teachers from across the country who wanted to work in this new experimental school with all the latest facilities, including a black American teacher who was to eventually teach me the British Constitution. I thought that was funny, an American teaching about British politics.

Everything was going fine, I was enjoying school, there were the usual nutcases who would bully the other kids for their dinner money, but I either stayed clear of them or when I had to fight them behind the bike sheds I'd win some and lose some but they soon got to know that I wasn't worth the trouble and there were much easier pickings to be had.

My dad, mum and me aged seven in Cephas Avenue

My whole life was to change one Sunday morning in 1963. My dad was bringing me home from Lewisham to my nan's on the tube when I started to complain about pains in my legs. By the time we reached Stepney Green station, I could hardly walk and didn't feel too good. With a struggle we got to my nan's house and my dad told her I wasn't feeling too well and was given an aspirin and sent to bed.

The next morning, when I woke up, I couldn't move my legs at all and the bed sheets where wet from me sweating all night. My nan called a doctor who examined me and immediately called for an ambulance to take me to the Mile End Hospital. I had never been inside an ambulance before and although I was as ill as I was feeling, I quite enjoyed the ride.

What started out as a bit of an adventure was to become a bloody nightmare. The first few days I remember being forced to drink pints of iced cold water around the clock because apparently I had a temperature of 104 which was dangerously high and this treatment was the hospital's way of trying to reduce it. I normally liked drinking water but not gallons of the stuff particularly when I couldn't get out of bed for a piss!

I had lots of different doctors looking at me but nobody could diagnose what was wrong. So someone came up with the bright idea of giving me a lumbar puncture. This involved pushing a very long needle into my back and drawing fluid from my spine. It was one of the most painful things I have ever experienced in my life. Eventually a specialist diagnosed me with rheumatic fever. After the first week I was moved into a side ward with three other children all of whom had been diagnosed with the same illness. The room was to become known as the rheumatic room.

I had to have injections of penicillin every day and was seen by lots of different doctors and specialists. I still couldn't move my legs and was convinced I'd be paralysed for the rest of my life. Christmas was getting close and I desperately wanted to be home for that special time. No chance! I was far too ill so all I had to look forward to was being stuck in a room with three strange kids and no television.

The nurses in the hospital were very kind and as we got

nearer to Christmas more and more people would arrive with toys and sweets from different charities, but I still had the prospect of never walking again and no television.

Then just before Christmas Eve, a miracle happened, a giant television was delivered to our room. When I asked where it had come from, all the nurses would say that it was from an anonymous donor.

Whoever they were, we were all eternally grateful to them. It was a big bastard too, fantastic.

I was only to discover many years later that my parents had bought it for the hospital on what was called the *never-never*, otherwise known as hire purchase. That meant them paying for it over a number of years because they couldn't afford to pay cash, and in those days they were a fortune and this one was even bigger than the one we had at home. When I asked them many years later why they'd never told me they'd bought it, they said so I wouldn't hog it all to myself and the three other kids had a say on what they wanted to watch. What heroes!

THAT WINTER WAS one of the coldest in London for decades, with deep snow which made it even harder for my family because my father couldn't work the stalls.

I'd been in hospital for some six weeks and although I was feeling better I was still confined to a wheelchair as I couldn't walk. One day as a treat the hospital arranged for some of us sick kids to go and see a film in the library next door. I think they were showing *Lassie Come Home*. I'll never forget as we were being pushed in our wheelchairs to the front row, some kids at the back started shouting "Look at those cripples! Where did they come from?" One girl in a wheelchair, aged about seven or eight, on hearing this started crying and I thought *great is this what I would have to put up with for the rest of my life?* Needless to say I didn't really enjoy the film but wished I could have got out of the chair and wallop the ones responsible.

After about two months in hospital I managed to walk short distances and my parents were told that with rheumatic fever there was a 50-50 chance as to whether it had damaged the heart or not and if it had, there wouldn't be much chance of living past thirty! At this stage they weren't sure if it had damaged my heart valves.

When you're twelve years old, thirty seems such a long way off, but I was to be one of the lucky ones and was later told it hadn't affected my heart but I'd still need to take penicillin tablets for the next five years and that I wouldn't be able to do any sports like football, rugby or boxing - which didn't worry me, particularly with some of the arseholes we had at my school.

As I gradually got better, I was moved into a general children's ward, which made me feel better and I started to believe I wouldn't grow up a cripple.

One day as I was lying in my hospital bed, I heard a strange noise, it sounded like a *thump-thump* across the wooden floor.

I couldn't make the noise out at first, then I noticed a young girl about four or five years old running around the ward. She was laughing and screaming at the same time. I still couldn't work out what the strange noise was, then I looked down at her feet and she had none! Instead there were just two stumps where her feet should have been. I'd never seen anything like it before. It didn't seem to worry her as she tore around the ward at 100mph being chased by a nurse.

I later discovered that she'd been abandoned in the snow and had caught frostbite in her feet, meaning they had to be amputated.

I felt so sorry for her and made great friends with her. It was a sight I'd never forget as long as I lived and when I was older, I sure would have liked to get my hands on the bastard who'd left her out in the snow in one of the coldest winters that London had seen in over twenty years.

AFTER SOME THREE months I was discharged and went back to Stepney Green Comprehensive. It felt strange going back to school after such a long break and I'd fallen behind in maths and science classes which were two of the subjects I least liked. I never did catch up and never took my 'O' Levels in those two subjects.

At this time, my parents were friendly with one of the managers of the Lewisham Odeon which in those days not only showed films on one giant screen but also held pop concerts. The Beatles were now a massive hit worldwide and were going to hold a concert there, needless to say all the tickets sold out quickly and I couldn't get one. My parents spoke to the manager who they regularly went to drink with in the Mid Kent Tavern and he got a ticket for me.

I had a brilliant seat near the front of the stage and was really looking forward to seeing my favourite group at that time. The cinema held about 2000 people and the atmosphere was electric, and what the organisers did was to keep teasing the crowd by announcing The Beatles and opening the curtains to an empty stage, so when they did appear the whole place erupted with the noise of girls in the audience screaming, which was absolutely deafening. From the moment they came on stage to when they left I never heard a song. I've never been to a concert since where during the whole performance it was just one long scream with girls fainting.

When I got home and my parents asked me if I'd enjoyed the concert, I told them that I hadn't heard a single bloody song because of all the loud screaming.

SCHOOL WAS GOING PRETTY WELL but I never had any real friends except one Jewish boy whose name was Stephen. He lived in some flats near the school with his mum. I never saw his dad. Stephen was very clever and we made good friends although at that time, being Jewish, his family never mixed with non-Jews and I was never invited into his home. Stephen like me was a loner and also, being overweight with all his mum's good Jewish food, would get picked on and bullied a lot.

Although I'd been told not to do any sports because of my rheumatic fever, I'd heard of a new mystical sport called Judo and wanted to try it! At that time in the East End boxing was favoured by most kids for defence. I'd tried it but had never much liked it. So I thought this could be the way to deter bullies. So I dragged Stephen with me to our first Judo class which was held in an old Victorian school in Bancroft Road, which was the grammar school I hadn't gone to.

We were the only two there plus a black belt instructor who I fear was past his sell by date. Stephen hated it but I enjoyed learning the moves especially *ippon-seoi-nage*, which is a shoulder throw. We were about fourteen years old and swore we wouldn't tell anyone at school for fear they might take the piss out of us.

I attended the classes regularly but eventually found a better club in Lewisham that my dad took me to at weekends.

I enjoyed school, except for the bullying, partly because of my size, the school made me a prefect.

One day in the school playground one of the more aggressive, mad bullies jumped onto my back, I immediately swung into my Judo training and threw him over my shoulder onto the floor in front of his mates. I don't know who was more shocked, him or me; after that incident the bullies all steered well clear of me because they'd never seen anything like it before and didn't understand how I'd managed to throw their friend with such force onto the ground. Judo at that time in England was very much an undiscovered form of self-defence.

I was nearly seventeen old years and had managed to get GCSE's in History, The British Constitution (God Bless Mr Pandy from America!) and in English (considering my terrible spelling). I was the only one to pass English in a class of 42 pupils. I don't know who was more surprised, me or the head master, Mister Taylor, who came down personally to my class, called me outside to give me the good news and then had the cheek to ask me if I had a relation on the examining board! I think he was joking...

I still helped my dad on the stalls in my free time and I'll never forget one day when helping him a big flash car pulled up and a big guy in a smart suit walked over. I went to serve him and my dad pushed me away which I thought was odd. The guy asked my dad how much the bunch of bananas hanging up was. My dad took them down and offered them to him saying no charge.

The man replied no let me pay for them which was ten shillings and six pence saying we all have to earn a living.

My dad had fought in the Second World War, in the jungles of Burma with the 14th Army and the Gurkhas against the Japanese. He was a tough sod and yet this was the first and only time I'd really seen him scared. I found out later that evening that the man in the car was Ronnie Kray of the notorious Kray twins who were big time gangsters and ran the East End and most of the West End with protection rackets and other scams. My parents and family would often drink in one of their clubs, *The 3Rs* on the Mile End Road. The East End being a violent place there were fights in many of the pubs at weekends, but no one dared start any trouble in any of the Krays' clubs.

My Dad's mum lived in East Ham and I later found out that the Krays had freed Mad Frankie Mitchell from prison and for a few days had hidden him in a house belonging to another stall holder from Whitechapel Market called Lenny the Book, who sold secondhand books and for his regulars he would supply dirty magazines, from under the counter. His pitch was near my dad's.

Frank (The Mad Axeman) Mitchell was a giant of a man who even the Krays were wary of as he was quite mad by all accounts so they murdered him and he's supposedly holding up the Bow Flyover encased in concrete. Poor old Lenny ended up in prison for harbouring an escaped convict, he never really recovered. At that time no one refused the Krays. Eventually, after Ronnie Kray had murdered George Cornell in the Blind Beggar pub for calling him a fat poof, their reign of terror came to an end with both of them both dying in prison. My family and many others in the East End always maintained that they only hurt other criminals who threatened their business.

The reason for Ronnie Kray's visit to my Dad's stall was to let him know that if he heard anything, to say nothing... not that he was likely to. The house they'd kept Mad Frankie in was only a few doors away from where my Dad's Mum lived.

My dad in uniform of the 14th Army taken in Sumatra December 1945

TWO

THE LYCEUM

I WAS NOW NEARLY seventeen years old and all my life I'd wanted to join the army on a three-year short service commission.

I had all the necessary qualifications to join except bloody maths and science. So I stayed on at school to study for my 'A' levels much to the annoyance of my dad who wanted me to go and work with him on the stall, but my mum was having none of it and swore that I would never end up working in the market.

I started the first year of my 'A' levels but was getting itchy feet and wanted to go out to work and earn some money. So I looked at my next option which was to join the Police force. That idea really pissed my dad off who like most of the people in the East End hated the cops.

The problem with that idea was my short sightedness (I'd had to wear glasses since the age of eleven). At that time the police didn't accept anyone who wore glasses, so once again I was fucked.

After a few months of studying for two 'A' Levels, I'd decided I'd had enough of school and needed a job. My mum would not under any circumstances let me go work for my dad in the market, so I found a job as a trainee manager with Caters Supermarkets. They were the Tesco's of the time and had a chain of stores. I joined their store in Bromley, Kent, and then moved to their store in Catford because at this time I was living with my parents in Lewisham and all the other pretend cockneys south of the bloody river.

My job in Caters consisted of working for a few months in different departments, such as cheese, bread and bacon. By now I was big for my age and strong. I still went to Judo a couple of a times a week, so when I was working in the bacon department lifting three or four sides of pigs on my shoulder it proved to be no problem for me. I never worked in the butchery department, which was considered a skilled job. There was always rivalry between the two departments.

There was one big bastard who worked in the butchery who was always taking the piss, but I knew I couldn't have a fight with him without losing my job.

So one day, I challenged him to an arm-wrestle. All the years of helping my dad on the stall and the Judo had made me strong, particularly in the arms and although I was big for my age, this guy made me look small! But I was confident of giving him a run for his money, as I'd never been beaten at school.

So we squared up to each other and decided on the best of three arm wrestles. All of his mates came to cheer him on and they were expecting an easy win for him. Arm wrestling is not just about strength it's also about psyching out your opponent. Once we got to grips and he realised I was no pushover he'd already lost I took all three pins and earned a lot of respect from everyone considering no one had ever beaten him before. Years later arm-wrestling was to play a major part of my life.

Barry, who I worked with in Caters, told me of a good friend of his called Dick, who owned his own business which turned out to be a small rented shop in Forest Hill where he sold secondhand furniture and other bits and pieces. He was also a black belt in Judo and had been captain of England's junior Judo team as a schoolboy. This was someone I was dying to meet. So it was arranged for the three of us to go to the *Lyceum* in the Strand for a night out.

The *Lyceum* holds 2100 seats and is a West End theatre in the city of Westminster on Wellington Street, just off the Strand. It dates back to 1765. What's unique about it is that it has a balcony overhanging the dress circle. From 1871 to 1902 Henry Irving appeared at the theatre especially in Shakespeare (which I never liked at school). Henry Irving's ghost is reported to still haunt the place with many sightings over the years by members of staff, although I'm pleased to say I wasn't one of them, but later did witness some strange goings on. The building closed in 1939 and was set to be demolished but it was saved and converted into a Mecca ballroom in 1951, the year I'd been born. It was now famous for hosting the Miss World contest, and live TV performances of *Come Dancing* which is now known as *Strictly Come Dancing* by the BBC.

Like most teenagers at the time we ended up as wallflowers just watching girls dance together on the dance floor around their handbags.

It was for us quite expensive to go to the *Lyceum*, as the drinks were West End prices. So after a few excursions Dick who was always tight with his money (he used to switch the engine off on his Dormobile at the top of any hill he found himself on and let it roll down to the bottom to save petrol), Dick came up with the idea of asking the *Lyceum* if there were any jobs as doormen. So we made a few enquiries and the manager Pete Smith agreed to see us. I knew they wouldn't give me and Barry a job as bouncers because we wore glasses, so we took them off for the interview. It wasn't really an interview, we stood on the front door and the manager looked us up and down.

Barry was tall for his age, Dick was a medium build and I was considered at that time a giant although I was only seventeen years old and legally wasn't supposed to be allowed in until I was eighteen, but I looked older and what really helped was Dick having a card that confirmed he was a black belt in Judo which was really something at that time. Much to our surprise the three of us were given the job of looking after the *Lyceum* and asked if could we start the following Friday. The pay was okay, nothing special, but we were convinced that working as doormen we could pull all the birds we wanted.

They told us our title was door supervisors and the head supervisor was a guy called Dave Troop who I didn't care for as he was a bit smarmy and weedy. They told us to wear white shirts, black trousers and they would supply the jacket and bow ties to wear.

So the following Friday we turned up for our first night's work before they opened, Dave took us backstage to fit us with our jackets which turned out to be old Band jackets, a dark red with a little sparkle. They couldn't even find one to fit me as I was so broad. "We've got no chance of pulling wearing these we look like bloody clowns!" I remarked to Dick.

Now the *Lyceum* was a big venue, with eighteen fire exits and it could hold nearly 3000 people. Ray McVay was the resident band, who had a supporting group. We were told if the lights flash on and off that that was the signal that there was trouble on the dance floor and to get down quickly and sort it out. The place started to get busy and the three of us stuck close together and walked around. The problem was once the band started playing they lowered the lights and I couldn't see a bloody thing without my glasses on so me and Barry followed behind Dick like two blind mice.

After half an hour of walking around and trying to look hard in the soppy jackets we were wearing I said to Dick "Where are the rest of the doormen?" They then told us it was just us three! So that's why we got the job so easily because they had no security, as all the previous doormen had been sacked the week before for fiddling on the door. I thought this is great as none of us had worked in a club or pub before and had no training. Talk about being thrown in at the deep end.

I thought that's great if there's a big punch up, but then I thought Dick could sort them out no trouble with a black belt and Barry could look after himself and I knew I was strong as an ox.

So all was going well, until halfway through the night the dreaded lights went on and off and a fight started on the dance floor, right in front of the stage. We were on the balcony and had to run down the stairs in half light, so I grabbed Dick's coat tail and Barry brought up the rear. I swear if anyone was watching us we must have looked like the Marx Brothers.

When we got down to the dance floor, there were two guys punching the lights out of each other, I grabbed one and he started swinging at me so I ducked and swung him around, then I saw another guy coming from my side so I threw a punch and caught him good on the jaw, only problem was it was poor Barry, without my glasses and in the confusion I'd punched him by mistake. We threw the two of them out of the side exit and that was our first fight as door supervisors. Barry complained bitterly to me after asking why I'd hit him. So I told him when I get stuck in, to steer clear. I asked Dick why he hadn't used any Judo on them and his answer was he didn't need to because I'd sorted it out.

At the end of the night, Ray McVay, the resident band leader who was watching from his perch on the stage, told Pete Smith how well we'd done and from that moment on our jobs were safe. So, over the next few weeks, the *Lyceum* built up a team of doormen. Some were better than others in a fight but I always thought there was strength in numbers and we got our own black jackets to wear, sod those maroon ones. I was a natural on the door and quickly learned to spot potential troublemakers and soon earned a reputation of knowing how to handle myself. I was often throwing out troublemakers who were twice my age which I thought was funny as legally I wasn't supposed to be in there but this was in an age before computers and photo id.

After a few months working in the *Lyceum*, Dick and I had saved enough money to go on holiday together. By then Dick owned a Mini Countryman estate and suggested we go on a touring holiday along the South Coast and into Wales. He told me he had a nice tent that slept two so we could save money on bed and breakfast.

So off we went and on the first day we stopped at a nice camping site with some nice big tents in it. I'd never seen Dick's tent before and was excited to see it once we'd erected it and there lay the problem, as he didn't know how to put it up and after a lengthy struggle with everyone watching us making total prats of ourselves we finally got the thing up. I wished we hadn't – I could have died of embarrassment. It turned out to be an old army camouflage tent, which didn't look great amongst all the other posh tents on the site.

The weather wasn't great and that night it started to rain and the bloody thing leaked like a sieve. I could have killed him. The next day I couldn't get off the site quick enough.

AFTER A FEW DAYS IN BRIGHTON, we found a local pop festival who were hiring security men. So off we went thinking great idea for some petrol money and pull a few hippie birds who believed in free love.

The festival took place on Plumpton race course and turned out to be the forerunner of the very successful Reading pop festival. It ran for three to four days and the money was okay. I wasn't much interested in the bands playing but thought this is going to be a bit of fun. All was going well with no real trouble then we heard that a gang of Hell's Angels were on their way there and we were not to let them in as they didn't have tickets.

The intelligence had come from the police, who warned

the organisers that if they got in, there could be serious trouble. The organisers hired extra security, they got about fifty men from the local rugby club who looked the part and also a couple of vans with Alsatian dogs, so with the rest of us, there must have been over 150 security men. So I'm thinking if they want to start any trouble we were more than a match for them.

The local police weren't interested in getting involved at the event because it was being held on private land, so it was up to us to stop them.

We then heard it was the Windsor chapter of the Hell's Angels that were coming, who at that time were considered the most dangerous bikers in the UK, and who were associated with guns, drugs and protection. They were even suspected of committing murder. Dick wanted to leave before they came and I didn't blame him, but I was enjoying myself too much and told him to wait a bit and see if they showed up or not. We didn't have to wait long as we heard them long before we saw them.

There was a narrow road leading into the site and in the distance we could see a huge cloud of blue smoke from their bikes. It reminded me of Custer's last stand and a band of approaching Red Indians like in the pictures I'd watched in the ABC. There was even, behind me, an old geezer on a white horse who maybe thought he was General Custer. The organiser of the festival, a nice guy named Harold Pembleton, who I was told also owned the famous Marquee Club in Wardour Street, had told us earlier in the day not to let them in as they'd not bought tickets and were trouble.

The noise of fifty or sixty Harley Davidsons was unbelievable but I'm thinking there must be about 160 of us and only fifty or sixty of them so we should be able to stop them.

We lined across the road blocking it and waited. They suddenly appeared from around a bend moving slowly towards us in a close pack. I found myself in front of our line who were edging back as the bikers moved slowly towards us. I found myself face to face with a guy who was obviously their leader as he held up his arm for his gang to stop behind him. They sat on their bikes letting them tick over and I had to admit they looked a fearsome bunch.

I said to him in a loud voice that they couldn't come in. He smiled at me and asked "Who's going to stop us?" I looked him straight in the eye; he was by now three yards in front of me and I replied "We will". He grinned again at me which was beginning to annoy me and asked me again "Who's going to stop us?" so I said "Us". He then said to me "You'd better look behind you first". I smiled this time and said "I'm not going to fall for that old trick". He said "No, go on take a look", and something told me he wasn't kidding and the hairs on the back of my neck stood up as I slowly turned around to see all the rest of the security at least thirty yards behind me standing behind a fence including my mate Dick!

So here I was facing down a bunch of Hell's Angels stuck in the middle of the road on my own. Shit! I'd never been much good at running because of my size and I didn't fancy my chances of beating a Harley Davidson back to the safety of the fence first. My heart sank and I wished for a big hole to swallow me up. Five minutes earlier I was in front of a 150 strong team and now I was stuck out on my own like the Lone Ranger, I really thought I was going to die here and still a bloody virgin!

I thought there's only one thing I can do and that's to front them out for what it's worth. So I said to their leader "I don't care about the wankers behind me", trying to sound as confident as possible under the circumstances and said "You're not coming in here". He says who's going to stop us? I said "Me if I have to", by now I was really angry and embarrassed by all the other wankers who'd left me stranded on my own. He stared at me for what seemed ages, smiled again and shook his head. He then slowly turned on the seat of his bike to look back at the rest of his gang and shouted in a loud voice "He's the only one with any bollocks, no one touches him!" With that they revved up their bikes and the noise again was deafening.

My feet froze to the ground and I couldn't move my legs. I thought again I'm going to die here, seventeen years old and still a virgin.

The group of bikes then split into two and roared either side of me and I disappeared in a cloud of blue smoke. I closed my eyes and hoped when I opened them I would still be standing and not waiting outside the pearly gates.

I've got to give respect to their leader for saving my life that day, for the rest of the festival there was an uneasy truce but the bikers never caused any trouble. I was furious and went back to Dick and the others and shouted why had they left me on my own? Dick said he'd shouted to me to come back with them but with all the noise of the bikers I hadn't heard him.

Harold Pendleton, the organiser, had been watching everything from the side and came over to me and shook my hand and said that was the bravest thing he'd ever seen. I replied "Yeah, and the stupidest". He said the following year he was moving the festival to Reading and I could have any job I wanted. I said thanks I'll think about it as long as there's no Hell's Angels. He was a true gent and we became good friends, I never had to pay to go into his club because he knew he could rely on me if there was any trouble.

The next year he moved the festival to Reading where to this day it is still held every August Bank Holiday. That day I learnt a very valuable lesson when facing overwhelming odds.

"NEVER BACK DOWN".

THREE

BOW STREET

As I worked the door of the *Lyceum* I got to know a lot of the policemen who were stationed at Bow Street, and we used to let them into the place free for obvious reasons.

As I got friendlier with some of them, I told them that it had always been my ambition to join the Force but as I wore glasses I couldn't join. They told me about the special constabulary, telling me that they accepted people who wore glasses, and that they had the full powers of a police officer.

Now this sounded a great idea, so I made a few enquiries, went for an interview and was accepted subject to me passing my training at Catford Police Station just down the road from where I lived in Lewisham. The training consisted of learning basic law, arrest, learning the phonetic code etc, and some basic moves in unarmed combat.

One day, they sent down to the station an instructor in unarmed combat to teach the class a few moves, by this time I was an orange belt in Judo and was regularly holding my own against black belts, when he pointed to me to come out and join him. I didn't tell him about my Judo training so when he grabbed me I immediately swung him over my hip onto the floor.

Needless to say he wasn't best pleased with this and asked me where I'd learnt that move from. I told him I had some Judo training and he queried why hadn't I told him. I replied because he hadn't asked.

My group consisted of a very mixed bunch; some were quite old while others just didn't look like policemen to me and reminded me of Dad's Army! Anyway I finished the training and was given a date to go up to Scotland Yard to be sworn in by an assistant commissioner and collect my warrant card. I was told I wouldn't get my uniform until a week later but that I'd been accepted at Bow Street Police Station which was just up the road from the *Lyceum* opposite the Royal Opera House and next to Bow Street Magistrates Court.

This was one of the proudest moments of my life and I felt ten feet tall.

Bow Street was famous for the Bow Street runners, which was an early voluntary Police Force established by Henry Fielding, a magistrate, to fight the increasing lawlessness in the area. From 1832 the Metropolitan Police Force was created by Sir Robert Peel (becoming known as Peelers) which operated a station house there.

On my way back from Scotland Yard after being sworn in, I noticed some street gamblers in Irving Street, just off Leicester Square. These guys I despised because they used to cheat tourists out of their money. They operated what is known as the three card trick where they'd shuffle the Queen in between two other cards. They always had a member of the gang standing amongst the crowd, who'd bet and find the Queen to encourage the others in the crowd to gamble, who they then cheated. They were difficult to arrest because they always had lookouts at each end of the road to warn of any approaching policemen. They also knew the plain clothes police as well.

As I walked down to Trafalgar Square it was my mate on duty, PC Peter Crow, the one who'd told me about the specials. I told him about the gamers in Irving Street and that I'd just been sworn in at Scotland Yard. He was pissed off because he didn't like them either but said he couldn't get near them in uniform. So I came up with the suggestion of what about if *I* arrested them? He said as long as I got the cards they were using and the cardboard box they used as a table I could bring the guy to him and he'd handle the arrest.

So, I casually walked up to the crowd watching the gamer working his tricks then I stepped out of the crowd, grabbed his wrist, the cards and money and placed him in an arm lock (a variation of ude-gatame), so he couldn't run away and cautioned him, which is basically telling him his rights in court. I then marched him down to Peter Crow in Trafalgar Square who called up a Black Maria (a police van) to take him and me to Bow Street Police Station. By this time I'm feeling pretty pleased with myself as I'd made my first arrest, a good one too, and I was only eighteen years old.

When we got to the station Peter started filling out the arrest form and I'm thinking this is a great start to my career as a special when all hell broke loose, a chief inspector appeared not looking at all happy and shouted at me and Peter, asking how had a special constable who'd only just received his warrant card that day and didn't even have his uniform yet managed to nick an experienced gamer? But the arrest was good and the gamer got a hefty fine the next day in Bow Street Magistrate Court.

I was told in no uncertain terms not to arrest anyone else until I'd received my uniform and finished my beat training which involved going out with a regular Police Officer learning the lie of the land around Bow Street, which consisted of the Strand, Leicester Square, some of the Embankment, Covent Garden Fruit and Veg Market and all the roads in between.

With the Special Constabulary, you only had to work a minimum of four hours a month but if you saw someone breaking the law, you could place yourself on duty and have the full powers of arrest as a regular policeman. Which really pissed off a great number of regulars especially as a great number of specials looked like misfits in uniform. I was lucky as there was only one special sergeant who came on duty once in a blue moon and one other special constable who was long past his sell-by date. Like many others, he only covered ceremonial duties like the Lord Mayor's Show, Trooping the Colour and the Cenotaph Parade, all of which I enjoyed but I wanted more. So I found some weeks I did thirty to forty hours in a week and could come and go as I pleased, sometimes doing a double shift when I had a day off from the *Lyceum*. Many of the PC's there knew me from the door but there were still some that wouldn't talk to me and shunned me in the canteen.

That was all to change one evening in Leicester Square.

I was out on patrol one evening when a call came over the radio that assistance was needed at the *Talk of the Town*, a well-known cabaret spot on the corner of Leicester Square and Charing Cross Road.

I was nearby so I answered that I'd go. When I got there my mate Peter Crow and another PC were talking to this big guy who was standing on the steps arguing with them. They'd been called there because he'd tried to leave without paying his bill. He was being cocky saying you can't touch me because I'm standing on private property, and was acting like a big villain. Peter seemed unsure what to do and in the meantime this guy is taking the piss out of us big time. So I thought I know what to do and I grabbed him and pulled him off the steps onto the pavement and said now you're not on private property and under arrest! With this he kicked out and caught Peter hard in the bollocks. I grabbed him, spun him around and put him in a stranglehold while Pete's mate called for a van to take him to Bow Street. Poor Pete was in agony and all the while this guy was swearing at us and doing his best to get out of my stranglehold, but as strong as he was he never stood a chance even black belts in Judo who I practised with couldn't break my grip.

We bundled him into the police van and took him to the station and while he was being charged, he begins fighting again like a lunatic. I'm standing there, watching four PCs trying their best to hold him down and getting nowhere so I turn round to the duty inspector and asked 'do you want me to hold him?' The Inspector looked at me and smiles and says if you want to, thinking I'm going to get a smack from this guy. So once again I span him around and put an arm lock on him (another variation of ude-gatame) and as much as the bastard struggled he couldn't move and with the others we march him down to the cells for the night to appear next morning in the magistrates court and I'm thinking what a tosser all this because he thought he was so hard and could walk away without paying his bill. The funny thing was that when they searched him they found hundreds of pounds on him. After that incident, word quickly spread through the shifts what had happened and the few PC's who wouldn't talk to me soon realised I was a valuable asset to have around when there was any trouble.

Poor Peter was sore for a few days after but soon recovered and was telling everyone how I'd saved his life which was a bit embarrassing. The guy who'd attacked him had a record for violence and next day got a two year suspended sentence. I thought that this was lenient because in those days attacking a police officer was a serious offence.

Things changed a lot for me after that incident. Whenever I went on patrol, the Black Maria, and even the area car (which was a souped up Rover V8 and considered a real treat to ride in) would come looking for me to join them, knowing that I was someone on board who would be useful in a punch up.

One evening, I was on patrol down the Strand on a midweek night and it was unusually quiet. I hadn't bumped into any other PCs. I hadn't noticed any cars on patrol and there was none of the usual chatter on the radio. In fact it was like a ghost town. Then my radio came to life and the station asked for my position. I thought great some action at last. I replied where I was and the operator said I should come back to the station, I explained that I'd only just left the station. He then said if I didn't want to be the only policeman on patrol then I should come back to the station now.

Now, this was something really strange. It had never happened to me before, for there to be no police patrolling that side of the West End, so I'm thinking it must be something very serious. I walked back to Bow Street as fast as I could. When I arrived at the station I asked the duty sergeant what was up and he said I should go down to the basement and see for myself. I'm thinking had someone I knew died or had some prisoners escaped? So I walked down the stairs to find it full of the whole shift. A duty inspector, two sergeants and ten PCs. Eight Rows of chairs had been laid out and a screen put up and at the other end a cine projector had been set up, which was showing blue films that had been confiscated by the vice squad in an earlier raid in Soho.

We sat there all evening with the others, shouting lewd remarks drinking tea for the rest of the shift with not a single PC patrolling some of London's most famous streets that evening. The films were 8mm as this was decades before video and it was a serious offence to be caught with pornography in those days, and here I was eighteen years old sitting in the basement watching my first blue films with a room full of policemen!

A few weeks later, I was on patrol with the only other special stationed at Bow Street, who was a nice enough guy but quite old.

A call came over the radio that someone was causing a disturbance at a local hostel, not too far from where we were patrolling. I said we should take the call but he said the place was known for trouble and we should steer clear. I said he could do what he wanted but I was going. It was specials like him that only wanted to look nice on parades and never get into any rucks, which gave us a bad name. I went off on my own and got to the place just in time to see a guy running off. The manager of the hostel told me he'd been the cause of the trouble because they were full up and didn't have a bed for him.

I started to follow this guy who was about a street in front of me. I shouted at him to stop because I wanted to question him, but he looked back at me and started to run. I ran after him and I could just about keep him in sight when he turned a corner and disappeared. By the time I got to the corner he'd disappeared so I stood for a moment getting my breath back and thinking where could he have gone?

Then across the street I noticed a pub, so I walked over and went inside – and sure enough he had his back to me and was standing at the bar. So I walked over and tapped him on the shoulder. With that, he swung around knocking my glasses and cap off. I grabbed him as I fell back onto a table full of glasses knocking everything over, women in the pub began screaming and the guy was on top of me. I immediately went into my Judo training and swung my right leg over knocking him onto his back with me now on top of him. I placed my right hand on his throat and with my left called to the station on my radio. Now at this time the Police had a code that if you asked for urgent assistance everyone no matter what they were doing even police from outside the area would come to help. Now this guy couldn't move because of my hand and weight on his throat so all I asked for was assistance to take him back to the station.

Within minutes, all I could hear was police sirens coming

to my location from every direction. The pub door then burst open and at least ten policemen charged in. They grabbed the guy off me and bundled him outside into the van. Fortunately my glasses weren't broken and I was none the worse for wear. The duty inspector came over to me and asked what had happened, there were two sergeants with him, one I knew, who liked me. I told them exactly what had happened and explained I didn't call for urgent assistance. He then told me he'd been in the canteen when my call came over the radio and he said the place had erupted with everyone rushing out to my help.

He said he'd never seen anything like it before and because it had been me who'd asked for help, everyone had thought I was in serious trouble.

The publican then came over and told the inspector what he'd seen and that the guy had assaulted me. He then asked the Inspector who was going to pay for all the broken glasses and table. This inspector knew the game and this pub like many others had after hours drinking because at that time pubs had to close by 11pm and if he didn't want to lose his licence in a raid then it was better if he forgot all about it.

When I got back to the station, everyone kept asking me if I was all right and I had to reassure them that I didn't have a scratch on me. The CID who I knew said to me they were arresting him for assaulting me and would put me on the charge sheet as the assisting arresting officer, and that I was to be in the magistrates court in the morning, and they'd give the evidence.

So next morning, I'm sitting in court with them and they bring the prisoner in. I hardly recognised him as his arm was in a sling and he had a big black eye and I'm thinking

I never did that and I actually felt sorry for him. He looked a right mess.

The magistrate, who was called a stipendiary, which I think was an ex-barrister, was listening to the CID giving their evidence and he kept looking over the top of his glasses at the prisoner. He then interrupted the CID and stopped them from giving their evidence and asked if the special who was assaulted was in the court. My heart sank and I'm thinking I'm going to get blamed for beating up this poor sod while I haven't got a mark on me. So with great trepidation I stood up in court and replied it was me your honour. He then looks me up and down over the top of his glasses and asks me if I was okay and not injured. I couldn't believe it, here's the prisoner standing there like he'd done ten rounds with Henry Cooper and he was asking me if I was okay? So I replied yes, thank you sir and he then asks again are you sure?

Then he turns to the prisoner who'd just been released from prison two days before for assaulting a policemen and gave him eighteen months suspended jail sentence, warning him that if he appeared before him in court again then he would surely go back to prison for a long time. With that the poor guy limped out of court and probably went to hospital instead of prison.

One evening, quite late at night, a call came over the radio, asking if anyone could go to the Strand near the law courts as someone had reported that a man was lying on the pavement.

As I was quite close I replied I'd go.

I walked down the street and saw someone lying face down on the floor. I'm thinking at that time of the night he's probably drunk and had passed out. So I turned him over and as I did I saw that half of his head was missing and his brains were dangling out. I retched and nearly threw up. This guy was as dead as a dodo. I called the station and asked for an ambulance which came quite quickly and confirmed he was dead which was pretty obvious. The duty Inspector and sergeant arrived who called the local coroner to take the body away. Until an autopsy had been performed, they had to treat the death as suspicious. Like I'd seen in many American films they chalked the outline of where the body had been found and gave me orders to wait for forensics to come and examine the scene. They told me under no circumstances to let anyone walk over the crime scene. Being midweek at 1am in the morning in that particular location, that was pretty unlikely.

So, I stand there waiting for someone to come and relieve me. It then started to rain so I moved into a nearby doorway for shelter. After a short time the rain had washed away all the chalk marks and I'm thinking what the hell do I do now? At that moment a guy suddenly appears looking the worse for drink walking straight to the spot where the body had been found. So I stepped out of the doorway which frightens the life out of this chap and I say to him excuse me sir can you please walk this way indicating a route around where the body had been found, bearing in mind by now there's nothing there, not even the chalk marks. He takes a deep breath, straightens himself up and with exaggerated steps, just like John Cleese doing one of his silly walks, walked a bit unsteady to where I'd pointed. He then stops and asks "Is that all right officer?" thinking I'd asked him to walk in a straight line to see if he was drunk. I said "Yes okay", then burst out laughing. I think after all that had happened that night and seeing this poor guy with half his head missing this was the anti-climax I needed.

THE *LYCEUM* WAS a diverse place for events, ranging from boxing dinners to the BBC televising live *Come Dancing*, to the ballroom holding Miss World events and dancing. It was also hired for private functions and all night live rock nights.

One day, Lord Snowden had hired the *Lyceum* for a photoshoot. He had various models parading around in different gowns for effect, and he'd brought in two smoke machines which was something quite new at the time and after taking some shots decided to start them up. Now the *Lyceum* is a large auditorium and they weren't producing enough smoke for his liking, so he asked them to be turned up to maximum, and after about half an hour the smoke inside was quite thick and he asked for them to be turned off. Unfortunately they got stuck and being diesel-powered they couldn't be unplugged. So they kept churning out more and more smoke until it was like a scene from an old black and white Charles Dickens film. The *Lyceum* had eighteen fire escapes, and we opened all of them but it made very little difference. Then someone remembered that, before the war, a large section of the roof was rolled back above the dance floor so people could dance under the stars as a gimmick.

So, half a dozen of us marched up onto the roof and an old boy called George, who'd worked there as a handy man for many years, knew where to look. We found the metal trapdoor which was fitted on rollers but hadn't been used in over twenty years and had rusted badly. So we got some oil and grease and inch by inch slowly moved it back. Then after a lot of effort it slid about halfway across. The gap was about 15 foot by 12 foot, and with that the smoke inside shot out the hole in a giant column of black smoke about twenty feet into the air. It was a hot summer's day on a Friday afternoon at lunch time and the Strand was packed with workers on their lunch break. All they could see was a column of smoke coming out of the roof of the *Lyceum*.

Within minutes, the sound of sirens filled the West End and because the *Lyceum* is a listed building they sent eighteen fire engines which brought the Strand and the nearby roads to a standstill. We went down to the front door to tell the firemen there was no fire. The chief fire officer then asked who was responsible for all the trouble, and at this point a very red-faced Lord Snowden came out to offer his apologies. He was very well known at the time being the husband of Princess Margaret and instantly recognisable.

The fire chief in front of all of his men laughed out loudly and Lord Snowden went even redder. Needless to say because of who he was and the power Mecca had at the time with the press none of this ever appeared in the papers. It wouldn't be the last time Mecca used their influence to cover up what they considered bad publicity.

THE *LYCEUM* WAS NOW BECOMING famous for its versatility. It wasn't just being used as a dancehall but also for various functions such as Miss World and private dinner parties. One reason was because it could comfortably seat six hundred people plus.

One evening, there was a VIP dinner dance with Prince Charles attending as guest of honour. Naturally it was a black tie event. The Prince duly arrived with two armed special branch officers. When they arrived they went into panic mode as there'd been a serious breakdown in communication. They'd arrived in lounge suits and not dinner jackets and bow ties. So the Prince told them they couldn't go inside and would have to wait for him on the front door. The Prince wouldn't budge on the matter and they were panicking, so they asked Pete Smith, the *Lyceum*'s General Manager, who was the best security man he had and without any hesitation he told them me!

So they took me to one side and explained what had happened and told me I was now responsible for the Prince's safety, to follow him wherever he went and keep three yards behind him at all times. They told me that if anyone made a move on him to take them out even if it was an old granny. So I said that's all well and good but what happens if I hit someone by mistake? They said I wasn't to worry about that and if that was to happen they would take care of it.

If truth be told, I felt immensely proud to be responsible for the Prince's safety. The *Lyceum* had hired extra security for the evening to cover all eighteen exits. So I went inside and did my duty and followed the Prince around for the rest of the evening. It turned out a quite normal event with no one attempting any attack on him, much to my relief.

At the end of the evening I took my place on the front door and as the Prince was leaving he suddenly stopped, looked me in the eye and said in his posh plummy voice "You throw people out, don't you?" I could feel myself going bright red but couldn't resist replying "Only the ones that upset me, Sir". With that he smiled and left.

I think it was his way of letting me know he knew I'd been given the job of following him around all night.

It was the first time in my life I'd been given the job of looking after someone really famous, but it wasn't to be the last.

FOUR

MECCA

Things were going well with my job in the 'specials' and at the *Lyceum*.

I made friends with London's first black policeman, Norwell Roberts. He was a funny guy with more of a cockney accent than me! Being London's first black policeman wasn't easy for him and many of the white officers at Bow St wouldn't talk to him as there was a lot of racism at that time. So I think he was grateful that I'd made friends with him and invited him to the *Lyceum* for a drink.

There were some policemen at Bow St who told me they didn't like him, not because he was black, but because of the superior officers letting him get away with all sorts of infringements, such as wearing his helmet on the side of his head and not wearing a tie which was against police regulations. The reason he got away with these infringements was because the senior command didn't want any bad publicity if they punished him and also didn't want to be seen as racist. There were a lot of policemen who gave him a hard time but in all fairness he brought a lot of it onto himself because of his behaviour.

Anyway I still liked him!

One day, when I was working on the door at the *Lyceum*, I got a call from the General Manager Pete Smith to see him in his office. I'm thinking what I have done now? I went up to his office and he asked me to sit down and told me that he'd been watching me closely. I'm thinking to myself it can't be me fiddling on the door like some of the other doormen because I didn't do that. He then told me that the *Lyceum* had booked a lot of promotions and there was a vacancy for a full time Box Office Manager and would I be interested in the job. The wage was £18 per week which was £3 more than I was getting working in the supermarket, which by now I was fed up with anyway. So I jumped at the offer and at 18 years old, I became the youngest Box Office Manager in Mecca's history at their busiest branch in the UK.

I gave a week's notice to Caters Supermarket and joined the *Lyceum*'s management. Pete Smith was the General Manager and he had working for him an Assistant Manager called Alan Hopkins, who had a habit of sticking his chin out whenever he was making a point. Hence Dick use to call him 'The Chin'. Dick had nicknames for everyone, Barry he used to call 'Silly Dilly' who in honesty was a bit dipsy and he nicknamed me 'Winnie' after Winston Churchill, because of my love of cigars.

Two weeks into me taking the Box Office job at the *Lyceum*, Pete Smith hired the venue out to a private company for a reggae night. The company had booked Desmond Dekker as top of the bill along with some other reggae bands.

Desmond Dekker had, at the time, a number one single in the charts called 'The Israelites', which Dick and I loved so I was looking forward to seeing him perform live.

On the night of the performance there were a lot, and I mean a *lot*, of people coming in. The capacity of the *Lyceum* was about 2700 and I estimated at least 3500 people were inside that night. The problem was we had no control over how many tickets were being sold and the organisers, who were Greek Cypriots, were greedy and had oversold the tickets to earn more money. We knew it was going to be busy and hired extra security for the night but twenty doormen were nowhere near enough for that amount of people in a building with eighteen fire exits plus the front door to cover. We soon lost all control. More and more people were flooding in because their friends were opening exits to let them inside with no tickets.

I was getting reports of prostitutes selling themselves inside some of the exits and of drugs openly on sale. The extra security we'd hired soon lost all interest in doing their job and Pete Smith was nowhere to be found. I thought this was a great start to my career after only two weeks in the job and was really angry that Mecca could let something like this happen.

There were at least two people knifed inside and one man stabbed to death outside. There were some really nasty characters walking about that night and because the majority of the audience was black if you tried to sort them out the rest would gang up on you.

Desmond Dekker came on last and I took a dozen of my best men to the front to try and keep the crowd from getting onto the stage. As soon as Desmond Dekker came onto the stage, the crowd went wild with excitement and started pushing us back. We were trying our best to keep them in check and made a cordon in front of the stage by linking arms with each other but one very large black woman who I swear must have weighed at least twenty stone broke through our cordon and rushed forward to Desmond Dekker on the stage. Dekker's trademark at the time was to wear a neck scarf and this woman grabbed his neck scarf, knocked him over and fell on top of him. I rushed to pull her off him, but by now Desmond Dekker had lost consciousness, not just because of her weight on top of him but because the neck scarf he was wearing must have had a slip knot and by her pulling on it she was slowly strangling him.

I undid his neck scarf, picked him up and carried him off the stage. By this time he was slowly turning blue so I started to give him mouth to mouth resuscitation, something we had to learn to do on first aid courses in 'The Specials'. An ambulance finally arrived and took him to hospital. I'm pleased to say he made a full recovery and went on to make a good living from that one hit song.

The next day there was not one word in any of the newspapers about the serious assaults that had taken place inside the *Lyceum* nor of the guy being stabbed to death outside. Such was the power of Mecca's publicity machine. It wouldn't be the last time I was to witness the UK's biggest entertainment group cover up as what they saw as bad publicity.

BBC TELEVISION often filmed episodes of *Come Dancing* from the *Lyceum*. It used to amuse me how the couples would glide around the dance floor, smiling with looks that butter wouldn't melt in their mouths, when very often backstage they'd be arguing with their competitors and sometimes would even sabotage their rivals' costumes!

The show was presented by Michael Aspel who would follow me around the ballroom to find someone to talk to. He was a real pest and at times I would do my best to avoid him.

By now the *Lyceum* was becoming the number one venue in the UK for rock concerts and many famous bands would play live there.

On one such night, I was standing on the door and a guy walked in with a guitar on his back with another man and girl. I was standing at the stairs that led into the foyer and this guy was asking one of the doormen if he could come in. They told him he had to walk around the outside of the building to the stage door. I heard his name as he was about to walk off, so I called him back and asked him who he was? He replied "David Bowie" and as a joke I made out I hadn't heard of him and said "Are you the same David Bowie who sings *Space Oddity*". His face lit up that someone had recognised him and replied, "Yes". I then said to him, "Well it's your lucky day" and he replied, "What do you mean?" I said "I love that song and you can come in this way on one condition". He asked "What was that?", and I replied, "If you sing Space Oddity for me". He then asked me what my name was and I replied "Les", so he said "Okay" and went inside.

During the course of the night, I'd forgotten about my cheeky request until in the middle of his gig when I heard over the loudspeakers in the foyer, "And now, this next song is dedicated to Les on the front door" and he sang *Space Oddity* for me.

A top man who kept his word and I was very sad when, many years later, he died.

On one of the very rare occasions when the *Lyceum* was closed for the evening, I was given the job of waiting for the Night Watchman to hand over the keys. He was a funny little man from Malta called John.

I'd told Dick I'd be there alone until midnight and could he pop in to keep me company, as there was no radio or TV to watch. He agreed to come.

He arrived about 7pm and we sat there bored out of our minds when he suddenly come up with an idea to pass some time. "I know Winnie, I'll make an Ouija board!"

This was years before *The Exorcist* film was released and I'd never heard of a Ouija board before. Dick told me it was easy to make. He found some card and scissors, cut it into squares on which he wrote the alphabet A to Z, then two other pieces with Yes and No. He placed all the cards into a circle and put the Yes and No opposite each other. He then went over to one of the bars and took a wine glass which he blew into three times and placed it upside down in the middle of the circle.

I was watching all of this with amusement, wondering when the trick would begin. He sat at the table opposite me and asked me to place my finger tip on the upturned rim of the glass and he did the same. He then said "Spirit, Spirit in the glass is there anyone there?" and I'm thinking what a prat! The glass then slowly starts moving around inside the circle, with Dick asking different questions and not really getting any answers. I'm thinking to myself this is quite clever how without me pushing the glass he's making it move around the table.

He then asks me to ask the spirit in the glass a question, so I'm thinking, okay, I'll play your game and ask if there were any evil spirits here. Dick becomes angry with me and says, "You shouldn't ask questions like that!" Before I could reply the glass shot over to the Yes card, comes back into the middle of the circle and then moves erratically. I'm thinking this is bloody clever how Dick is moving the glass around without me pushing it. Dick then says to me all seriously "Change the subject Winnie!" I'm thinking you're not going to frighten me and I say "Spirit, spirit in the glass, if there are any evil spirits here who are they?" With that the glass shoots around the cards and spells out 'DEVIL' then moves back to the middle of the circle like a tornado and explodes!

You've never seen two grown men move so fast, knocking over the table as we bolted for the back door. He's shouting at me saying I'm so stupid for asking such a question and I reply saying he was even more stupid for starting this in the first place. We must have been standing outside at least an hour in the cold before we plucked up enough courage to go back inside. I told Dick we had to clear up the mess before the night-man arrived. So I picked up the broken pieces of glass from the floor and I noticed the stem of the glass had snapped in half. When I placed the two pieces together there was a crack in the shape of a lightning bolt, something I've never seen before or since.

After we had cleared up the mess, we both stood outside the back door in the street waiting for John the night-man. There was such a bad atmosphere inside we were too scared to wait inside for him.

When John turned up for the keys I tried to sound as casual as possible and walked inside with him. He immediately said, "What's happened here?", sensing that something bad had occurred. I played the innocent and pretended I didn't know what he was talking about. I gave him the keys and he said "Don't leave me here alone, why's it so cold in here?" I replied "Don't be silly, you must have been drinking!" and left him there to it.

Dick and I couldn't get out fast enough. It taught me a valuable lesson not to mess with things you don't understand. It was the first and only time I played with an Ouija board but it wasn't to be the last of many strange happenings in that old building.

THE *LYCEUM* HAD NOW STARTED to hold all night hippie parties which started at midnight on Friday and went on until 6am on Saturday morning.

That started to attract some of the top groups in the world such as Black Sabbath, Deep Purple, Pink Floyd and it was great to hear Procol Harum singing a Whiter Shade of Pale. It was also amazing to watch the Crazy World of Arthur Brown singing 'Fire' which was one of Dick's favourite songs. I also saw the Moody Blues, Marc Bolan and heard one of my favourite songs, 'Born to be Wild' performed by Steppenwolf, as well as many other great bands.

One band I wasn't so keen on was Black Widow which, as part of their act, performed black magic rituals on stage including sacrificing a live chicken. They generated a lot of publicity at the time and were booked to play at the *Lyceum*.

As a publicity stunt, they'd contacted Alex Sanders who was known as King of the Witches in the UK with his beautiful wife Maxine who used to appear naked next to him on stage. We'd been warned that they might cause trouble and I was told by Pete Smith that if they tried to kill a chicken during their act with Alex Sanders on stage then I was to cut the lights and power off to the stage.

On the night they performed there were a lot of press in the audience waiting for them to kill the chicken. I was waiting at the side of the stage ready to turn off the electricity if they tried anything stupid. Sure enough, during their act, Alex Sanders and his wife, who was completely naked under a see-through dress, came on to the stage and started to perform a black magic ritual. At that moment Sander's wife Maxine dramatically fainted on stage and I cut the power to the stage.

As I did this the lead singer of the group tried to stab me with a sword he had on stage as a prop which I luckily managed to dodge but it only missed chopping my ear off by inches.

I then jumped onto the stage and picked up Maxine to carry her backstage to the dressing rooms. She really was a beautiful woman with long blond hair, and this was the closest I'd been to a naked woman and as result I got a hard-on!

This time the press got the story they wanted but no pictures because I'd cut the electricity off and the stage was blacked out before they'd had a chance to kill the chicken.

ONE DAY, Pete Smith called me into his office and told me

he'd hired the *Lyceum* all night to a group of musicians who wanted some privacy and no press to jam together. He asked if I could keep an eye on them all night and make sure they didn't burn the place down! I was intrigued to see who was wealthy enough to hire the *Lyceum* for the whole evening without selling any tickets. I was told by Pete Smith that there would be maybe ten to fifteen hangers-on with this group.

During the evening the group's roadies stacked the stage with amps and equipment for them to practise on. There were only three musicians in the group; Eric Clapton, Jack Bruce and Ginger Baker. The ten to fifteen hangers-on turned into a crowd of about thirty people amongst which were the usual number of groupies.

This was the original lineup of the super group, as they were known, called Cream. They'd previously broken up and were now thinking of getting back together to reform Cream.

This session was to be strictly behind locked closed doors and it was my duty to make sure no press infiltrated the session. Pete Smith told me to keep any of their friends off the balcony in case any of them got too high on pot and tried to jump off thinking they could fly. As one poor girl from an earlier concert, high on LSD, had come out of the *Lyceum* and jumped off Waterloo Bridge thinking she could fly. The poor girl drowned and once again Mecca's publicity machine had managed to keep the story out of the newspapers.

The night started about 11pm after all their roadies had set up their equipment. The group spent an hour or so doing their sound checks and setting up and everyone was smoking pot which was usual at that time. I didn't say anything to them because, as there were no members of the public present, there wasn't much point. That however didn't mean I condoned it, and when I was asked by various members of their party would I like a joint I politely refused and told them I hadn't smoked since I was five and got flashbacks of my mother giving me the cigarette to smoke and making me sick!

As the night progressed the music got better and better. They were playing not to a crowd in a concert, but playing what they enjoyed and it was truly exceptional music.

Ginger Baker was amazing on drums - by now I'd seen a lot of good drummers playing in concerts at the *Lyceum*, but boy this guy was good!

All three members of Cream were high on pot and playing out of their skins. Some of their friends had now drifted off to the balcony and were bonking merrily. I let them get on with it as I was too busy listening to some of the best music I'd ever heard. By now, there were clouds of pot drifting over and around the stage.

At about 4am, I noticed someone walk over to one of the exits so I followed him and was confronted by a large man with bright ginger hair and a bushy ginger beard. He turned around to me and said, "Hi, you've been looking after us all night?" I replied "Yes just doing my job". He then looked down at the floor where a crate of milk had just been delivered. He bent down and from the crate picked up a jar of fresh cream and stared to drink it completely off his head. The cream dribbled down his bright, ginger beard and he started to laugh and said "Look, Ginger Baker drinking fresh cream" and burst out laughing. He then said to me to have a drink for looking after them and pulled a note out of his pocket. I told him as management I wasn't allowed to accept any tips, but he was having none of it and pushed the note into my top jacket pocket.

With that he ran off laughing high as a kite with cream dribbling down his beard. I thought, sod it, I'm not going to run after him and took the note out of my pocket, it was a brand new £20 note which had only recently been released by the Bank of England. My jaw dropped open as my weekly wage then (which was considered good at the time) was £18 for the week. He'd just given me over a week's wages as a tip! I liked his drumming even more after that.

Sadly it wasn't to be until decades later that they reformed as Cream for a comeback concert at the Royal Albert Hall in May 2005 with tickets selling on eBay for over £1000 each! The tickets for all four shows sold out in under an hour and I bet the music they played wasn't as good as I had heard that great night at the *Lyceum*.

FIVE

LED ZEPPELIN

THE NEXT BIG concert the *Lyceum* booked was Led Zeppelin, who were one of the biggest groups in the world at that time.

The tickets quickly sold out and we were expecting a capacity crowd of over 3000 people. I was really looking forward to seeing them play live as they were one of my favourite groups.

On the day of the concert, they arrived with one of the biggest sets of amplifiers and equipment I'd ever seen. It was a Sunday in October 1969.

The roadies set up their equipment which took hours, then did all the normal sound checks. The doors were due to open at 7 pm and they were scheduled to play about 8pm. During their rehearsals they were one of the loudest bands I'd ever heard and such great musicians.

All seemed to be going to plan until mid-afternoon when Jimmy Page's guitar amp stopped working. At first the roadies and our electrician looked at it to try and fix it but had no success. Now this was on a Sunday afternoon and in those days there were no shops open to get the amp fixed, or buy a new one. So this was a major disaster as he couldn't play and he didn't have a spare amp. Everyone was panicking and making calls to different people who may be able to help.

Eventually, I was told that Jimmy Page had spoken to Ronnie Wood of the Rolling Stones who'd agreed to lend Jimmy one of his. Ronnie Wood lived somewhere in the country and we had to find transport to go to his house, pick it up and bring it back to the *Lyceum*.

They eventually found a flat back lorry and driver to go and collect the amp. Pete Smith asked me to go with the driver and help bring it back, the problem was it was now late Sunday afternoon and the clock was ticking!

So, off I go with the driver who told me he knew where to go. He got lost on the way, losing us more time. We finally found the house but Ronnie Wood had been drinking or smoking pot and had forgotten we were coming. After a few more phone calls to the *Lyceum* he got to speak to Jimmy Page and agreed to let us take the amp.

By now, it was already dark and I knew we would never get back to the *Lyceum* by the time the doors opened. It was really getting late and I was thinking there would be a riot with over 3000 fans if Led Zeppelin didn't get to play.

Led Zeppelin had been announcing to the waiting fans what had happened but the fans were getting impatient. We eventually arrived at the *Lyceum* after 9pm and pulled the lorry round to the back exit nearest to the stage. When the back door was opened the cheer from the crowd inside nearly blew me off my feet.

We quickly got the amp down the stairs and on to the stage. The roadies connected and tested the amp and the group were ready to play the concert. Pete Smith asked me for extra protection to stand in the wings on stage. Led Zeppelin already had their own bodyguards who were standing in the wings who I found to be rude and aggressive. One of their bodyguards standing next to me had his jacket undone and I was shocked to see he was wearing a shoulder holster with a gun inside! I couldn't believe it because at that time even London's police were unarmed.

I immediately went and told Pete Smith the General Manager what I'd just seen. He just shrugged his shoulders and said to me, "They're Led Zeppelin". So I replied, "What if they try to shoot a fan that gets onto the stage?" He then told me, "That's why you're there, to stop them!"

The concert went on till after midnight without any trouble and I was privileged to hear some great music, but why they had armed bodyguards on stage in London, was totally beyond me.

THE *LYCEUM* WAS BECOMING KNOWN as the 'in' place for live underground music as it was known then. Now it's called heavy metal or heavy rock. It also became a magnet for drug pushers and we were constantly on the lookout for them. Mecca was seriously worried that they might lose their license if ever there was a police raid. It never happened because the Managing Director of Mecca, Eric Morley, had friends in high places within the police force, as I was later to discover.

We used to beef up security for the concerts on the lookout for people who were involved in pushing drugs. There was one guy in particular who I didn't like and thought might be involved. So, one night during a concert when they were working, I followed him with one of my guys who I could trust into the toilet where we grabbed him and sure enough his pockets were full of pills and bags of pot. I put him into a stranglehold position while my guy emptied his pockets.

We then forced him to flush all of his drugs down the toilet. There were tears in his eyes as he watched hundreds of pounds-worth of drugs go down the pan. He pleaded with us to take some for ourselves and offered us money to let him go so I replied by giving him an extra hard slap and threw him out onto the street. I then told his boss, Tony Barnes, who I liked what had happened and he was shocked and told me he'd make sure the guy never worked for him again.

ONE MONTH later the Rolling Stones were booked to play a double concert, one in the afternoon and one in the evening, which was unusual. On the day of the concert I thought it was funny seeing Mick Jagger sitting with Pete Smith drinking tea like he was at some garden party. It wasn't the image I had of this wild man of rock but I was still looking forward to seeing him play live. Ticket sales for the afternoon concert weren't a sell-out which I think surprised everyone and to be honest their performance, I thought, was a bit disappointing and flat. Maybe it was because it was a Sunday afternoon and they never really got the crowd going. Nonetheless they more than made up for it when they played the evening show. We'd placed a row of crash barriers in front of the stage to stop fans getting onto the stage and I had some of my best doorman with me standing behind them.

The evening show was a sell-out and the Stones were on form, with Mick Jagger strutting his stuff on stage in complete contrast to the earlier afternoon performance. Maybe Mick had something stronger in his tea for the evening show?

ONE OF MY all-time favourite groups were a band called Ten Years After, who had a top ten single from their album called 'Love Like a Man'. Their lead guitarist Alvin Lee was considered by many at the time to be the fastest guitarist in the world, so I was more than pleased when I heard they were going to be playing at the *Lyceum*.

Pete Smith knew how much I liked them and as a reward asked me if I would like to assist in the lighting box on the night of their concert. I jumped at the offer. The week before the concert our electrician Paul Reading showed me how to operate the various spotlights and our brand new liquid kaleidoscope.

On the night of the concert, I was nervous but delighted at the prospect of operating the light show for Ten Years After. The night went well and I had a perfect view of the stage from the lighting box and that night didn't have to worry about any idiots getting onto the stage. The music was brilliant and I'll never forget their live rendition of 'Love Like a Man' or the brilliant guitar work of Alvin lee.

Normally on the rock concert nights, there wasn't any real

trouble - it was mainly hippies getting high, sometimes trying to take their clothes off or fly off the balcony. There were even cases sometimes of fans being so out of it they would lie on the floor and masturbate to their favourite song!

One night however, things didn't go to plan. I was standing on the door during a concert when someone rushed over and said there was trouble in one of the boxes. The *Lyceum* being an old theatre had, like most London theatres, boxes on either side of the dance floor which seated between 6-8 people. These boxes were reserved for V.I.P's and on this particular night a big guy, off his head on drugs, had broken into the box and threatened to throw the people inside over the edge if they didn't get out. I ran up to the box with two other doormen and was confronted by a giant who reminded me of a boxer called Brian London.

The three of us grabbed him and walked him down an exit corridor to throw him out. The two doormen had hold of his arms and I was walking behind him, but he was a big fucker and broke free from one of the doormen holding him. He then picked up some iron bars from the floor which had been left behind by some builders who'd been working there during the day. As he lifted them up above his head he caught the seam of my brand new dinner jacket, ripping it all the way from my pocket to my armpit.

That distracted me enough to take my eye off him, which gave him the chance to smash me over the head with the iron bars. I was already angry about my new jacket being torn and I wanted to kill the fucker. As high as he was he looked shocked that he hadn't knocked me out and looked down at the iron bars he was holding, dropping them onto the floor and running like hell for the exit with me chasing after him.

The golden rule of any doorman is to never chase after someone into the street, but I was so angry I'd lost my temper. Never being great at running I soon lost sight of him and as I was walking back towards the exit looking at my poor ruined jacket I started feeling wet drops on my head and thought *Oh great that's all I need now, it's started to rain'*.

When I got to the door the other doormen and Pete Smith all crowded around me asking if I was okay. I said "No I'm not look what the bastard has done to my new jacket!" They then asked me the same question again, if I was all right. Then I suddenly realised that it hadn't started raining but that it was blood pouring down my head from where he'd hit me with the iron bars.

Fortunately I didn't need any stitches and one of my doormen who knew first aid cleaned me up. With all the money that Mecca had earned from their dancehalls, bingo halls and ice rinks they refused to buy me a new jacket, the tight bastards!

THE *LYCEUM* USED to hold some very prestigious award and ceremonial nights, one of which was called the Carl Allen award and on this particular night Princess Margaret was guest of honour. There were a host of V.I.P's attending and we brought in extra security for the night. One of the first to arrive was Robert Maxwell, the owner of the Daily Mirror, who arrived with his wife who was covered in diamonds. Years later he was found to have robbed the pension fund of the Daily Mirror worth millions of pounds, and later mysteriously died in a boating accident.

While I was standing on the door, I noticed what looked like a tramp wearing a big army overcoat and balaclava walking towards us. I told the other doormen to watch him and not to let him in. As he got to the door he took off his balaclava, shook his head and a bundle of long blonde hair fell down to his shoulders. He undid the big army coat and was wearing an immaculate dress suit underneath. He then took from his pocket a very large Cuban cigar and placed it into his mouth. I instantly recognised him, it was Jimmy Saville. He then took off his gloves to display a variety of rings that he was wearing on both hands. He then turned to each doorman, took off the rings on his right hand to shake the hands of the doorman, then replaced them then turned to the next doorman and repeated the procedure with each and every man standing there, myself included.

He then cracked a joke that if we needed any help to come inside and fetch him. Jimmy Saville had worked as an Assistant Manager and DJ for Mecca in Leeds. He was one of the very special guests on Princess Margaret's list of VIP's for that evening. It wasn't until decades later and after he'd died, that he was found to be a serial paedophile. He wasn't the only known paedophile to visit the *Lyceum*.

Jonathon King, who was very well known in the music business, used to come to concerts and functions with a young boy always in tow. I really detested him and asked Pete Smith if I could bar him from coming in but was told no, because he was too important to the music scene at that time, even though many other people were aware he was a nonce.

I let him know on a few occasions that I didn't like him one bit and tried my best to provoke him to hit me, so I would have an excuse to bash him up, but he wouldn't take the bait because he was, as us cockneys say, "all mouth and no trousers".

Again, it wasn't until many years later that justice finally caught up with him and he was sent to prison for sex with underage boys. I'm sure and hope he got all he deserved in prison knowing how child molesters are treated by fellow prisoners and screws alike. He was truly a nasty piece of work.

ONE OF THE new doormen who I became very good friends with was an ex-Royal Marine called Alan. We used to go out for a drink after work and I got to know him really well.

One night, when he was a bit worse for wear from drinking, he drove me past a building in the West End and asked me if I knew what it was. I knew a lot of famous landmarks in London from the specials and my love of history, but this was one I didn't recognise. It had a high metal-gated fence and was floodlit, so I was thinking maybe it was an embassy. He then told me it was the headquarters of MI6, the spy organisation for the UK. I asked him how he knew this and he told me he'd done some work as a chauffeur for a film director who he frequently drove over there. He said that the guy he used to drive for took him all over Eastern Europe, supposedly looking for locations but never actually made any films. It was fairly obvious to me that the man he was talking about was probably using the film locations as an excuse to spy. Alan was a lovely man but, in all honesty, a bit thick.

One evening when we were working together at the *Lyceum*, we got a call that there were two men at the bar upstairs causing aggro with the waitresses, so we ran upstairs, saw the two men and told them that they had to leave. They were both holding glasses in their hands and without any warning the one closest to Alan punched his glass into Alan's face.

While his mate threw his glass at me which shattered on my chest, I looked down at my shirt expecting to see it covered in blood, but to my surprise there wasn't a drop. But poor Alan's face was covered in blood.

When the two men saw that I wasn't injured, they made a run for it, but I wasn't going to let them get away. In the meantime one of the waitresses had pushed the panic button behind the bar which alerted the doormen in the foyer that there was trouble upstairs. By the time the doormen had run upstairs to the balcony the bastard who'd glassed Alan had got away but I'd managed to jump onto the guy that had thrown the glass at me. I tore into him with several good punches and soon knocked him semi-conscious. When the other doormen saw the state Alan was in, they dragged his mate downstairs and gave him another good pasting to get him to reveal his friend's name who'd glassed Alan before the police arrived.

The glass had been punched into Alan's face with such force it had gone through his cheek and cut his tongue inside his mouth. Needless to say he had to have many stitches which left him badly scarred for life. I was much luckier and escaped with only a round of bruises on my chest from the rim of the glass that had been thrown at me.

When Alan fully recovered, which took several weeks, he told me he'd served with the Marines in some of the world's most dangerous places such as Aden and Oman and had never been injured. Now he was scarred for life after working at the *Lyceum* for only two months. The two men who'd carried out this vicious assault had only recently been released from prison for GBH. Now they were both back in prison where they belonged.

Mecca, for a change, actually had some sympathy for Alan and his horrific injuries and offered him a full time job at the Ilford *Palais* as an Assistant Manager.

BECAUSE OF THE long hours we worked I lost touch with Alan, until one evening a Detective Chief Inspector from the C.I.D at Bow Street came to see me at the *Lyceum*. He asked me if I'd seen or had had any contact with Alan. I told him I hadn't seen Alan since he'd taken the job at the Ilford *Palais* and what was the problem.

He told me that Alan had disappeared off the face of the earth and his friends and family hadn't heard anything from him. The police had gone to his flat where he was living in Ilford where all of his clothes were still hanging in the wardrobe. Mecca told the police that Alan had also not collected two weeks' of wages from his job which I must admit was certainly not like Alan. The D.C.I. told me he'd come back and talk to me once they'd made more inquiries.

A few weeks later the D.C.I. came back to the *Lyceum* and

told me in confidence that he'd spoken to special branch who'd informed him that they'd received information that Alan had gone on a job with the 'film Director' and that they'd lost all contact. The DCI who knew me from Bow Street then said to me, "You know what's happened to him" I replied "I can guess". I was told to keep my mouth shut about our conversation and unfortunately I never heard from Alan again. He never did collect his wages or clothes which would have been difficult if you're stuck in some dungeon in Eastern Europe or worse.

Shortly after that incident I got called into Pete Smiths office to be told he'd been instructed by Mecca to cut down on his wage bill and I was to be transferred to the Café de Paris in Coventry Street.

I knew this was a load of bollocks! The real reason was a few weeks before he'd called me into his office during which he'd sacked his Catering Manager, Mr Lovejoy. I had liked Lovejoy a lot and we'd spent a few nice drinking sessions together in the *Lyceum*. Pete Smith wanted me to throw Lovejoy out of his office and the building because he didn't have the balls to do it himself as Lovejoy was a tall man and Pete Smith was only small. I refused to carry out his orders and Lovejoy had told Smith what he thought of him in no uncertain terms.

So now Pete Smith got his revenge by getting me transferred to the Café de Paris.

SIX

THE CAFÉ DE PARIS

I HAD TRULY LOVED my job at the *Lyceum* listening to some of the top bands in the world play.

It was my kind of music. Now I was to become the Box Office Manager of a small basement club that held a maximum of six hundred people.

The Café de Paris had its history like the *Lyceum*, but was nowhere near as old. The place had opened in 1924 and apparently someone called Louise Brooks had made history by introducing the Charleston dance in December 1924. The club had been owned by Marlene Dietrich before the Second World War. It had been a favourite place of the Prince of Wales who often dined there with Cole Porter and the Aga Khan which was all well and good but this was the last place on earth I wanted to work in. Now it was full of fuddy-duddy wannabes who thought they were on *Come Dancing*.

The place held tea dances and all they played in the evenings were waltzes and foxtrots. After what I'd experienced at the *Lyceum* this music was pure hell for me to listen to. The General Manager, who was perfect for the place as he spoke and dressed as if he'd just stepped out of a 1920s time machine, said to me he couldn't understand why Mecca had sent me there as they only had one till, one cloakroom, one doorman and never any trouble! I was sure I was going to die of boredom in this bloody place!

After a few weeks of working there, I got to know some of the regulars who'd been going there for donkey's years. They were pleasant enough people but so boring. Even in the afternoons for the tea dance the women would come dressed in ball gowns and their partners in suits and dinner jackets.

In the afternoons they would play records of the waltzes to dance to, and it used to drive me crazy. So I asked the manager one day if I could DJ and that I'd often done this job at the *Lyceum* at the end of the evening for the last thirty minutes. He said to me I could try it, but I must only play records that the punters could dance to in time. So the next day I brought in some of my own records and in the middle of the tea dance session I started to play Led Zeppelin and Black Sabbath at full volume.

It was worth the bollocking from the GM, just to see the look of horror on the faces of the dancers - it nearly gave some of them a heart attack!

It was, without doubt, a very uncomfortable week after carrying out this incident and the punishment for this dirty deed (which I still laugh about to this day) was to spend a week as Night Watchman looking after the building when it closed. This was all well and good except for the fact that during the Second World War on March 8th 1941 the café was bombed soon after the start of a performance. Two bombs had fallen down a ventilation shaft killing over fifty people on the dance floor including the band leader Ken 'Snakehips' Johnson and some of his band and staff, with over one hundred people injured.

After the bombing, the club didn't open again until 1948 but it became well known again playing host to Frank Sinatra, Grace Kelly, Tony Hancock, Noël Coward and many others.

I'd already been told by some of the staff that had worked there a long time that they'd experienced strange noises and sensations which they couldn't explain.

For sure I wouldn't be calling Dick to this place to keep me company with his bloody Ouija board! When I worked all night, there was a very eerie feeling in the place, which would send chills down my spine. All because I'd tried to introduce some new music to the old sods and liven the place up.

I HAD NOW SPENT five miserable months at the Café de Paris and was seriously thinking about quitting when, one day, the Area Director, a nice man called Michael Woods, came down to see me.

He started by saying he was sorry that it hadn't worked out between me and Pete Smith, who I knew he didn't like anyway and that he knew I was unhappy working in the Café de Paris. He told me a position for Box Office Manager at the Hammersmith *Palais* had become available and if I was interested in taking up the job.

I already knew through Mecca's grapevine that they

couldn't keep Box Office Managers there because of the trouble they were getting on the door and he'd come to me offering the job hoping I could go there and sort it out.

So I played it cool and let him know that I knew about the trouble they were having at the venue. I told him it was also a long way from where I lived in Lewisham, but I'd take the job if they gave me a pay rise. He looked a bit shocked and said he'd think about it and let me know.

The very next day he came back and said that Mecca had agreed to give me an extra £5 per week. To be honest I think I would have paid him just to get away from the Café de Paris and I certainly knew that the punters wouldn't miss me and Black Sabbath!

So the following week I moved to the Hammersmith *Palais*.

SEVEN

THE HAMMERSMITH PALAIS

The Hammersmith *Palais* was built in 1919 at the end of the First World War by a pair of American entrepreneurs called Booker and Mitchell as a purpose-built ballroom for dancing and new jazz bands to play.

It certainly never had any of the character of the *Lyceum* or the Café de Paris, but it was Mecca's largest ballroom in London and could hold nearly 4000 people which made it a bit of a nightmare to fill. The resident band playing there was Ken Mackintosh. The General Manager was a big Scotsman called Mr Robinson who fancied himself to be a bit of a James Bond. He was married to an ex-dancer who was very attractive. There was an Assistant Manager named Phil Anderson, a Catering Manager and Assistant Manager, and an old boy called Joe Beckett, who was a general dogsbody.

On my first night working there, I wanted to suss out how good the other doormen were, and to see if they were on the fiddle. It was a quiet mid-week night and I suddenly found myself on the door alone. They'd all pissed off inside and I was thinking to myself this is a good start, when a really big guy who'd obviously been drinking walked up to the front door. I opened it a few inches with my foot firmly wedged behind it. I thought *I will be nice and polite on my first night working here* and said "Sorry sir, you can't come in." He then replied in a slurred voice and a thick Irish accent "Why not?" so I told him because he'd already had too much to drink. With that he said "Fuck you, you English bastard!" and spat in my face.

If there's one thing that sends me into a rage, it's someone spitting at me. I totally lost it, pulled the door back and with all my strength slammed the heavy door into his face. The pavement outside the *Palais* was at least fifteen feet wide and I knocked him back the whole width. He fell backwards into the road in front of a bus, fortunately the bus stopped in time but this fucker was out cold. The bus driver got out and I shut the door.

Hammersmith police station was only a few doors away from the *Palais* and two policemen ran out from the station and called an ambulance. After the ambulance took him away they came over and asked me if I'd seen anything. I told them he was drunk and had fallen into the road. That satisfied them, as there were no other witnesses, so they put it down to just another drunk passing out.

What I didn't know at the time was that the Catering Manager had been watching all of this unfold behind me while he was standing on the stairs. He came over and said to me that he thought I'd handled the situation well, but I replied "All in a day's work, and the bastard shouldn't have spat at me".

By the next day he'd told the rest of the management and the other door staff. I soon found out that some of the doormen were on the fiddle and got rid of them, while the rest by now knew I was no pushover and could be relied on in a punch up. The problem with the door at Hammersmith *Palais* was that there had been no one really controlling it. The Assistant Manager Phil was a real softy who'd let anyone in, including underage kids, which I soon put a stop to. After a certain time at weekends I would enforce a couples only rule to keep the drunks and hopefully the troublemakers out.

Once the other doormen saw how I ran the front door I soon earned their respect and they never left me alone on the door again. We still had our share of trouble on a Saturday night and there were some vicious punch ups, but fortunately none of us got injured.

I'D ONLY BEEN THERE a couple of weeks when I attended a weekly Manager's meeting. This was to discuss how to bring business into the dancehall. During the meeting I said we have a perfect venue here for a rock concert. That was something they'd never tried before and had stuck to just a dancehall.

The General Manager Mr Robinson said that there'd be too much trouble if they held a rock concert. I told him that I'd worked at the *Lyceum* and generally that wasn't the case. They then asked me who should play there and I immediately replied The Who.

At that time The Who were one of the biggest rock bands in the world. The other Managers sitting around the table all burst out laughing, saying why would The Who play here? But I'd done some research and knew when the members of The Who were teenagers that they used to go to Hammersmith *Palais* to dance and it had always been their ambition to play there.

So I told the rest of the Managers about this and said if Mecca contacted the group they'd come and play and it would be a sellout.

So the most powerful entertainment group in the country did what they were good at and booked The Who to play the Hammersmith Palais. The tickets sold out in a couple of days and we were expecting a capacity crowd of over 4000 people.

On the day of the concert, the Palais started putting up crash barriers in rows like you see in amusement parks, to funnel the people inside. I soon stopped that idea and told them just to cover the dance floor with carpet, open the doors and let the fans in.

Michael Woods, the Regional Director who'd got me the transfer to Hammersmith Palais, strode over to me with a big smile on his face and congratulated me for my idea of booking The Who and organising the entry for the fans.

Robinson, the General Manager, had been panicking before the concert asking me whether he should hire extra security in case there was a riot and the place got wrecked. I told him we only needed a few extra security and that they were only needed to keep a lookout for any drug pushers.

One of my doormen was a very experienced ex-policeman and I put him in charge of that job. Robinson was becoming a real pain in the arse running around the place panicking. Michael Woods took him to one side and told him he should listen to me because of my experience at the *Lyceum*.

We placed crash barriers in front of the stage while I and a few other security men stood behind them for the performance. I was pleased that the group never brought with them any armed bodyguards!

After a few warm up bands, The Who finally came on stage to a massive cheer from their fans. I thought Led Zeppelin were loud, but I swear The Who sounded even louder that night.

They were absolutely brilliant, with Pete Townsend jumping all over the stage playing out of his skin. I'll never forget the moment when during one of theirs songs, I looked over my shoulder to see drummer Keith Moon hit the rim of his drum with a drumstick which he sent spinning in the air above his head at least fifteen feet, while he carried on playing with his left hand and without looking up reached up with his right hand, caught the stick above his head, bringing it down onto the drum, exactly in time to the song they were playing.

If I hadn't seen it with my own eyes, I wouldn't have believed it. By now I'd seen many famous groups play live but without doubt after that performance, Keith Moon was the best drummer in the world, even better than Ginger Baker. The Who were the most exciting rock band on the planet!

Pete Townsend finished the gig in typical style by smashing his guitar up on the stage. At least he didn't try to stab me with it like the prat from Black Widow had.

The concert went off without any trouble and was a huge success. Later that evening I was backstage when Pete

Townsend and Roger Daltrey asked if I'd been the one responsible for booking them. I replied that, "Yes, it had been my idea". They both thanked me, shaking my hand, saying how much they'd enjoyed playing in the ballroom they used to dance in as teenagers. I felt really privileged that one of the greatest rock bands of all time had gone out of their way to look for me and thank me. Top men, top band!

WHILE I WAS WORKING at Hammersmith Palais, I got very friendly with Phil Anderson the Assistant Manager. He was a bit of a strange character who spoke quite well and I think had come from a wealthy family.

He used to sometimes take me after work to a drinking club in Dean Street in Soho. Long John Baldry, the singer who'd split his trousers on TV, was one of the regulars who also frequented there. At that time there weren't too many places you could get a drink after 11 o'clock at night, so I was grateful at times to go there with him.

After my second visit there I noticed that there were no women, so I asked Phil where were they? He just laughed and told me "It was a club for homosexuals." I went apeshit with him and now it all made sense to me why whenever I went there the men inside would stare at me and there wasn't any skirt.

Needless to say I never went back and I also had suspicions that Phil used to buy drugs from a man who used to come into the club with a very large white dog. It was dangerous for me to be seen drinking there, especially being a Special Police Officer.

I WAS STILL CARRYING out my duties as a Special at Bow Street, which was my first love. One day whilst on patrol I saw the gang of three card gamers up to their old tricks. I was in uniform and knew I wouldn't be able to get near them to stop and arrest them, which was really frustrating for me. I started walking down to Trafalgar Square where an Inspector and Sergeant were on duty. I told them what I'd seen and they said that they knew that they were operating there, but couldn't do anything as they didn't have any plain clothes Police Officers available to arrest them.

So I came up with the idea of perhaps going home and changing into civvies, coming back and arresting them? The Inspector replied that while he was on duty he didn't have a problem with my plan. So I jumped on a train at Charing Cross to Lewisham, where I lived with my parents. I quickly changed and came back, all in under an hour.

By now all the gamers knew my face and before I could get anywhere near them they'd pack up and run away. So I waited on the corner of Irving Street out of their sight, wondering how I was going to get close enough to them to make the arrest.

At that moment, a large group of tourists came ambling up Charing Cross Road, then started to walk down Irving Street towards Leicester Square. I waited in a doorway until they got level with me, then ducked into the middle of the group out of sight of the gamers. As the group of tourists got close enough to the gang I jumped out and grabbed the guy who was cheating the crowd with his cards. Because I had no radio on me I had to move fast and I immediately placed the guy with the cards into an arm lock and walked him down to the Inspector and Sergeant waiting for me in Trafalgar Square. As I walked him down to the square I heard one of his gang shout out "Don't go with him, he's only a Special". This made me angry and I twisted his arm even harder so he couldn't run away.

The guy shouted back to his mates, "I can't move, he's breaking my arm". He turned around and said to me, "I'll give you £25" (which at that time was over a week's wages), if you let me go." I told him to shut up and that he was lucky I didn't charge him with attempting to bribe a Police Officer. He then asked me why not take the money, all the rest of your lot "take a bung." I could tell by the tone of his voice that he was telling the truth and it made me feel sick thinking which one of my friends at Bow Street had been taking bribes from these bastards.

Much later, I discovered that the corruption went from the very top, to the bottom.

This time I didn't get a bollocking for the arrest and the next day, the gamer received a big fine which his gang paid for.

Outside the court the gamer told me that the boss of his gang wanted to know if there was anyone in their gang who'd upset me and if there was they'd get rid of him to keep me off their backs. They just didn't understand that I despised what they were doing to tourists and ordinary members of the public. I told him to tell his boss that I would go on arresting them as long as they were operating on my patch. Shortly after that incident the gang moved on to Piccadilly Circus and became a problem for West End Central Police Station.

Shortly after going back to work at Hammersmith Palais, I got a terrible shock when I was told that Phil, the Assistant Manager, had been found dead in his flat from an overdose and had left a suicide note.

He'd once told me that he'd been shunned by his strict Jewish family for being homosexual. He had even made a pass at me one day in his office, which I'd responded to by knocking him over to the other side of his office.

After that incident I kept my distance, which now made me feel really guilty because he really was a harmless nice guy, but just mixed up in the head with no real friends.

The more I thought about Phil's death, the angrier I became. I made the decision that I would at least try to get the guy who I thought was responsible. I knew that the man with the white dog had been his regular pusher at the club that Phil had taken me to. So now I was going to do my best to make him pay.

For the next few nights I parked near the club to watch out for this man and how he operated. Sure enough he went into the club every night to sell his drugs to the punters inside. He would then move onto other clubs in the area. The dog was always with him, not for his protection but for new potential customers to recognise him as a pusher.

After watching him for a few nights and waiting in my car outside the club, he came out and I slowly followed him down the road until I saw a parked police car. I then ran over to the car and showed them my warrant card and told them about my suspicions. They were more than happy to stop and search him as well as looking under the dog's collar for hidden drugs. Unfortunately they didn't find anything as he'd probably sold them.

The guy recognised me from the club and realised I'd been following him. The two uniformed officers found during their search a diary which contained the names and ranks of police, including a Detective Sergeant from West End Central. The other two officers then carried out a check over the radio on this guy and information came back that he had a record as a convicted drug dealer. They told me it had been a good "stop" and they thought that the man had had a very lucky escape.

The drug dealer then started shouting at me that I'd be sorry as he knew a lot of people. I was used to being threatened in my job on the door and told him to piss off and that I would be keeping a close eye on him, and that next time he might not be so lucky.

Much to my surprise this bastard was right. Within a few days of me stopping him, I got summoned to the Divisional Assistant Commander's office in West End Central Police Station. I knew this was going to be serious. I went into his office and he gave me an ultimatum, either resign or move out of the area to another police station. I knew they couldn't sack me because I hadn't done anything wrong. I asked him why I had to move and he told me he couldn't tell me and that I'd never know. I realised I'd become a danger to a few corrupt officers in that area and they wanted me out of their way. The drug dealer I'd stopped was working around Soho with the protection of a few senior officers.

Back at Bow Street when my friends found out what had happened they went mad, some even petitioned the Chief Superintendent for me to stay, but it was too late as my fate had been sealed and I had to move on to another police station.

As it happened a few years later Operation Countryman unearthed major corruption in the Vice Squad and Drug Squad in the Metropolitan Police. Several officers went to prison, others resigned and I heard that the officer who'd interviewed me at West End Central had also been transferred to a small police station in the countryside.

It didn't help me. I was heartbroken to leave Bow Street and all the friends I'd made there.

EIGHT

"THE CAT'S WHISKERS"

AFTER HAVING WORKED at Hammersmith Palais for six months and sorting the door out, Michael Woods told me about a new flagship venue that had been launched in Streatham called *The Cat's Whiskers* and they were looking for a box office manager.

I knew that this place had previously been known as the Streatham Locarno and had been notorious for trouble. Mecca had no choice but to close it, or lose the license as it was so bad.

Mecca had completely refurnished the old Locarno, spending a lot of money on deco and new carpets. They wanted to turn it into south London's *Talk of the Town* with cabaret acts at the weekends and a new 2am drinking license.

Once again I knew Mecca were having trouble there, so I got another pay rise to £35 per week which made me the highest paid box office manager working for Mecca and the youngest.

I didn't know what I was letting myself in for.

I told Mr Woods that before I took the job I needed a short break. I'd heard of a special subsidised trip that Mecca were offering their managers and their families to New York for four days, and I was determined to go there.

My mum loved travelling and was more than happy to come with me once I told her about it, it was now 1970.

We flew to New York with Freddie Laker airways, who later went bust. We stayed in a hotel near Central Park. While I was there I wanted to take the opportunity to visit the New York Police. The first opportunity I had I went to a local precinct and showed them my IPA card (International Police Association) to the sergeant at his desk.

It felt like walking straight onto a film set. The sergeant was very friendly and loved having a police officer from London visiting them. They took me upstairs to a room where they processed their prisoners and introduced me to two detectives, who were wearing shoulder holsters with their guns inside. They showed me a cage in which they locked their prisoners while they did their paperwork. They told me a few weeks before a prisoner had escaped, grabbed a gun and had killed two policemen before he was then shot dead. I was relieved that to know while he was telling me this story they didn't have any prisoners in the cage just then.

One of the detectives was a giant of a man, with hands like shovels, who they said they sent to anyone they didn't want in town to tell them to politely *leave*.

They took me for a ride in one of their squad cars around New York. It was a great experience I'll never forget, even though I didn't have a gun! All of the police in New York asked me the same question: "Was it true that the police in the UK didn't carry guns and only carried a small stick". When I replied yes, they just shook their heads in disbelief.

While I was in New York I also visited the night court. This was a court that was open 24hrs to try and shift the backlog of people who'd been charged with crimes. As I sat in the public gallery I couldn't help smiling when every time a defendant and detective stood in the dock, the detective looked like more of a criminal than the person charged!

I WENT with my mum to the statue of liberty and didn't realise till I got there that it was hollow with some 300 steps inside. We climbed to the top and had great views of the bay. But, for me, one of the best experiences was taking a helicopter ride over the city. The helicopter was called a whirlybird. The pilot sat in the front with two passengers, next to him. The front of the helicopter looked like a giant goldfish bowl.

My mum was a bit nervous to say the least and the pilot told us he'd flown missions in Vietnam. He looked and acted a bit crazy and years later, whenever I watched *The A Team*, I would think of the character 'Howling Mad' Murdock. What an experience as we flew over Central Park and in between the skyscrapers. As I looked out the side window I could see people sitting at their desks working. Then I'd look up to see another twenty or thirty floors above them. When we landed my mum told me she'd never fly in a helicopter again but I loved it.

We didn't get much sleep in the four days we were there, with the sound of sirens from police, fire engines, and ambulances going off all the time. At that time there was a lot of rioting taking place in Harlem. It was a great trip which I'll never forget, and I was ready now to start work at *The Cat's Whiskers*.

ON MY LAST Saturday working at the Hammersmith Palais, I was called onto the stage by Ken McIntosh, the famous band leader, who introduced me to a crowd of over two thousand people. He said "You all know this man from the front door, who's been spat on and abused but who's made this a safer place for you all to enjoy yourselves" and, much to my surprise, instead of getting a load of boos which I was expecting, I received a resounding applause from the crowd. Ken then asked me to say a few words to the biggest audience of my life, totally unprepared. I quickly managed to think of the right things to say and got even more applause. He then presented me with some LPs as a going away present, which I thought was nice of him. Until that moment I'd never realised how much my job had been appreciated by the general public.

The following Monday, I started work at *The Cat's Whiskers* in Streatham.

The Cat's Whiskers held around 1200 people depending on what type of function it was hosting or six hundred if it was a sit-down dinner. There were two bars on the balcony and a restaurant, and three bars downstairs. In the foyer there were two box offices and a cloakroom.

They also employed one of the biggest and hardest teams of bouncers I'd ever worked with. There were fourteen of them and even though I was just under six foot and weighed sixteen stone I was one of the smallest of this lot and the youngest!

There was Eddie, who was the oldest one of the group at forty years old. He was an ex-police sergeant from Glasgow and as hard as nails. He later taught me some very useful Aikido holds that he'd learned in the police. He wore false front teeth which had been knocked out in numerous punch ups on Saturday nights in Glasgow. He used to take the false teeth out and put them in his pocket before a fight which we all thought was hilarious and took the piss out of him for. Then there was Terry Daily who was an ex-professional boxer, who'd won thirty-one of his thirty-three fights, and he'd also sparred with Muhammed Ali. He was now working as a scaffolder. The smallest bouncer was Reggie Pullman, who was an ABA (amateur boxing association) London champion.

There was another ex-policeman who came from Newcastle who was too fond of his Newcastle brown ale, which had led to him being sacked from the force. Another one was an ex-Coldstream Guardsman. There were two Maltese brothers, John and Micky, and a 6'6" giant who had a second Dan black belt in Judo named John. There was also Ray Curzon, an ex-RAF military policeman who'd worked at Mr. Smith 's club in Catford where there'd been a shooting. There was another Judo expert who had a 3rd Dan black belt. Then me, who was in charge of this lot and was the youngest.

A truly formidable team who later in times of trouble, even

with all their considerable skills, still struggled with some of the troublemakers there.

The General Manager was Bob Shackle and the Assistant Manager Gordon Hall, along with a Catering Manager and his Assistant Manager. Bob Shackle used to walk around the place in a white tuxedo, full of stories of his exploits from the Second World. In one story he was a Para jumping behind enemy lines, then the next minute he'd be on a submarine, then fighting in the desert. One thing was for sure. Whenever there was any trouble he was nowhere to be seen! But I liked him and he had a great sense of humour.

The Head Supervisor was Johnnie Haines who didn't like me because he saw me as an obvious threat to his job as I'd taken full control of the front door. That meant any fiddling that went on would now be much more difficult with me in charge.

The Cat's Whiskers hadn't been open long but already there'd been some serious trouble. The problem was its late night drinking license which was attracting some of South East London's worst villains and troublemakers like a magnet. It had become a real alternative to London's West End and was a really nice place, with some good cabaret acts at weekends with a lot of attractive women coming in.

I'd been working there for less than two weeks and the doorman treated me with suspicion because I wouldn't leave the front door until it had closed making it impossible for them to take any backhanders to let people in. Friday nights were always the worst for fights when the local chaps would go out to get drunk and pull a bird. Saturdays were more for couples and a bit calmer.

On only my second Friday working on the door, one of the customers came running up to me shouting that Terry was in trouble downstairs. I took my glasses off and ran downstairs to the dance floor. I'm thinking to myself if our best man, an ex-professional boxer, was in trouble then what the fuck was I supposed to do?

As I got to the bottom of the stairs I saw a man built like a brick shithouse with his back to me. He was threatening Terry with a knife so understandably Terry was keeping his distance. I had no choice but to grab the man from behind and put him into one of my strangleholds. As I grabbed him and put my arm around his neck using all the strength I could muster, his right hand which was holding the knife came over his shoulder and missed my ear by inches. This fucker was trying to stab me in the face, so I hung onto his neck for dear life. I was shouting at Terry to knock him out, but he only gave him a couple of jabs which had no effect. In the meantime I could feel this guy's muscles straining through his jacket and for the first time in my life I was slowly losing my grip on him. This called for some drastic action on my part and I remembered a jujitsu move that I'd learnt but had never used before because of the dangers involved.

This guy had given me no choice in the matter as he was doing his best to stab me. It was either him or me. The move involved applying pressure onto a nerve point behind the ear. So I put all my strength into the move, and slowly felt the strength draining out of him.

By now some of the other doormen had arrived to help,

but it was still a dangerous situation because he was mob-handed with a group of his mates.

John the Judo teacher shouted at me to let the man go as I was killing him. There was an urgency in John's voice that made me listen, and by now we had enough doormen there to throw this fucker out. So I let go of my grip, pulled my arm back in readiness to hit him when he spun round. There was no need, as when I took my hold off him he collapsed to the ground like a sack of potatoes, unconscious.

I moved back into a corner waiting for the worst to happen. The man was out cold and as white as a sheet. Some of his mates ran over to him and I heard one of them say he wasn't breathing and dead! The only thought that went through my mind was that if it went to court then, it would have been a clear case of self-defence as he had a knife and I was unarmed and just trying to do my job.

I honestly didn't feel any remorse whether he was dead or not, as he'd tried his best to stab me in the face. What seemed like ages passed, when suddenly the guy, who was out cold on the floor jumped up as if he'd been electrocuted! I thought to myself oh no here we go again, what am I going to do now? This guy still white as a sheet looked around with glazed eyes and just slumped forward into his mates' arms. It took two of his friends to hold him up, one under each arm. They took him out of the club still semi-conscious.

After they'd taken him outside John the Judo teacher asked me what had I'd been doing and that I could have killed him. I shrugged my shoulders and replied "Just defending myself and that the other doormen should have got there quicker". I asked Terry why he hadn't hit the guy after I'd grabbed him. He said because he could see that the man couldn't move, which didn't feel like that to me at the time.

Some days later it got back to me through the grapevine that the man with the knife was an ex-professional boxer and bouncer from Battersea In south London and a small time villain who'd never been knocked out in his life. That made me even angrier knowing that an ex-boxer and bouncer was carrying a knife around with him. He might never have been knocked out before, but hadn't come across the Clayden strangle.

After that incident I won the respect of the other doormen and the thanks of Terry who could easily have been stabbed that night, the word also quickly spread amongst the regular punters about what had happened that night. They were totally mystified how a slightly overweight man wearing glasses had knocked out cold one of the hardest men in Battersea without even throwing a punch. Judo at that time was not so popular and was somewhat of an unknown martial art.

After that incident whenever the other doormen saw me take off my glasses and Eddie take out his false teeth there would be a groan as they knew that it was all about to kick off.

MECCA WOULD BOOK some of the country's top cabaret acts to perform at weekends in order to add some class to the place. Some, like Keith Harris and his puppet duck Orville didn't last more than ten minutes on the stage on a Friday night, with many others fleeing the stage in floods of tears. The crowd on a Friday would either boo them offstage or just ignore them because they wanted to get back on the dance floor so they could pull the birds. It got to a stage where the doormen would place bets before the act went on stage on how long they'd last, the one exception to this was a comedy duo from up north called Little and Large. They were the only act that lasted the full thirty minutes without being booed off stage.

They were really funny with their impersonations and after their act I'd have a drink with them at the bar, and they never stopped cracking jokes. They'd played up and down the country in some rough places but both agreed that *The Cat's Whiskers* was the roughest place that they'd ever performed in.

I was very happy when these two really talented men got their own TV show, going on to become one of the country's favourite comedy acts.

The Cat's Whiskers not only attracted a lot of the local villains from south London, but also members of the Chelsea football team, who liked to come in on a Friday night and sometimes stay until after midnight drinking, before playing the next day! Some of them even smoked cigarettes.

The Chelsea football team were one of the top clubs in the country, but it never failed to amaze me how much some of them would drink and smoke at the bar and I'd watch them on TV the next day running around the pitch.

One of their players who I didn't like was Peter Osgood who was considered a legend at Stamford Bridge. I found him to be flash and arrogant. The first time he came to the door he went to walk in without paying, just ignoring us on the door. I knew who he was, but I still stopped him and made him buy a ticket. On another occasion he made to walk in without wearing a tie. We had a strict dress code on the door which he knew about, but thought he was above that, and could just walk in and ignore it. So I wouldn't let him in until he'd borrowed a tie from one of his friends. The rest of the team were okay and used to buy me a drink and have a laugh and a joke, but not him. Even with the team of doormen we had at *The Cats Whiskers*, there were still some serious fights and there wouldn't be a single Friday night going by without at least one punch-up or more.

One such night we had a pitched battle with about thirty yobs who we'd stopped on the door from coming inside. It spilled out onto the street which wasn't good for us because it left us open to arrest if the police were called, which is exactly what happened that night. The fight had turned particularly vicious and some of the yobs were badly injured. As the police arrived mobhanded, they saw one of the Maltese brothers fighting on the pavement and they arrested him, putting him in the back of one of their vans.

The fight was so bad the police didn't have enough men with them to guard him in the van and told him to sit there until they came back. It was a real riot outside with blood and bodies flying everywhere. I'd watched the police take him to their van, then leave him as they went to try and stop the fighting, I slipped out from the front door, and went to the back of the police van and said to my man "What are you doing sitting there?" he replied because the police had told him to. I told him to get out of the van, fortunately the police hadn't had time to handcuff him. I told him to take his bowtie off and lose himself downstairs in the crowd which was nearly a 1000 strong.

Afterwards, when the police came to me on the door to ask me where he'd gone, I just shrugged my shoulders and said "No idea, I think he ran off that way", pointing down Streatham High Street.

Many years later I bumped into Maltese John in the west end. He was carrying a machine gun and wearing the full uniform of a Metropolitan Police Officer! He told me he'd joined the police and was now a marksman in one of their elite units called the Diplomatic Protection Squad. He still remembered the night I'd got him out of the police van, and couldn't thank me enough.

Another night I was standing on the door with the rest of my team, when a smallish guy looking a bit worse for wear came to walk in. I told the doorman not to let him in and he walked off. About an hour later I noticed he'd come back to the door to try and come in. I told the doorman to watch him, and as he got to the door he pulled out a plastic squeezy bottle and sprayed all of us in the face with a liquid. I immediately felt a burning sensation and ran into the toilets to splash cold water onto my face. I was thinking that it might be acid and I'd be scarred for life. Thankfully it wasn't and later turned out to be a strong mix of ammonia.

Ray the ex-RAF policeman had managed to trap the man's hand in the door, so he dropped the bottle. This little shit managed to pull his hand free from the door, then ran out to the road and stopped a taxi which drove him off into the direction of Brixton.

I ran outside into the street and managed to get the taxi's

number. I then called the police and explained what had happened. The police stopped the taxi in Brixton and arrested him, having the bottle as evidence with his fingerprints on, it appeared to be a straightforward case.

The police told us that he had a long criminal record and was a nasty piece of work. We were all thinking that was the end of it, but then found out that this man was an enforcer for a big time villain called Joey Pyle, who was an associate of the Kray twins. These were real gangsters who would shoot you as soon as look at you and we were open targets standing on the front door. Soon after starting my job at *The Cat's Whiskers* I started to wear a boxer's box, which is a plastic box inside leather padding that you wear over your pants inside your trousers to protect your balls if you got kicked or punched below the belt. Nevertheless I didn't think it would stop shotgun pellets.

After a week or so we got a message that Joey Pyle wanted a meet-up to talk about what had happened to his man. He turned up at *The Cats Whiskers* with a couple of his henchmen and I went to the bar with them and the Assistant Manager Gordon Hall. He told us that the man who'd thrown the ammonia at us did work for him but that night he'd been acting on his own. In Joey Pyle's own words he thought the man was out of order for what he'd done, and was willing to let the matter drop because he liked coming in *The Cats Whiskers*. This was a huge relief to us as we had enough problems without upsetting the local Mafia.

The man who'd thrown the ammonia pleaded guilty and got eighteen months in prison. I'm glad to say we never saw or heard from him again.

Shortly after this incident happened I got a call to see Bob

Shackle in his office, and when I walked in he asked me to take a seat and that he'd received a request from Mecca's head office to ask me if I would like to join a special security team to look after the Miss World contestants for two weeks. I replied "Yes please!!"

Boy, I didn't know what I was letting myself in for!

NINE

MISS WORLD

The Miss World competition was the most-watched beauty contest in the world, with up to forty countries taking part. It had hundreds of millions of people worldwide watching the final on television.

I had to go first to Mecca's head office for a meeting with their head of security. He was an ex-policeman who I immediately took a dislike to, he had shifty eyes and no personality. He came straight to the point and asked me if I'd be interested in being a bodyguard for two weeks amongst a team of seven security men, looking after the competitors.

I didn't have to think too long to give him my answer about looking after some of the most beautiful women in the world for two weeks.

It was November 1971, and I was 20 years old!

The Miss World event was Mecca's flag ship. They hosted the event in London and the final was to be televised live from the Royal Albert Hall. Many people think that the girls came the day before the final to take part in the competition. That's not the case, as Mecca brought all of the contestants two weeks before the final to take them to various events to generate maximum publicity before the final. Everyone likes a picture standing next to a beautiful woman!

The other six security men and I had to go back to Mecca's head office, where our duties were explained to us. As I looked at the other six men I thought to myself that one or two looked like they might be able to handle themselves in any trouble but the rest didn't impress me. They were a mix of managers from other branches and not trained bodyguards. I wished that I had my team from *The Cat's Whiskers* with me to work with, but then again what trouble could a bunch of girls cause?

We were told by Mecca that they'd booked the whole floor of a hotel in Grosvenor Square where we'd be staying for the two weeks. They told us wherever Mecca took the girls we would go with them.

They also told us in no uncertain terms that if any of us were caught having sex with the contestants we'd be sacked immediately. So, I'm thinking that this could be the most difficult part of the job - locked up for two weeks in a hotel with some of the most beautiful women in the world and no touching.

We all moved into the Britannia hotel in Grosvenor Square where Mecca had booked the whole of the second floor. I was given a nice double room to myself and told I could order anything I wanted from room service except alcohol.

I thought *This was the other side of life and I loved it*! I don't know who was more excited, the contestants or me.

Our duties we were told was to stick like glue to the contestants wherever they went and to keep the press at bay, except when there was an organised photo shoot. Mecca divided up the girls between the seven of us and I had six or seven girls allocated for me to watch. Wherever we went we travelled in a luxury coach.

The first day we were taken to the Savoy Hotel for lunch. There were a lot of celebrities there including Roger Moore who I loved to watch in the TV series *The Saint*. I couldn't believe I was sitting down in the Savoy and having lunch with all these famous people, as well as some of the most beautiful women in the world. I was in seventh heaven. I thought if there was any trouble here then Roger Moore, 'The Saint', could sort it out. I was really looking forward to eating lunch in such a famous place. We were served five courses and I can honestly say it was one of the worst lunches that I'd ever eaten! I was thinking that their chefs could benefit from my grandmother who was a great cook. When I got back to the hotel, I went straight to my room and ordered some sandwiches from room service, as I was starving.

That morning I'd left my room in a rush and had left some clothes on a chair, but when I returned they were gone. This is a good start, I thought, someone's nicked my clothes. I began looking around the room and opened the wardrobe and there were the clothes I'd left on the chair.

They'd been cleaned and pressed. I'd never stayed in a four star hotel before let alone a five star. I phoned my mum and told her what had happened, and she asked me if she could come round with some of her dirty clothes to be cleaned. I told her I didn't think Mecca would appreciate that, knowing what tight bastards they were. She then asked me how beautiful were the girls taking part in the competition. I told her "Honestly mum I've seen more beautiful women walking down Whitechapel market."

The next day, Mecca took us in two coaches to the officer's mess of the Household Cavalry in Horse Guard's Parade for sherry. The room was full of officers wearing their smartest dress uniforms. They'd put out an impressive display of the regimental silver. I found it amusing how the officers swarmed around the girls like bees around honey. I noticed standing on the other side of the room, a tall distinguished-looking gentleman who I immediately recognised as Lord Mountbatten. He was moving around the room speaking to different people and eventually came over to me to ask me what did I do? As I was wearing a suit he didn't realise I was just a bodyguard. I told him what an honour it was to meet him, especially as my father had served during the Second World War in the 14th army in Burma.

Mountbatten had been their commander-in-chief. When I told him about this he shook my hand and with a distant look in his eye replied to me "They were a brave bunch of men."

It had been a very hard war against the Japanese in the jungles of Burma. He became known as Lord Mountbatten of Burma. When I told my father the next day about my meeting he couldn't believe that I'd spoken to his old commander-and-chief.

I was shocked and saddened some years later on the 27th of August 1979 when the news broke that the evil bastards from the IRA had murdered this great man by placing a bomb on board his fishing boat, killing Lord Mountbatten, his two grandsons, Nicholas (14) and Paul (15), as well as his eldest daughter and her husband. That's what the IRA did in those days to innocent people.

In the evening we were taken to the London Palladium to see a show. The top of the bill was Val Doonican, who nearly sent me to sleep with his music and singing. He was a bit different to Led Zeppelin.

The last act to come on stage was a camp comedian, who I'd never heard of before. I couldn't stop laughing at his jokes and was so impressed I called my mum to tell her about him the next day I told her I think this guy is going to become a big star. She asked me what his name was. I told her Larry Grayson.

Wherever we went with the Miss World girls it was a big success and created a great deal of publicity. By now I was getting to know all of the contestants and really liked them except for one or two, who were real prima donnas.

The next big event Mecca organised for us was to have lunch inside the House of Commons with some selected MPs from a cross section of all of the political parties. Now I thought at last I'm going to have a dinner to remember - I wasn't wrong!

We arrived at the House of Commons and they gave us a short tour around the building, which was particularly interesting for me having studied the British Constitution at school. We were then shown into a private dining room, which had been set up for the lunch.

I sat in between Miss New Zealand and Miss America, who I particularly liked. Sitting opposite us was one of the many MPs, who were sitting around a very long dining table. There was some nice fine wines on the table, but the bodyguards weren't allowed any alcohol, which I agreed with. I thought at least I'm going to get a nice lunch.

The Member of Parliament sitting opposite us, like most of his colleagues, was guzzling the drink like there was no tomorrow and getting a bit worse for wear. Many of them were flirting outrageously with the girls which was beginning to annoy me as the girls were just trying to be polite. if these are the people who are supposed to be running our country, then God help us!

Then this prat of an MP sitting opposite us says to me in a very sarcastic tone "Oh that's a nice shirt you're wearing" taking the piss out of me trying to impress the two girls I'm sitting with. So I replied "Actually it's not my shirt" that shocked him and he asked me "Well, whose is it?" and I said "It's my father's, but it's my turn to wear it today" and with that the two girls sitting either side of me burst out laughing and almost choked on their food, while this sad sod goes bright red and shuts up for the rest of the meal.

Once again I was to be very disappointed by how terrible the food was. I'd obviously been spoilt by my gran's great cooking. At the end of the meal the waiters entered the room carrying large silver dishes with bottles of brandy and Cuban cigars. Now if there's something I enjoy it's a good cigar and a glass of brandy, like my namesake 'Winnie'. I thought this would make up for the disappointing food they'd served us. I couldn't believe it when the waiters went around the table offering the cigars and brandy only to MPs and deliberately missed all the bodyguards out. I wouldn't be booking a table to come back here and that I could get better grub at Pellicci's café on Bethnal Green Road!

The next day the head of security called me to his office and told me to take Miss Switzerland by taxi to the Swiss Centre in Leicester Square for a VIP visit and photoshoot. Miss Switzerland was a very good looking woman with a great body so I was chuffed at being her personal bodyguard for a couple of hours. Her English wasn't that great and the fact that we were travelling alone together and not in a big coach, she thought I was someone important. Inside the taxi she started touching my leg and with that she started thanking me for all the nice things Mecca were doing for her, she then leaned across the seat and gave me a kiss full on the mouth. Most men would think they were in heaven, except that she had terribly bad breath!

When we arrived at the Swiss Centre we were both treated like royalty and they really put out the red carpet giving us lots of gifts and souvenirs.

Many of the girls were very naïve and didn't speak much English, some hadn't even travelled outside of their own countries. It did make me wonder what some of them had done to get into the competition?

United Kingdom
Marilyn Ward

Marilyn is a 22 years old blonde from Hants, where she can ... Her statistics are 34-24-36 and she is 5'7" tall. Marilyn is very sporty and has played hockey for Hampshire. She loves riding during her spare time and cooking her best recipe is ...

Aruba
Maria Bruin

Maria is a Bank Clerk and during her spare time she enjoys bowling, basket ball, swimming and dancing. She would like to see Madame Tussauds and some of London's musicals. She has five sisters and four brothers. Her statistics are 35-25-36 and she is 5'5" tall.

One of the girls I got on really well with was Miss U.K., Marilyn Ward, who unlike some of the other contestants was a very clever girl. She was two years older than me and we shared a love of Tommy Cooper. She used to sit next to me on the coach when we were travelling to events and loved my impersonations of that great comedian. On one occasion when we were going to a VIP event in London, she asked me if the dress she was wearing wasn't too daring. It was a long white evening dress which had a slit from under her arm going down to her ankle. It clearly revealed that she was not wearing any underwear, which was very bold at that time. I told her she looked great in it and she was very happy. The next day a photo of her wearing the dress appeared on the front pages of all of the tabloid press, and it really did cause quite a stir.

At the time there was a lot of controversy over South Africa's apartheid rules. So Mecca, not wanting to be seen supporting that country's regime, came up with the bright idea of having a white Miss South Africa and a black Miss South Africa.

The two girls got on surprisingly well and there were no problems between the two of them. All the tabloid press wanted to make a story of this and tried their best to get a photo of the two girls together which Mecca didn't want under any circumstances. So I was given the job of keeping them apart, but they couldn't understand Mecca's decision and nor could I. I felt sorry for them when every time we went outside to an event they couldn't even talk to each other in public.

One evening Mecca took all of the contestants to the *Sportsman Club* in Tottenham Court Road which Mecca owned. The word had got out that the Miss World contestants were going to be there and the place was packed when we arrived. There were far too many people inside for just seven bodyguards to control, and we were losing sight of some of the girls.

I was looking around the crowd when I noticed Miss South Africa, a tall blond, being hustled by two men. She gave me the eye that she wasn't comfortable so I pushed my way through the crowd and said "Hi Monica, we have to go now." These two guys were having none of it and blocked our exit. They told me to get lost and that this sexy bird was going with them and who was I? I told them that I was her bodyguard and gave them a hard stare. They replied, "What can you do? There's two of us." And true enough they were big fuckers but I stood my ground and fronted them out. I told them if they didn't move they'd get seriously hurt, thrown out and I'd make sure they would lose their membership to the club which was owned by Mecca. They could see I meant every word, they thought about it for a minute, then backed down and walked away. Monica gave me a big kiss on the cheek and told me from now on she'd call me her Tarzan!

Gibraltar
Lisette Chipolina

19 years old. Lisette's ambition is to succeed in life. She loves playing tennis and whilst on this, her third visit to London, she would like to see some of our latest fashions. Her measurements are 35.24.36, she is 5' 4" tall and works as a Bank Clerk. Lisette can speak English, Spanish and French.

South Africa
Monica Fairall

Monica is a student and amongst her many interests she enjoys music, yoga and flying. Her ambition is to become a pilot. She speaks English, Afrikaans and Zulu. Her measurements are 35.24.36 and she is 5' 9" tall. During her stay in London she hopes to see as much as she can.

By now we were about half way through the contest and I was having the time of my life. On one of the rare nights Mecca hadn't booked us all to go to an event we spent a very enjoyable evening in the hotel. We weren't allowed any alcohol but that didn't stop us from dancing and watching T.V. I had a dance with Miss Brazil, Lucia Tavares Petterie; she wasn't the most prettiest of girls and a bit shy. She told me that if she won the competition she wanted to become a doctor and go back to Brazil to help the poor. I really liked her and wished her good luck. I had a real laugh watching TV and dancing with Miss USA, a really nice girl from Texas called Brucene Smith.

United States of America
Brucene Smith

Brucene hopes to become a teacher of elementary education. She is a student at the University of Texas. Her statistics are 35 25 36 and she is 5' 7" tall. Amongst her interests are swimming, sailing, drawing and reading.

Yugoslavia
Zlata Petkovic

17 years old Zlata is still a student. She speaks English and French besides her native Yugoslav. Her favourite hobby is acting and she has starred in a film that was shown at the Cannes Film Festival. Zlata has not been to London before and she would like to see as much as she can.

So after a really enjoyable evening I went to my room to sleep. At about 1am I heard a soft knocking on my door. I jumped out of bed wondering who was in trouble and I opened the door to one of the contestants from the Caribbean standing there in her bathrobe and I asked her what was wrong? She smiled at me, and let her bath robe fall open to reveal that she was completely naked underneath. She then said to me "I can't sleep, can you help me?" so I opened the door wider and said to her "You'd better come inside."

I knew I was risking everything if I got caught, but in those days there was no CCTV in the hotels. I just couldn't resist this beautiful woman asking me for sex.

We spent all night making love and she crept back to her room, which fortunately was opposite mine at about 5am.

Later that morning I went for breakfast and felt like I was walking on air. I had a big smile on my face and some of the other security men asked me what I was smirking about? I just replied "Nothing". I'd just sat down for breakfast when I got a call to go and see the head of security. I walked into his office and with a very serious look on his face he told me to take a seat. He asked me if I'd read the morning newspapers, I said "No not yet" he then told me that Mecca had a serious problem. I started to panic thinking about what had just happened that night. He said to me "Leslie this is very, very serious - it's on all the front pages of the press". I was doing my best to look calm, but inside my stomach was doing somersaults, I was thinking how on earth could the press have found out about what I'd done the night before? I knew that they were always on the prowl looking for a story, but how had they acted so quickly? Had the girl sold her story? I was trying not to look guilty.

I couldn't bear the suspense any longer and asked him, "What's on the front pages?" He then told me that the IRA had threatened to kidnap Miss Ireland, June Glover, if she didn't leave the competition, the reason being that she was a Protestant. A wave of relief flooded through me that it wasn't me on the front page telling the story about what I'd done with one of the contestants.

Then the thought struck me, why is he telling me all of this? So I replied "Yes this is serious." He then tells me that

Mecca wanted me to look after Miss Ireland for the next few days.

I knew that the IRA didn't make idle threats and this wasn't the usual bunch of gangsters and hard nuts that I had to deal with in *The Cat's Whiskers*.

Miss Ireland had told Mecca she wouldn't leave the competition because of the threat, and I respected her courage considering who had made the threat. I also knew that she wouldn't stand a chance if any of the other six security men took the job. Which they probably wouldn't have anyway because of the danger involved.

So I said to the head of security "Okay, I'll take the job on two conditions: first I want treble wages." I knew how tight Mecca was and was surprised when without any hesitation he said "Okay". (Maybe he thought I wouldn't live long enough to collect them?). He then asked me what the second condition was. I replied "I want a gun". He nearly fell out of his chair and repeated "A gun, why do you want a gun?" I replied "So if they try anything I can shoot the bastards with pleasure". He answered "You're mad, I can't get you a gun!" I replied "I must be mad to take the job, you don't think Judo is going to stop machinegun bullets do you?" He went onto explain "I can't get you a gun, even the police don't carry guns." Which was true at that time. I replied "But you're Mecca, you can do anything you want." He shook his head again and said "No, no you can't have a gun."

So I took the job of looking after Miss Ireland who'd been threatened by the IRA, and I was totally unarmed. He then told me that over the next few days wherever the contestants travelled to in the coach I was to follow with Miss Ireland in a black cab. I thought great, so if they try one of their tricks to blow us up, only we get killed and no one else!

The IRA threat that morning had been the headline in most of the newspapers in the country. The next morning there was a follow-up column on the front page of many newspapers saying in response to the IRA threat to kidnap Miss Ireland, Mecca had hired a special security team to protect her!

I had to laugh when I read that thinking I know I'm big but I had never been described before as a team. Once again Mecca's powerful publicity machine had done its work.

For the next few days I was running on pure adrenaline waiting for something to happen and wondering how on earth I was going to stop any attack on my own with no bloody gun! By the end of three days much to my surprise and relief nothing had happened. I had lost half a stone by the end of it through nervous energy, worrying about the threat and totally losing my appetite. To this day I still don't know why the IRA never carried out their threat, it just wasn't like them, but nonetheless I was very glad that I hadn't had to face the bastards. It was to be some years later until they did catch up with me.

June Glover: Miss Ireland

By now the two weeks were coming to an end and the Grand Final was to take place in The Royal Albert Hall and would be televised around the world to a massive global audience. The day started early at the venue for rehearsals. Eric Morley, the managing director of Mecca, was firmly in charge as he'd done this many times in the past. He was on top form, shouting and swearing at everyone when the tiniest thing went wrong. The staff there were genuinely scared of him. He knew me from the *Lyceum* and gave me a nod in recognition. He even asked me if I could move his car which was in the way of some delivery lorries and gave me the keys to a brand new Jensen interceptor!

There was a huge buzz of excitement as the contest drew nearer. I then got called to go and see Mecca's head of security. I thought to myself here we go again, what now? He took me down underneath the Albert Hall where, to my astonishment I saw miles of winding corridors and tunnels. It was a real catacomb. He then told me that Mecca had received a bomb threat from women's lib. This was the organisation that had infiltrated the audience the year before and had flower bombed the host Bob Hope on stage. They considered the Miss World contest to be degrading for women, and I knew that some of them were dangerous fanatics capable of anything. They'd telephoned Mecca two hours before the contest was due to start, saying that they'd planted a bomb underneath the Albert Hall and knowing full well that it didn't give enough time to search everywhere.

The head of security asked me what I'd do in such a situation. He was an ex-police sergeant, and I'm thinking why's he asking me? I told him the obvious thing to do was to call the police who could send extra men and sniffer dogs trained to look for bombs. He replied that if he did that then there was a good chance that the police would postpone the event and I said that's what should happen, as we didn't have enough time to conduct a proper search. He said Mecca would never agree to that because of all the various satellite links that had been booked for all the different TV companies around the world and that they'd lose a fortune. I told him people's lives are more important than money.

Mecca chose to ignore the threat and the contest went ahead as planned. Fortunately there was no bomb, but Mecca wasn't to know that and in my opinion had taken a risky decision based on profit.

The contest was a huge success and one of the girls I'd danced with, Lucia from Brazil, won the contest, which I was happy about because she was really one of the nicest girls in the competition and I hope she achieved her dream of becoming a doctor, which she later did in Brazil.

Lucia Tavares Petterle: Miss World 1971

One of the judges was Peter Wyngarde, who was a big TV star at the time and played Jason King in a TV series called *Department S*. he played a James Bond-type character who knew all about martial arts. When I was in the lift with him on my way out of the Albert Hall we heard a very loud demonstration outside from Women's Lib.

Peter Wyngarde was visibly scared hearing the commotion going on outside and said to me in a very effeminate voice "I hope we're going to be all right!" I smiled and told him not to worry as that's why I was there, to protect him.

In the evening we all went to the *Lyceum* for a gala dinner and dance. This time we were allowed to drink and dance with the contestants. It felt strange for me dancing and enjoying myself after working there. There were lots of celebrities present. Before the event the head of security had asked me if I knew any men I could trust to beef up the numbers of bouncers. So I'd told him to get in touch with my Judo club the LJS.

In the evening it was nice to see some of the black belts from my Judo club who I regularly practised with. I also told him about Dick who'd joined the police force the year before, and got him a job for the evening. He loved chatting up Miss Israel, Myriam Ben-David, who was a gorgeous woman who'd served as an officer in the Israeli army.

Dick told her we'd fought in the Six Day War in Israel and even got me to show her a big scar on my chest, which I'd got from an operation when I was a baby. He told her that I'd been wounded, to try and impress her and get her into bed. It was all bollocks of course, but she believed every word.

Myriam Ben-David: Miss Israel

Now THAT THE contest was over many of the girls paired off with different men at the end of the evening, taking them back to their rooms at the hotel. By this time Mecca didn't care what happened as the contest was over, and after being virtually locked up for two weeks many of the contestants wanted to have some fun before returning home to their countries and I couldn't blame them.

The next morning Mecca held a big press conference for the winner and afterwards at the reception I was introduced to the Mexican Ambassador to London by his daughter who I'd got to know very well. She told him that I'd been responsible for protecting her. He insisted that I visit his country as his guest in gratitude for looking after his daughter.

I regret that I never took him up on his offer. The next day instead of being in sunny Mexico I was back in cold rainy Streatham at *The Cat's Whiskers*.

TEN

SECURITY EXPRESS

Coming back to *The Cat's Whiskers* after all of the hype and glamour of Miss World was a real anti-climax.

The fights on a Friday night were becoming more vicious and even in the weeknights I wouldn't work without wearing my boxer's box for extra protection. It proved invaluable, when one night in a fight someone kicked me hard in the bollocks it brought tears to my eyes, but the box stopped me from collapsing and the look on the guy's face when I smiled at him was pure magic.

On another evening a fight broke out on the dance floor while I was upstairs on the balcony. I ran down to stop it and got punched hard in the face. The punch felled me like a tree and while I was on the floor I actually saw stars flash in front of my eyes. Now I know why they show them in cartoons when one of the characters get knocked out. For what seemed like ages, but what was perhaps no more than a minute, I lay there half-expecting someone to put the boot in. I didn't wait for that, and instead jumped up to see the guy who punched me, fighting with a doorman. I ran over and punched him hard in the face, his nose burst like a ripe tomato and sprayed blood over everyone close to him. We then managed to throw him and his mates out the front door. His shirt was covered in blood. He shouted at me that he'd be back with a shotgun to shoot me. I told him he'd better make sure that he shot straight, because otherwise I'd kill him.

We were used to being threatened on the door, and if we took every threat seriously, we wouldn't be able to do the job.

About two weeks later, the guy I'd punched came up to the door to talk to me. The other doormen recognised him, and were waiting for him to start trouble. He said to me that he shouldn't have got involved in the fight and he was sorry, he told me that he liked coming in and didn't want to be barred. There was something about him that I believed. He then said I had broken his nose in three places, and that he'd already had a broken nose. I told him that his punch had fractured a bone in my face and that I had to go to hospital to get it checked out after the fight, so I made that even.

He then told me that his wife and his friends were waiting outside and wondered if they could all come in. I told him yes, as long as they all behaved themselves. The four of them went to the Box Office to pay, and I said that they could go inside without paying, as my guests. This surprised some of the other doormen, but they knew better than to question me. I told the other doormen that if he was man enough to apologise he deserved a second chance.

The man became a regular and sometimes I'd let him and his mates in without paying. It paid dividends one night, when a very bad fight broke out downstairs in one of the bars. There were at least a gang of thirty-odd men fighting with the doormen, and it looked like they'd get the better of us, when the guy, who I'd now made friends with and about six of his mates, waded in on our side and tipped the balance in our favour. Together we gave the other gang a good hiding.

After a few weeks I noticed that this guy hadn't been coming in, which was strange as he liked the place so much. So I asked around amongst some of the other villains I knew, and they told me that this guy and his mates had been caught in Brighton holding up a jeweller's shop with shotguns and had been sentenced to twelve years for armed robbery. It sent a shiver down my spine thinking back to the night he'd threatened to come back and shoot me. This was a dangerous criminal who could have easily carried out his threat.

THE FIGHTING on a Friday night had got worse, with little Reggie Pullen an ex-flyweight ABA boxing champion, getting half of his ear bitten off, and another one of our doormen who had a 3rd Dan black belt in Judo getting badly beaten up, and never returning to work. I started to lose some of my best men, because Mecca were just not paying enough for the risks we were taking. The other perk of the job was that we were given some complimentary tickets which gave free entrance to family and friends. Some of the doormen were selling the tickets to make up their wages, which I knew about and turned a blind eye to. One of the punters who knew about this and had been barred for fighting, grassed us up to Mecca, who held a big investigation and came down on a Friday night with some other doormen, from one of their other dance halls, to question us all, including Bob Shackle, the General Manager.

It was completely over the top for Mecca to behave in such a way in response to a few comps being sold. The people being let in free were still spending money at the bar and in the restaurant. When I was at the Hammersmith Palais I had to deliver hundreds of complimentary tickets to local companies in the area, to get people in!

By now I'd had enough, and resigned in disgust. All of the doormen, once they knew of my action, also took off their bow ties and quit as well. The Assistant Manager, who I'd got on well with, also quit, going on to open a secondhand car site in Rotherhithe with a local villain. Bob Shackle transferred to Tiffany's in Shaftesbury Avenue.

A week later Mecca called me to their head office and offered me the position of Assistant Manager at *The Empire*, Leicester Square; but I'd seen enough of this company which, in my opinion, just didn't know how to look after or reward their staff, so I told them to stick their offer.

ONE OF THE doormen at *The Cats Whiskers*, Ray Curzon, who was an ex-RAF policeman, had told me of a company called Security Express, who he'd worked for in the past. He told me that they were always looking for men, because of the high risk of getting shot. They used to deliver and pick up cash from banks and local businesses including supermarkets. He said the pay was good and that I should give them a try. So I went along to their headquarters in Curtain Road, East London, and applied for a job as a guard.

Because of my size and experience in Judo and the Specials, they gave me a job there and then. Most of the time, I was sitting in the back of an armoured van, with bulletproof glass, either reading a book, or sleeping. When the van pulled up outside a bank, I'd look through a small window on the side of the van, and wait for the guys to come out, with the bags of cash. I would then open a trapdoor at the back of the van, so they could throw the bag in. I would then transfer the bag into a locked safe inside the van. So if anyone tried to rob us, they not only had to break into the armour-plated van, but also into the locked safe inside. So what would normally happen in a robbery, the villains would attack the guards as they came out of the bank while they were making their way to the van. They'd then usually shoot the guard in the legs if he refused to hand over the money.

I felt quite safe sitting in the back, and the pay was better than I'd been getting at Mecca. All was going quite well, until some bright spark in the office looked at my CV and decided I was wasted sitting in the back of the van and would serve them better on the Bank of England run.

This involved me driving a ten-ton armoured lorry on HGV plates from the vault at Security Express, delivering cash into The Bank of England. The lorry carried one million pounds in cash, which was divided into two steel cages. At that time, this was the maximum amount of cash that any insurance company would cover. It was less than a ten minute drive from Curtain Road to the Bank of England, but because of the cash involved, we had to radio a coded message to the City of London Police three times during the ten minutes. If we missed even one of the calls to the police, they had in place a plan to close down the City of London by road blocks.

When I drove the lorry to the entrance of the Bank of England there was only inches to spare on either side of the arch that I had to drive through. Once inside the courtyard, there was no space to turn the lorry around, so you had to drive onto a large metal plate, which then spun the lorry around, so the back was facing the door where the two steel cages with the cash in were taken into the bank to be deposited in the vault.

In the beginning it was quite exciting work and I used to fantasise about how it would be possible to carry out a successful robbery. I'd never seen so much money before, only in films. It's quite different when you're standing next to one million pounds.

After a while I soon got bored with the monotony of it, and asked if I could be transferred back to the vans. The money was good, and even with the overtime and working Saturdays I was still working fewer hours than when I was with Mecca. But truth be told, I was missing the clubs, so I started to go to the *Astoria* in Charing Cross Road. It was a large club on two floors, and I soon became friendly with one of the doormen, Colin Jarvis, who lived in Peckham.

He told me his late father was a Romany Gypsy and had been a horse trader. Colin was a real character and like me loved a laugh and a joke.

One night when I was drinking in the *Astoria* I noticed what looked like some trouble on the balcony upstairs. There were about a dozen men arguing with the bouncers, one of which was my mate Colin. There were only three doormen, who were hopelessly outnumbered. It looked ready to kick off and there was one guy in particular who was mouthing off. So I stood next to him, I was smoking a cigar, and I started to blow clouds of smoke into his face. He began coughing and looked round at me, and asked who I was. I smiled at him and replied, "I'm with them", pointing to the other bouncers. Experience had taught me that if you stand up to a bully, they'll often back down. With that, to my amazement, the group he was with backed down and left the club. Colin told me he'd never seen anything like it before and it had reminded him of a standoff between two gun slingers. After that incident I never had to pay to go in and used to get quite a few free drinks.

As I got to know Colin better, he asked if he could come with me to Judo practise, at my club, the London Judo Society, or LJS, as it was known at the time, in Vauxhall. I said "Sure" - by now I was a brown belt and could beat most of the Black Belts there. I was simply too strong for them, and could move surprisingly fast for a big man.

The club was run by ex-policeman, George Chew and Eric Dominie, who was an ex civil servant; both real gentlemen and it was a pleasure to train there. I would try and go at least three times a week.

When I first joined and walked into the dojo, I saw three flags hanging up. One was a Japanese flag, one the Union Jack, but the other I didn't recognise. When I asked what country this third flag had come from, I was told Jordan. I asked what did Jordan have to do with Judo? They both laughed and told me that King Hussain of Jordan was their honorary president and whenever he was in London he'd come to the club to practise as he was a 3rd Dan black belt.

Dick used to come and train occasionally and the club was considered to be the second best in London. The British Olympic Judo team often practised there as well. Colin tried to take Judo up, but never really mastered it and remained a dirty street fighter. He was a real scrapper.

I was earning good money with Security Express, and still living at home with my parents in Lewisham. I didn't have any overheads to worry about, so when the opportunity arose to go to Moscow for a short trip, I jumped at it. I asked my Mum if she wanted to go and she said she would love to.

ELEVEN

MOSCOW

My Dad didn't like flying and had the stalls to run so he wasn't interested in coming with us.

At that time in 1972, Russia was in the middle of the Cold War with the West, and because I was still in the specials I had to put a written request to special branch before I went. I then had to be interviewed by a senior officer, who asked me why I wanted to go to Moscow? As if I was a spy or something. I told him that I liked travelling and wanted to see what it was like. He looked at me as if I was some kind of traitor and shook his head. I didn't care and was determined to go.

I finally got permission from the police, and me and my Mum flew to Moscow. It was in February, and Moscow was just as I'd imagined it, covered in snow and freezing cold. We stayed in the Intourist Hotel near Red Square, and the food was bloody awful! On every floor, there was an old lady sitting in a chair, who would be normally knitting, and every time we left the room, or arrived back to the room, she would put her knitting down and write the time, in a little notepad.

Because of my experience on the doors, in the clubs and in the Special Police, I knew that every time we left the hotel we were being followed by plain-clothed security men. There were very few tourists in those days. The first time we went to their Metro I was gobsmacked. The platforms were carpeted, there were crystal chandeliers hanging from the roof, and icons on the walls, it was immaculately clean. A far cry from what I was used to on the dirty London Underground. We visited the Moscow State Circus, which was truly amazing.

One morning I left the hotel for a walk across Red Square with my usual shadow in tow. I saw the back of a long queue of people which snaked around the corner of a large building. The queue of people were standing in the snow, and the temperature was well below zero. I was intrigued to see what they were queuing for. I'm thinking, is it bread? Or maybe fur hats like the Russians liked wearing? So I walked on the outside of the queue to the front, and couldn't believe what I saw. There was a guy with a small barrow selling Ice-cream!

They were queuing up in the freezing cold, standing in the snow to buy bloody ice-cream!

The trip to Moscow was about nine months after we'd visited New York. There couldn't have been such a greater contrast between two countries and such a difference in cultures. Every time I walked across Red Square, small kids would come up to me, and ask if I had any ball point pens, and would offer in exchange small enamel red stars. This really was a case of the have and have nots and the other side of life.

The climax of the trip was to visit the Bolshoi Ballet performing Swan Lake. My mum loved the ballet, opera and ice-skating. So she was really looking forward to seeing the performance. On the night of the performance I put on my best evening suit, which I'd bought from the Pierre Cardin shop in Charing Cross Road for the Miss World contest. My mum wore a lovely evening dress; she used to make all her own clothes, being a top machinist for Mr Grunberg.

We set off to the Tchaikovsky Hall, to watch the performance. On our arrival, the place was packed, and there were at least three thousand people there. I went to the bar to get a drink, before the performance started, and while I waited to be served, I had the feeling everyone was staring at me. I looked down at my evening trousers to check if I'd left my flies undone, but no they were fine. Then I realised that all the men at the bar and in the foyer, were wearing Military uniforms from the Army, Navy and Air Force, and I was the only man there wearing an evening suit and smoking a large cigar which I had bought in New York. I felt like James Bond, in *From Russia with Love*!

We went inside, and my Mum had tears in her eyes as she watched the performance. It was an experience we both never forgot.

TWELVE

CRACKERS

When I returned to London, I went to see Colin at the *Astoria* to tell him about my adventures in Moscow. He told me about a disco club in Wardour Street called *Crackers* who were looking for doormen and that I should give it a try.

Crackers was a disco in a basement, with a pub next door. The front door was at street level, with one small box office and a flight of stairs leading downstairs into the club. There were two bars inside, a small stage and a small dance floor. Its capacity was 600 people, a far cry from some of Mecca's ballrooms.

The place was owned by Bob Wheatley who also owned the *Circus Tavern* in Southend and some other pubs. He was considered a bit of a hard nut from the East End.

As I was missing the club scene, and life was pretty boring at Security Express, I decided to give it a try. So one evening I went along, and standing on the door was a man called Mark. He wasn't big for a doorman, but had a broken nose, and looked like he could handle himself in a fight. I told him where I'd worked, and he said, "Okay, we'll give you a try".

So, I started working weekends, when the club stayed open till 3am on Fridays and Saturdays. The extra money was good and, together with my wages from Security Express, gave me enough cash to buy a nice car. I found a right-hand drive 1965 convertible Mustang with a 5.5 litre engine. It needed a re-spray and a new roof, which Ray, my old mate from *The Cats Whiskers*, sorted out for me, as he was a good mechanic and body sprayer. It was white with a black stripe, and black electric hood.

I felt like the King of Saudi Arabia when I drove it through the West End with the top down on nice evenings. Strangers would often stop me, and ask if it was for sale or if they could take a picture of it. I'll never forget one day, when I was driving it to work at Security Express. As I was about to drive into the yard, the MD of Security Express was driving out in his Jag and nearly crashed it looking at me.

I heard later he started to ask questions, on how could I afford such a car on a guard's wages. He was told that I worked part-time in a West End club and was living with my parents. The few times I saw him after, I could see the look of jealousy on his face.

The arrangement of working weekends at *Crackers*, and the odd night in the week, suited me. I could go to work at Security Express the next day, and have a kip in the back of the van!

Crackers was relatively easy to work in after *The Cats Whiskers*. There wasn't too much trouble, mainly drunks trying to get in after the pubs closed. I got to know Mark who was a strange character and didn't talk much. Over the following weeks, he told me that he had been an enforcer for a protection racket up north, and had spent five years in prison for arson. Most of which he spent in solitary confinement. He told me that he'd converted to judaism in prison because the food was better!

One night, we were both standing on the door, there were just the two of us working, as it was a quiet mid-week night. A couple with a very big, very tall man, came to the door. We could see that the tall guy had been drinking, so we politely refused him entry. The tall guy, who must have been at least six foot six, was having none of it, so he started swearing at us and offering us out to fight. I could see Mark was looking a bit wary of him, and couldn't blame him, as this guy looked real trouble.

I thought to myself, this calls for some drastic action, so without any warning, I grabbed the lapel of this prick's jacket, pulled him hard towards me, and smacked him half a dozen quick punches in the face. Both to me and Mark's astonishment, the guy ran off down the road. The couple who were with him, said to us afterwards that they were glad I'd punched him as they thought he was a big bully. This reconfirmed my philosophy that attack is the best form of defence, especially against bullies.

Picture of me in my Security Express Uniform next to my 1965 convertible right hand drive Ford Mustang.

THIRTEEN

SOUTHWARK POLICE

I HAD RELUCTANTLY TRANSFERRED from Bow Street Police Station to Southwark Police station on the Borough Road, off The Elephant And Castle.

I chose Southwark, because I'd got to know two specials from some of the ceremonies I'd attended. One was Cliff, an ex-guards officer, who was about ten years older than me, the other was John who looked like Brian London the professional boxer, but who in fact couldn't punch his way out of a paper bag!

I'd met these two when I'd attended the Queen's Birthday parade. I'll never forget the event. Just before the Queen came riding down on a horse along the Mall, we were all lined up on either side to keep the crowds back. There were guardsmen in ceremonial uniform, regular policemen and women, and a mixture of specials.

I was standing in line with a mixture of different men, when just before the Queen started riding down, there was a ripple of whispering coming down the line on my side.

Each policeman, or soldier, told the person next to them to look to their left. I was wondering what the problem was when the soldier I was standing next to said out of the corner of his mouth "Look at that woman, standing in front of the crowd who's wearing jeans". So I looked down the line, and there was an attractive woman wearing tight jeans, and the zip of her jeans had come undone revealing a crop of bushy pubic hair, which wasn't the same colour as her bright blonde hair! We were all trying our best not to burst out laughing, as the queen rode past the woman in the crowd, waving and smiling. I still don't know if the Queen was just being polite, or had like us, spotted the woman with her flies undone and was smiling to herself. For sure, Her Majesty had a perfect view, and would have got an eyeful!

After she'd ridden past, a police sergeant went over to the lady in question and discreetly told her about her zip being undone. I've never seen a woman look so shocked. She quickly did her zip up after going bright red, and then promptly disappeared into the crowd.

The specials at Southwark consisted of me, Cliff, John and a sergeant called Frank, who was a real embarrassment. The station covered London Bridge Station, Borough Market, The Elephant & Castle, and surrounding streets. This was no Bow Street, and the regular police never mixed with us, always keeping their distance. It didn't worry me when I was on duty, I just did my job.

I hadn't been there long, and was on patrol one night with John, when we were walking down the underpass below the big roundabout at the Elephant & Castle, when I saw a couple walking towards us who were smoking. I immediately recognised the distinct smell of pot as they passed us. I stopped them, and told them to put their cigarettes out. I then arrested them on suspicion of smoking pot.

After working at the *Lyceum*, I could spot a cannabis cigarette a mile off and recognised the distinctive smell they give off.

We took them to the station to be charged, and there was one really cocky policeman who started questioning me on how did I know it was pot. He suggested that I knew because I smoked it, and was really winding me up. I told him that I knew because I'd worked at the *Lyceum* for over two years. Then I had a go at him and said "Maybe you sold it to them?!"

The station sergeant who was a fair man, could see that this was getting out of hand and stepped in and said that the cigarettes would be sent off to the lab to be tested. If it came back positive then the arrest would stand. I knew they'd come back positive, because of how many I'd seen in the *Lyceum*. The results came back confirming that the cigarettes contained cannabis, and the couple were fined in court a few days later. The problem was that the police in Southwick were not used to specials making arrests for drugs, and had a low opinion of us.

The following week I was walking down the stairs with John in the station, and walking up was the Chief Superintendent. He stopped us on the stairs and asked if we were the two specials who'd arrested the people for smoking pot. I thought here we go again, another bollocking, even though I knew it was a good arrest. We replied "Yes Sir", and he then said "Well done lads that was a good arrest!"

"At last", I thought, someone here appreciates us.

On another occasion, I was out on patrol with John and a call come over our radios of a domestic disturbance, in a particular block of flats. The station told us the address and that it was on the third floor. Domestics, as they were known, could be tricky to handle when husband and wife got into an argument, often when they were drunk, and you'd go along to try and sort it out and often they'd both turn on the officers.

John answered immediately on his personal radio that we'd both attend this domestic. When we arrived at the address, I began quickly climbing the stairs to the third floor. John was hanging onto the bannisters as if his life depended on it, and was moving really slowly up the stairs, which I thought was a bit odd. I told him to hurry up, but he was painfully slow getting up to the third floor. When we finally reached it, I looked behind me to see where John was, and to my astonishment I saw him pressed up against a wall, hands outstretched like Christ. He was slowly inching his way along the wall. By now, I could hear the row going on inside the flat and couldn't wait any longer for John to catch up. I banged on the door, and sure enough a man and woman, both drunk, opened it.

I could see that no one was injured, and told them that if they didn't shut up I'd come back and arrest them and they'd be spending the night in a cell. That seemed to do the trick and they stopped rowing.

John was still pressed against the wall, with a look of terror on his face. I asked him what was wrong, and he told me that he had a real fear of heights. I said, "But we're only on the third bloody floor?!" He said that ever since he'd been a kid, he couldn't stand heights, so I asked him why the hell had he answered the call? When they told us it was on the third floor, especially in the dodgy place it was, where they could have easily opened the door with a knife. What a prat! After that incident, I tried whenever possible to go out on my own or with Cliff. I made quite a few arrests for drunk and disorderly, which got me a begrudging respect from the regulars at the station.

On another occasion I took a call to a disturbance at the Wimpy bar at the Elephant & Castle. As I was running down the stairs to the outside of the shop, I could see a guy threatening the staff inside.

As I walked in the guy, who had his back to me, was holding a broken plate in his hand and threatening the staff. I crept up behind him and grabbed his wrist in an aikido hold and twisted his arm far enough up his back, for him to drop the plate. I then put him in a strangle choke hold, until the Black Maria came and they took him off to the station and charged him.

After that, I always got offered a free burger and coffee from the Wimpy when I was on duty. By now, one of the station sergeants had started to call me "Buster". I didn't really understand that. On a couple of occasions, I was asked to ride in a plain police van, with special observation windows, when they were staking out places before a raid. This van was equipped to give anyone touching it from the outside a mild electric shock.

FOURTEEN

SECOND-HAND CARS

During this time I'd kept in touch with Gordon Hall the Assistant Manager from *The Cat's Whiskers*.

He'd gone into partnership with one of the small-time villains who had patronised the place called Phillip Roth, who came from a known family in South London.

They owned a second hand car dealership on Culling Road outside the Rotherhithe tunnel. It had a small office, showroom and enough space for about 15-20 cars on some land rented from the Council.

The site was in a rough part of Bermondsey, but the business was doing well as they sold anything from small cars to the local dockers, to Rolls-Royces to the local villains.

Phillip had got into trouble for drinking and driving and assaulting a police officer. He'd been arrested, and was now serving eighteen months. So Gordon asked me if I wanted to buy in and become his partner. I didn't know anything about car mechanics, or going to the auction to buy them, but I could drive anything after my experience at Security Express.

He told me he could handle that side of the business and that I could help him clean and sell the cars. Gordon wasn't very big and with Phillip being off the scene, he wanted me there because he was afraid of some of the local villains would muscle in on him for protection money. So, I asked my Dad if he'd lend me the extra money to buy in. He flatly refused, saying I was mad to trust them. He still wanted me to help him on the stalls in Whitechapel Market. My mum, who was still against that idea, lent me the money to go into partnership with Gordon.

Within six weeks, I'd managed to pay her back and give her £50 extra. I made sure I paid her in front of my dad to let him know it was a good business. Although I knew nothing about car mechanics, I found that I was a natural salesman, and most people preferred to deal with me rather than Gordon, who they felt was a bit too slick. I found that I was particularly good with making deals when people brought their cars in as a part exchange for another vehicle.

One day, a guy came in with a convertible Vitesse which was immaculate, except for the hood. I managed to buy it for £50, and got a new hood for another £25. It was a lovely little car, and very nippy, with a six-valve straight engine. I sadly had to sell the Mustang a few weeks before because the oil seal had gone on the engine and I couldn't find the part to replace it.

All second hand car dealers were considered by the public at that time to be crooks and true enough, Bermondsey had more than its fair share who were involved in a lot of dodgy deals.

I had to keep quiet about being a part-time policeman, and only Gordon knew. Otherwise the other dealers wouldn't have traded with us… or worse! After spending over five years in the specials, I'd become more and more disillusioned with my duties. The regular police at Southwick were nothing like the men that I'd worked with at Bow Street, and except for Cliff, the other two specials John and Frank were a real embarrassment, so I reluctantly resigned.

The regular police inspector, who was a nice, guy tried his best to persuade me to stay on, or even take a break and come back. He believed I was too good an officer to lose. But I decided I'd had enough, and resigned. I also felt there was too much of a conflict of interest from working on the car business, surrounded by crooks and working for the specials, even though I made sure we ran the site honestly and never cheated anyone.

Cliff went on to become Commandant of 'A division' in the West End, and to my absolute astonishment, they made John Inspector at Peckham Police Station. I hope for all of their sakes they didn't get too many calls to high rise buildings!

ONE DAY at the car business, we bought a vehicle from some traders, that we later thought might have been stolen because the engine number and chassis number didn't match. I called in the special police car squad to check out the car. They couldn't believe they'd received a call from a second hand car dealer in Bermondsey to check what was thought to be a stolen car.

They sent down two officers who spent a day going through the car checking everything to see if it was a ringer but after an extensive search they came to the decision that the car hadn't been stolen. They even said to us afterwards that we'd set them up to waste their time, bloody cheek!

FIFTEEN

DANKA

During this time I'd often go out with Colin and his new girlfriend, a tall attractive blonde from Yugoslavia.

She worked at the Middlesex Hospital, sometimes we went to a restaurant for a meal in Chinatown or to the cinema. As much as I enjoyed their company, I felt a bit of a gooseberry.

One day, he told me his girlfriend Fatima had a friend who she worked with in the hospital and we could all go out together. Her name was Slobodanka, which we shortened to 'Danka', and she was from Belgrade.

So a few days later, we went to the cinema and I was immediately smitten with this shy, attractive girl from Yugoslavia. As I got to know her better she told me that her dad was a lorry driver and they had a house in Belgrade that had belonged to her grandfather. He apparently had been a very wealthy landowner until after the Second World War when the communists had confiscated most of his land and he'd died of leukaemia shortly afterwards as a result of what the family believed was shock.

Her English was quite good and I used to help her revise for English tests, in the small room where she lived in the hospital.

One day, she told me she had an English test at a language school she went to and was worried that she might not pass. So I queued up all night with lots of other students, pretending I wanted to take the test. When one of the teachers asked me a question, I replied in a funny accent to hopefully convince them that I was a foreigner. I then sat next to Danka in the classroom, and when she wasn't looking I filled out the questions she didn't know so she could get on the course, which she did!

We soon got engaged and made plans to marry. I'd been working at the car site for over a year as well as on the door of *Crackers*, so I'd earned enough money for a deposit on a house for us. I was about £2,000 short and decided that the only way to get that sort of money quickly was to sell my half of the car site. Which I didn't mind as I'd fallen out with Gordon over a couple of deals he'd done behind my back.

When I told Mark about my plans, much to my surprise he said he was interested in buying my share. He'd recently had a couple of good wins at poker, which he played regularly at some unlicensed gaming clubs in the West End, plus he was fed up with working on the door.

So he took the car site over with Gordon and I was made the Head Doorman at *Crackers* with a nice pay rise.

I liked working at *Crackers*; I was left to run the door and didn't have to put up with the bullshit politics that I'd suffered working at Mecca.

Crackers had begun to become more popular and I persuaded Colin to join me on the door. He was a good right-hand man to have next to me to watch my back. There was also Mike Askey, who'd worked with me at the *Lyceum*. He was a clever man who was an insurance assessor who'd worked for a big company. He was a tall lanky guy with large sideburns and liked to smoke a pipe. We used to take the piss out of him telling him he looked like Sherlock Holmes. Mike worked part time on the door because he needed extra money to pay his alimony. I also had two brothers working for me and even got Ray from *The Cats Whiskers* to work weekends. So I built up a tough team of six hard men, who the regulars soon got to know if they upset them it would be a big mistake, and they would get barred.

I enforced a strict rule on the door that after 10.30pm it was couples only, and any doormen caught drinking or fiddling would be sacked.

With these rules in place, the news soon spread that this was a nice place to bring your girlfriend or wife at weekends and there was very little chance of any trouble. My philosophy was simple, if there was going to be any trouble let it be on the door, and if possible not inside, especially as all three exits were at the top of a long flight of stairs and it was hard work throwing out any drunken troublemakers.

During the week days, only Colin and I worked the door as it wasn't that busy and the two of us together could handle any trouble. On the quiet nights it would sometimes get really boring.

Colin, like me, enjoyed a laugh and joke, and one evening we were standing on the door bored to tears when I got the idea of making a false spider. I found a black bin liner, screwed it into a ball, tied some green hairy string I'd found around it so they looked like legs and took a roll of cotton from one of the girls working in the cloakroom. There was a lot of scaffolding outside the building where work was being carried out during the day.

So I threw this black ball over the scaffolding so it was out of sight and about eight feet from the door. We stood holding the cotton that was tied to this huge-looking spider, waiting for someone to walk down the pavement towards us. Then, just before they got to where the ball was hanging above their heads, we would let the cotton holding the ball go, so it fell down, suspended in front of their faces. If you were walking along Wardour Street, the last thing you'd expect would be a giant spider to drop down in front of your face. We were pissing ourselves with laughter at the reaction we got as girls screamed and ran away or couples would jump in shock. They all got the joke after and we had tears in our eyes from laughing so much.

Towards the end of the evening, a couple were walking towards us. The woman was about five foot tall and the guy she was with looked about six foot five. They really were an odd-looking couple. As it got to the point where we lowered the ball down, the cotton broke, so it fell onto the floor at their feet. The woman screamed and the guy with her ran across to the other side of the road while she jumped up and down on top of the fake spider. Colin's side was hurting with how much he was laughing, I've never seen anything so funny, especially when the woman told this giant of a man who'd run away it was just a black plastic bag!

On other occasions, we superglued a fifty-pence piece to the pavement and watched as people tried to pick it up. Another time, Colin got a £5 note, tied some cotton to it and placed it on the pavement, then stood out of sight inside the door, and pulled it out of reach when people tried to pick it up. Sometimes they would run inside the door chasing it, before they realised the joke we were playing on them.

One evening, we found in a doorway an old mannequin which one of the shops had thrown out. So we took the legs off and stuck them underneath a car parked outside the club. So anyone passing could only see a pair of white legs sticking out from underneath the car. We were having a great time, until someone called the police thinking there'd been an accident! When they turned up they saw the funny side and just laughed themselves and told us to take the legs away.

WE KNEW most of the local police from West End central and a few knew me from Bow Street. They knew we ran the club well, and there were no drugs allowed, which they respected. They would often come in with their girlfriends or wives. I also had in place on the door a policy of searching everyone before they came in.

It wasn't all laughs though. One evening a French guy came to the door who we refused to let in. He opened the jacket he was wearing to reveal the hilt of a knife stuck in his trousers. Colin and the other doorman to my right immediately jumped back, but I did the opposite and kicked him hard in the bollocks. As he doubled up I put him in an arm-lock and stranglehold. I banged his head against a parked car outside for good measure. I wasn't taking any chances, after seeing one of my guys earlier being stabbed in the stomach by a sixteen year-old girl.

The club called the police and a very young inexperienced, policeman came running down the street. He saw how I was holding this guy and told me to let him go. I told the policeman he had a knife on him and asked if he wanted to hold him? He soon changed his mind and told me to carry on holding him until the police van arrived. I heard that the next day the guy with the knife had been deported back to France.

By now, I'd got Danka a job as a cashier in the club's box office. With her working two jobs, and me now working five nights a week, plus the money I'd saved we got a mortgage on a house and made plans to get married. It was a nice three-bedroom house in Bostall Woods, Kent. It needed a lot of work to be done, but it had a nice garden and a garage.

We planned to get married on Sunday 15th August, 1976, in Christ Church, Lewisham.

We made arrangements for Danka's mum and dad to come over for the wedding. She had a big family, including a brother and sister. They couldn't all afford to come to England, so we decided that straight after we married we'd over go over to Belgrade and have a second ceremony there for all of her family and cousins.

Danka's mum and dad didn't speak any English but still had a great time in London. At the wedding Colin was my best man, and Fatima was one of Danka's bridesmaids.

Amongst some great food at the wedding, I made sure there was a large bowl of jellied eels from London's East End.

Me and Danka in a restaurant in Belgrade

After a few days' sightseeing around London, we all flew to Belgrade, with my mum and dad and Danka's parents. They lived in a big house in Belgrade on the outskirts of the city centre.

The people there really knew how to enjoy themselves. Once my dad had drunk a few slivovitzes, the local plum brandy, he soon relaxed and broke into song. They all loved his singing, even though they couldn't understand a word of what he was singing. They still recognised that he had a great voice. A bit like opera, you don't understand a word they're singing, but know that they can sing well.

Danka's family reminded me of the people of the East End. They left their doors open, and wouldn't let anyone leave their house until they'd eaten and drunk themselves full.

Danka and her family wanted us to get married again in one of their churches which was Russian Orthodox. But because I was Church of England they wouldn't permit it, so instead we went through the ceremony outside their church so the family could take pictures of us. It was a strange feeling, seeing Danka in her wedding dress only a week after our wedding in London.

The reception after was a magnificent affair, with over one hundred and fifty people attending. They were such lovely people, who I remain friends with, to this day.

SIXTEEN

PUNK

When we returned to London I went straight back to work in *Crackers*.

The venue was becoming busier and busier. My policy of couples only after 10.30pm, before the drunks starting spilling out after 11pm, together with keeping the age over 21, was beginning to pay off.

I remember I bent the rules for two young girls who used to beg to come in who I was sure were under 18. They told Colin and me that they had just started working on a BBC children's TV programme. They were both cheeky and I liked them. Colin fancied the blonde, but I told him she was far too young for a dirty old man like him. They became regulars to the disco, and they told us that their names were Pauline Quirke and her best friend Linda Robson.

Colin still got up to his tricks playing jokes on the door. There used to be an Indian selling hot dogs from his barrow on the corner of Wardour Street and Oxford

Street. One evening he asked Colin to keep an eye on his trolley while he went for a piss in the pub next to the Disco. Big mistake! While he was inside, Colin emptied a pot of red pepper that he used to carry around into the hotdogs. Colin always carried the red pepper in his pocket in case he ever got cornered, so he could throw it into the eyes of any troublemakers, temporarily blinding them while he smashed them. I relied on my boxer's box, which even on quiet nights I would wear for protection.

When this poor hot dog seller came out of the pub and saw some American tourists, waiting to be served he happily obliged them. They took one bite of their hot dog, then coughing spat it out. They shouted at this poor guy asking what the hell had he served them? Colin thought this was hilarious, but I actually felt sorry for the Indian.

Crackers was now being let out a couple of nights in the week to a couple of American entrepreneurs, who renamed it the *Vortex Club*. They started to promote live bands and the latest music rage, which was called Punk.

It was definitely not my kind of music, especially having seen who I considered some of the greatest rock bands perform live at the *Lyceum*. I didn't like the fans of this new music rage either, especially the spitting associated with it, something I particularly detested. But nonetheless I had a job to do, and as long as they didn't upset me I would put up with it.

Over the next few weeks, I got friendly with one of the musicians whose name was Stuart Goddard. He was really a nice guy and at least in my opinion could play a tune and didn't have a bad voice, which was much more than a lot of them that played there. A lot of the punk bands couldn't even tune their own guitars and they used to bring them to Stuart to tune them. Not that it mattered, as most of them couldn't sing or play anyway!

Stuart Goddard was known on stage as Adam from Adam and the Ants. He was honest and told me that his ambition was to play on *Top of The Pops*, become famous and buy his mum and dad a house. I said good luck to him, and he also asked me when he became famous if I could be his bodyguard because we got on so well. I told him to go on and make his first million and then give me a call. I was pleased when he did become famous, but he must have lost my number because I never did get a call as he'd promised.

Another singer I didn't mind and got friendly with was Siouxsie, of Siouxsie and the Bandshees. Me and Colin used to take the piss out of a funny little guy who thought he could sing like Elvis Presley. His name was Elvis Costello, who was a half decent performer.

By now, the *Vortex*, AKA *Crackers*, was becoming famous for promoting new punk bands: The Boomtown Rats, The Buzzcocks and The Stranglers were amongst just a few who played there. One evening we'd sold out all the tickets, over six hundred for a punk band. A few hours before we were due to open the doors I went inside the disco and saw two punks sitting down with their feet resting on two stools. It was something we didn't allow in the club, I could have ignored it, but in truth I didn't like them. So I walked over and told them to take their feet off the stools. They glared back at me then spat on the carpeted floor. "You don't know who we are?" I did know who they were but replied "You don't know who I am?". That shocked them a bit and looking confused asked "Who are you?" I then replied "I'm the man who's about to throw you out". With that, I grabbed these two skinny little punks by the scruff of their necks, lifted them off of the seats they were sitting on, marched them up to the back exit and threw them both out onto the street outside.

One was Johnny Rotten, the other Sid Vicious of the Sex Pistols. Within a short time the area manager of *Crackers*, George Taff, who I got on well with, came to me panicking, saying what had I done? I had to let them back in as they were top of the bill and we had sold out and they were due to play in a couple of hours. I told him I didn't have to let them back in the club, and explained about them spitting on the carpet.

He could have sacked me and let them in, but if he did that, he, knew that he wouldn't have any security for the night as the other doormen would have followed me to back me up. He kept pleading with me to let them in. But I was sticking to my guns and not budging. Then the Sex Pistols Manager, who I didn't like, Malcom McLaren came over to me and tried to bribe me with over a week's wages to let them back in. That only made me angrier and more determined not to let them in and I told him to piss off and stick his money where the sun don't shine.

George Taff then came over again to me and asked what did I want in order to let them back in? I said "Simple, an apology". He said "Les, you know what these punks are like, they won't apologise to you". I replied "Fine, then they don't come in".

After about half an hour, I was standing on the door when Johnny Rotten and Sid Vicious came up to me with their heads down, looking very sheepish, and mumbled that they were sorry. These two wild men of punk looked like two naughty school kids, so I just replied to them "Fuck off inside".

They played to a capacity crowd who enjoyed them spitting at them from the stage, unbelievable!

I just didn't get how this so called music was becoming so popular. On one of the punk nights, I noticed two men drinking at the bar who I instantly recognised as Roger Daltrey and Pete Townsend of "The Who". They'd come in to check out the punk scene. I went over to them and to my surprise they remembered me from the concert they'd performed from the Hammersmith Palais. They insisted on buying me a drink and told me how much they'd enjoyed playing there, and I told them how much more I had enjoyed their music than some of the shit I had to listen to here. They both laughed and we had a nice drink together.

On another punk night, I was inside the club when I noticed a tall skinny kid acting suspiciously. I kept my distance and wondered what he was up to. He was hanging around one of the lesser known groups who'd been playing earlier. I watched him casually pick up a guitar, which I knew didn't belong to him, and carry it outside into the street.

I followed him outside and caught up with him. I asked him what did he think he was doing, nicking someone's guitar. He tried to tell me it was a mistake, which was of course a load of bollocks. Any musician will tell you that the instrument they play is like a part of them and that they all know their own instruments.

He then pleaded with me not to hit him, but I was angry thinking how could another so-called musician steal someone else's living. So I gave him a tap on the chin, not too hard, to teach him a lesson. He collapsed to the floor crying like a baby. I picked him up and the guitar and marched them back into the club.

When I got inside, I found the kid whose guitar it was and, still holding the thief by the neck, told the kid I'd found this guy trying to steal his guitar. I couldn't believe it when he said how it must have been a mistake and how much he admired this other guy I'd caught red-handed trying to nick his guitar.

I just shook my head and said "That's why you're all called punks, because you are!"

The guy I'd caught trying to nick the guitar was the lead singer of a Punk Group that went on to become very well known in the scene. He personally became a millionaire from, in my opinion, not singing very well. It sure is a funny old world.

MIKE REED the comedian often used to pop down to the club to see his friend George Taff, the regional manager of Wheatley Taverns. He would always spend some time on the door cracking dirty jokes with me and Colin. The only PC in those days were Police Constables. He liked and acted as if he was one of the lads, a very funny man.

ONE QUIET, mid-week night when I was standing on the door on my own, a limo pulled up outside the club and a small man with spikey hair who I instantly recognised got out and went to walk inside, completely ignoring me without paying. I stopped him and told him to buy a ticket. He said very arrogantly "I'm Rod Stewart and I don't pay to go in anywhere". I shook my head and said "You do here mate". With that he turned round and got back into his limo. I thought you might be a good singer, but you need some lessons in manners.

Shortly after returning from Yugoslavia, my Dad started complaining of pain in his back. We all thought that he'd pulled a muscle lifting a sack of potatoes on the stall. He eventually went to see his doctor who sent him for tests at the local hospital.

When the results came back, they confirmed he had cancer of the liver. This was a quick death sentence with little pain, we were told by his doctor. He proved to be right as he died on December 7th 1976, 6 weeks after being diagnosed. He was fifty-one years old.

Before he died I heard him telling his friend on the telephone that he'd survived being wounded and getting lockjaw in the jungles of Burma during the war fighting the Japanese. Now, to finish up like this, he just didn't believe it could happen. He'd been a fit man who'd never been in hospital, but liked his drink and fags a bit too much. Although I'd always found him difficult to communicate with, I'd loved him to bits and was heartbroken.

At his funeral, the chief undertaker told me he'd never seen so many flowers at a funeral before. The punters from half the pubs in Lewisham where dad had sung for many years had sent hundreds of wreaths. They used to say that my dad had a voice that was between Frank Sinatra and Matt Monroe and could sing 'My Way' by Sinatra better than the original.

My dad had lived his life his way, working hard and playing hard every weekend and had now paid the price.

I found myself running the stalls just before Christmas, the busiest time of the year, on my own, with no idea of how to buy the fruit and veg from Spitalfields Market, which was the most important part of the business.

So now, against all of my mum's wishes I was running a fruit and veg stall in Whitechapel Market as well as running the door at *Crackers*.

Christmas was particularly difficult to celebrate with Dad gone,. It was hard, but I managed to get through it. I was relieved when it was over and hoped that 1977 would prove to be a better year.

SEVENTEEN

THE IRA

It was a Friday night, January the 28th 1977.

I was standing on the door of *Crackers* with Colin and another doorman, when five young men tried to come in. They were smartly dressed and hadn't been drinking. As they got closer to the door, I said "Sorry you can't come in". As I said it I thought, *why have I stopped them?* There was no logical reason, it was 8.30pm so we never had the only couples rule in place. Colin and the other doormen looked at me in surprise, but they also knew never to question my judgement on the door. Anyway now that I'd refused them entry, I had to stick with my decision.

Three of the men stood back and the other two came over to me and in a soft Irish accent, asked politely why they couldn't come in. I gave them the usual cock and bull story that it was members only and it took at least twenty-four hours to get membership. I also told them that they needed ID. The men never argued with me, they merely said "okay" and with that walked off and I didn't think any more of it.

That night it was particularly busy and we had a capacity crowd of six hundred inside the disco. There had been no trouble on the door and I was looking forward to getting out quickly at 3am when the place closed.

We closed the door at 1am, two hours before we shut. At about 1am I said to Colin "Come on mate, let's go inside and send one of the other doormen to come up and look after the door". At that moment there was a loud bang and the windows of the bank opposite blew out, sending shreds of glass towards me and Colin. Everything seemed to happen in slowmotion as the shockwave and glass hit us. When I recovered my senses I thought immediately that it must have been a gas explosion. I slowly looked down at my shirt, expecting it to be covered in blood from the flying glass but miraculously neither me nor Colin had been injured.

Just as I asked Colin what the hell had happened, a second explosion, even louder, ripped through the night, on the corner of Wardour Street and Oxford Street. This time, it blew the Indian's hot-dog barrow into the air, overturning it onto the road. The next minute a stream of water with hot dogs floating like an armada of brown ships went flowing past the door. I turned to Colin and said "These weren't gas explosions, they were bombs"". I locked the front door and said "We'd better go inside". As we ran down the stairs into the disco, we heard an even bigger explosion from outside, over the loud disco music. I was worried that if a bomb had been planted inside the club it would cause untold death and injury. My mind raced to think where a bomb could be hidden, if there was one?

The only place I could think of was possibly inside the toilets. We had one male and one female toilet inside the club. I immediately ran to the gent's toilet, placed one of my men outside to stop anyone coming in and started looking around inside.

I looked in the obvious place such as a rubbish bin. Then thought I better check on top and behind the two cubicle toilets. I found nothing there, that only left to look inside the cistern. So very slowly, with sweat dripping down into my eyes, I carefully inched off the lid of the cistern, looking for any possible wires. As I was doing this I thought I'm not getting paid enough for this, but at the same time I knew that if there *was* a bomb, there wouldn't be enough time for the police to come and defuse it. I also knew with the bombs going off outside, that the police would be stretched to handle the emergency.

I could have asked one of my other doormen to look, but I would never ask them to do anything I wasn't prepared to do myself. Which is why they followed me and respected me. To my relief the inside of the cistern was empty. I then had to go through the same procedure in the ladies' toilet, which was also empty. By now we heard a fourth explosion, the loudest, go off outside. I told the DJ to stop the music and turn the lights up and to make an announcement to the crowd that explosions were happening outside and that it was safer to remain inside the disco until we knew what was happening. It's strange sometimes how panic can pass through a crowd. There was a murmur from many inside that they wanted to leave. So I put two doormen on the front door and told them not to let anyone outside.

I then grabbed Colin and ran to the back exit to stop anyone from leaving there. I knew everyone had been searched before they'd been let in and I'd looked inside for any planted bombs and that it was a safer bet to stay inside until the police gave the all clear.

As Colin and I were standing halfway up the stairs on the back exit, a section of the crowd, about fifty strong, tried to leave. I shouted at them that it was safer to stay where they were.

With that, the loudest explosion of the night went off behind us in the street outside the back door. The bastards had planted four bombs outside and around the club in the hope that the people inside would panic and would run outside from the back exit, killing or injuring as many as possible.

The police eventually told us it was safe to let the customers out of the club. Then a very tall police officer came inside. He was wearing the uniform of a very senior officer. He asked in a loud voice "who's in charge here?!"

I thought after all what's just happened I don't need a bollocking from him! I replied "I am, Sir". He walked over to me took off his glove and shook my hand and said "You've done a very good job here tonight". I replied "Thank you, sir". He then asked me if I'd noticed anything suspicious earlier in the night. My mind immediately went back to the five Irish men who I'd refused at the door. He then asked me what did their accents sound like? I replied that all Irish accents sounded the same to me. He then asked me to concentrate and spoke to me in what I was told was a Northern Irish accent, then he spoke in a Southern Irish accent. I told him it sounded like the second one, from the South.

He nodded grimly, and said he thought that the five men who'd tried to come in were an IRA hit-squad, who in his words were "probably by now on the boat back home". He told me that I'd saved a lot of lives by not letting them in. He then asked me why I'd refused them entry. I told him I honestly didn't have an answer and that it was just a doorman's instinct. There was no real justification not to let them in, and to this day I still don't know why I said no to them, but I'm bloody glad I did!

I then asked this senior officer, if he could do me a favour? He was taken aback by this request and repeated back to me "A favour? What kind of favour?!" I asked him if he could make sure that no press took my photo or of any of my doormen, and to keep our names out of the press the next day. If that didn't happen, I knew it would leave us open to possible retaliation from the bastard IRA.

He thought for a moment and replied "That's a bit of a tall order". I then said to him "but you're a tall man". He was at least 6'5, he smiled, slapped me on the back and said "I wish everyone had your sense son, leave it to me".

The next morning, as I suspected, the bombing was the lead story on the front pages of all the newspapers. Not one single reporter had approached me or any of my men for a story. At the end of the front page of *The Sun*, it merely said the security staff at *Crackers* had done a good job! That was enough praise for me as I didn't want to be looking over my shoulder for any nutcase working for the IRA.

Sure enough this policeman who I later found out was Jim Neville, the Commander of the Metropolitan Police Bomb Squad, had kept his word to me. Top man!

That night had been the start of what the IRA called a soft target bombing campaign. Hitting banks, shops and discos, etc. One of their bombs that night had set Selfridges in Oxford Street ablaze. So indeed we were very lucky that night to have escaped with no injuries.

By the time we'd finished giving our statements to the police, I had no time for any sleep and had to quickly change and go straight to work in the market. It was a Saturday, the busiest day of the week. As I was busy unloading my van with fruit and veg, one of the other stall holders called Ginger, who sold toiletries, came running over to me with the Sun newspaper. He said, "Les have you seen the newspaper today?" I replied no and that I hadn't had time. He told me that he'd read about the IRA bombs going off in the West End and knew that I worked in that area. I replied, "Yeah, I know I was there!" He just shook his head in amazement and walked away. He could see I was in no mood for conversation, having had no sleep and the IRA trying to blow me up!

BY NOW I'D built up a small, but very professional, team at *Crackers*. They all knew that whatever the odds they faced we could rely on each other when it mattered. I had taught them the golden rule of all doormen, to watch each others' backs.

One evening when Colin and I were standing on the door, a Bruce Lee lookalike walked up to us, asking us if we had any jobs for a doorman. He spoke little English, but showed me an ID card stating that he was a third Dan black belt in karate. Now, this was someone I believed could be very useful in a fight, and he really did look like Bruce Lee who had become very popular. His name was Marc and he was a French Vietnamese. I liked him, so I gave him a job. I thought, his lack of English wouldn't matter too much if it all kicked off.

Colin and I tried our best to teach Marc some English, which was difficult. On the first evening he worked, we were having some trouble with four or five guys inside, who I wanted to leave. I thought to myself, this is a good chance to see if Marc could handle himself, so, mainly through sign language I explained to Marc that I wanted them to leave.

Marc walked over to the ring leader of this little group, who must have been at least 6'4, and stood in front of him, and in what sounded like a Chinese accent, says to the guy "You leave now", and points to the exit. Marc was about 5'5 and only came up to this guy's waist. The guy looks down at Marc and laughs at him. With no warning, and in a blur of speed that Bruce Lee would have been proud of, Marc flicks his fingers into this guy's chest. There was a delayed reaction as the guy looks down at Marc and then collapsed onto the floor, like a felled tree. The guy's mates just looked on in shock. I then walked over to them with Colin and said to the rest of his mates, "If you don't want some of the same, you better pick him up and leave"!

Colin said to me afterwards did I see what just happened? And how did Marc knock the guy down. I told him that Marc had jabbed his fingers, which were hard as nails into the guy's solar plexus, not only knocking the wind out of him but also paralysing his nervous system. A useful addition to the team I thought.

We got on really well with Marc and Colin, being his

usual self, used to take the piss out of him terribly, which frustratingly for him Marc never really understood.

After Marc had been working with us a couple of weeks, the Area Director, George Taff, came into the club. He could be a real pain in the arse at times, but was a nice guy. He hadn't seen Marc before, and called me over to ask me who he was. I explained that he was the newest member of the team. Taff went over and started to ask Marc questions, but Marc didn't have a clue what he was talking about. Taff then comes over to me and says "He doesn't speak a word of English, and can't work here", I pleaded Marc's case and explained that he was really useful to have in a fight. Taff was having none of it, so I asked for a few days to teach Marc more English, which he reluctantly agreed. He gave us just 48 hours to teach someone English, who even the School of Berlitz wouldn't stand a chance with!

Colin's now panicking, telling me what I already knew - that it was an impossible job, but we had to try. So, I began teaching Marc some easy phrases, parrot fashion, like answers to where the toilets and cloakroom were. Taff came back 48 hours later, and as he walks in Marc in his thick accent says to Taff "Good evening Mr George, you need toilet?" Me and Colin quietly groaned, that's it now, game over. George Taff is lost for words, and we plead for more time to work with Marc on his English. Taff wasn't such a bad bloke and muttering under his breath, agreed to give us more time. This was a really hard job as Colin and I didn't speak any French, and our Vietnamese was shit!

So the next time, Taff walks in Marc is on the door and says "Good evening Mr George, you need coat from cloakroom?", with that George Taff shakes his head, smiles to himself, and says no more on the subject. We knew Marc's job was safe.

ONE EVENING when it was quiet on the door, me, Colin and Marc were mucking around. Marc knew I was good at Judo and we were exchanging different moves, when Colin bet on me that Marc could break my stranglehold. Up until then, no one had ever broken it, so I took the bet with Colin, and Marc let me place my strangle on him. After he tried every trick he knew to break it, he failed. A very red face Marc conceded, and I'd won £5 from Colin. Colin really should have known better!

On another Saturday night, about twenty-five men on a stag night got into the club. They'd been very clever, coming inside in twos and threes before the 'couples only' rule had been enforced. As the night went on it was obvious they were there to cause trouble. They were taking their drinks onto the dance floor, which we didn't allow, and generally getting more and more rowdy and upsetting the other customers.

One of my doormen came up to me, and asked what we could do about them. There were only five of us working that night, with no Marc who had gone to a bloody English lesson at Berlitz! I told my guys not to panic and that I would think of something. He asked me again what we could do. I replied "divide and conquer". He looked at me as if I'd gone mad.

I remembered from history the famous Chinese general

Sun Tzu, who had written in his book *The Art of War* when facing superior odds, to divide your enemy and then conquer.

My plan was simple, to watch this gang of troublemakers carefully, and when one or two of them went to the toilet to wait outside, jump them and throw them out of one of our three exits. So, as soon as two of them went to the toilet, out of sight of the rest of their mates, we did exactly that. I guessed what would happen next. After a short while three of the group went to look for their mates, while the rest of the gang went on drinking and dancing. Again we grabbed the three and bundled them out of the nearest exit. Next, two more went to the toilet and again without too much trouble we managed to throw them out without the rest noticing.

Two more came up to the front door, asking if we'd seen any of their friends leave. We told them that they'd been feeling sick and had gone home. So during the course of about an hour we'd managed to whittle the gang down from twenty-five to five or six, who we easily managed to grab at the end and throw them out of a back exit so they couldn't meet up with the rest of their mates.

I sent a silent prayer of thanks to Sun Tzu for writing down his wise words, in *The Art Of War* over 2000 years ago, which had helped me throw out a gang of twenty-five men, without me or any of my men getting hurt or injured.

EIGHTEEN

RONNIE BIGGS

The Vortex was still hiring the club for their punk nights mid-week.

Two of the men who worked for them and helped organise the events were John Miller and his mate Fred Prime. I already knew these two from the Reading Pop Festival, which was held by my friend Harold Pendleton when I was doing security there. They were two crazy guys, who liked to joke, drink and smoke pot.

They reminded me of two, modern-day pirates. John told me he also did some body-guarding on TV and film sets and was very friendly with the actor Gareth Hunt who starred in *The New Avengers* TV series.

As I got to know John more and he trusted me, he told me that he and Fred had been in the Scots Guards together and had then joined the SAS. He showed me one evening on the door a really bad scar on his leg, which he said was a shrapnel wound he'd got fighting guerillas in Oman.

Another time he told me a story of when he was working

in Thailand and had met Oliver Reed. He said that the two of them had gone on a three day drinking binge together which, knowing Oliver Reed's reputation for drinking, which was already legendary I could well believe it. John told me that he'd got Olly so drunk that he'd taken him into a tattoo parlour and got them to put a tattoo on the actor's cock! I'm thinking I knew the stories of some of the mad things Oliver Reed had done while drunk, but had this really happened?

It wasn't until some years later, when I was at home watching the *Des O'Connor Show*, which was live, and he was interviewing Oliver Reed who had, as usual, obviously been drinking. Des O'Connor wasn't getting much response from Oliver, so Des asked the question "I hear you've got a tattoo in an unusual place Olly?" With that question Olly suddenly came alive, smiled and replied "Yes, on my cock". With that answer ITV went straight to a commercial break, but the damage had been done, and Olly's answer had gone out to millions of homes before the 9pm watershed.

ITV received hundreds of complaints the next day and it was widely reported in the press. Subsequently, ITV pulled the plug on the rest of the series on the *Des O'Connor Show*. They blamed Des for what had happened, saying that he shouldn't have asked such a question, especially when he knew he'd been drinking. I then knew that John had been telling me the truth of what he'd done.

A few weeks later, John Miller came over to me on the door with his friend Fred, and asked me if I wanted to go on a job with them and earn some extra cash. I've always been interested in extra cash, so I was all ears and asked him to tell me more. He said at that moment, he couldn't go into details, but was I interested in principle. I told him that he had to tell me a bit more before I could commit myself. He told me that someone high up in the establishment was funding the operation and that it involved a lot of money. He told me that he and Fred were impressed by how I handled myself in tight spots and would like me to join them on this job.

I said, "John you have to tell me a bit more about it", he then replied "Les, all I can tell you at this stage, is that it involves going to Brazil". I thought for a split-second before replying "Thank you, but no thank you". He could see that I'd made my mind up, and didn't push me, but asked "Why not?" I then replied "Because the last place on earth I want to finish up is in the nick in Brazil with you two crazy bastards!" With that reply they both laughed and never mentioned the job again.

Some months later, news broke out around the world, that some mercenaries had gone to Brazil and kidnapped Ronnie Biggs, one of the great train robbers. Biggs had escaped from a thirty year prison sentence many years before, and travelling to Australia, where his family later joined him. The police were closing in on him and he escaped to Brazil where the UK couldn't bring him back as there was no extradition treaty with Brazil at that time. Biggs was often in the news sticking up two fingers to the establishment, knowing that they couldn't do anything about it. This really annoyed many in the UK establishment.

Someone high up had put up enough money for John and Fred to go to Brazil, kidnap Biggs, and bring him back to the UK to face justice.

John and Fred had gone out to Brazil, and had made friends

with Biggs, which was easy enough as Biggs was only too willing to tell anyone who bought him a drink about his exploits carrying out what had up to then been Britain's biggest robbery. John and Fred had told Biggs that they were part of a film unit that wanted to make a documentary about Biggs' life and would return at a later date.

During this time they'd discovered where Biggs lived, and his daily routine, making plans to come back, grab him and take him back to the UK. I later found out that it was one of the members of the House of Lords who'd financed the operation.

John, with Fred and another one of their friends, returned to Brazil, and grabbed Ronnie Biggs from a restaurant and took him to a boat they had waiting. They'd known that it would be too dangerous to fly him out of the country.

I suspect that they wanted me to go with them so I could put Biggs in one of my infamous strangleholds and get him out of one of his favourite restaurants as quickly as possible. They'd chartered a boat and got Biggs on board, where they were going to take him to an island in the Caribbean where Britain had an extradition treaty so that he could be flown back to the UK.

The next day, the story of Ronnie Biggs being kidnapped from Brazil not only made the front pages of every newspaper in the UK but also became world-wide news. The story was on every TV and radio station around the world.

Everyone was asking the same question: who had kidnapped Ronnie Biggs? I knew days before the media found out but was keeping my mouth shut.

I wasn't in the least bit surprised, when I learnt that the boat that they had Biggs on had run out of diesel and had drifted ashore in Barbados. John and Fred were immediately arrested, and Biggs was held while the UK Government moved heaven and earth to move Biggs back to the UK to finish his prison sentence.

The problem was that Barbados at that time didn't have an extradition treaty with the UK. So once again, Biggs had escaped the net and was flown back to Brazil. Because John and Fred hadn't committed any crime in Barbados, they also were released.

Apparently, during the boat trip they'd smoked pot and had drunk with Biggs on board to keep him happy and had completely lost the plot!

There was uproar back in the UK amongst the criminal fraternity, who saw Ronnie Biggs as a loveable rogue and a bit of a Robin Hood character, who'd never hurt anyone. They thought it was a diabolical liberty that someone had gone to a safe haven and kidnapped him.

It was rumoured that certain gangsters had been so upset at this, that they'd put up a sizeable contract on John and Fred's' heads. When I heard about this, I was even more pleased that I hadn't joined them, especially as they didn't, to my knowledge, even get paid for the job.

It wasn't the last time John Miller made world news. Some years later he was filmed live on ITN television news, going to a small uninhabited island off Miami, supposedly to meet Lord Lucan, the peer who'd disappeared years earlier and was wanted by police in Britain for questioning over the murder of his Nanny.

Miller had told the press that he'd made contact with Lord Lucan, who'd agreed to surrender himself.

As Miller's boat came ashore and he walked towards a line of trees, shots rang out, the news camera went up in the air and John was shot in the chest! All of this was being televised live on the news. Fortunately for John he was conveniently wearing a bulletproof vest so he wasn't injured.

There was of course no sight of Lord Lucan, but John got £10k for his trouble I heard, not bad for one day's work!

NINETEEN

THE COURT

By now, I was working five nights a week, running the door at *Crackers* and four days on the stalls at Whitechapel Market.

I was determined to finish the house I'd bought, which needed extensive renovation work to make it comfortable for me and Danka, then hopefully to start a family. I needed all the cash I could get. Danka was still working in the hospital canteen during the day, and some evenings with me in the box office, selling tickets at *Crackers*.

The worst time for me was at weekends, when I would wake up at 5am to go to Spitalfields Market to buy the fruit and veg, then work all day in the market on my own in all weather conditions. I'd then have to pack the stalls up at 5pm, rush home, change, and be on the door at *Crackers* by 8pm, working until 3am. I would then go home for two hours' sleep, and then go through the same procedure the next day. It was a killer, and sometimes when I was inside the club even with the DJ playing loud music I would nod off standing up inside the club.

On one Friday evening at the end of the night, with the other doorman, I was asking people to finish their drinks and leave, There was a group of three boys and two girls sitting down inside, who we'd already asked politely to finish their drinks. They were not budging, so for the third time, I went over to ask them to leave. I was dead tired, and just wanted to get home for a couple of hours sleep.

After asking them again to finish up their drinks, as I was walking away I heard one of them say "Fat cunt". Big mistake. I spun around to this lanky kid of about nineteen and told him to get out now! With this he jumped up from his seat, still holding a pint glass in his hand. By now I had seen too many doormen scarred for life after being glassed. I didn't hesitate and in one quick move, knocked the glass from his hand with my left hand and punched him in the face with my right fist. With that the other doormen rushed over and Colin grabbed the guy who I'd hit from behind and placed two of his fingers inside his mouth and pulled.

This was a move that was particularly dangerous as you could easily rip someone's face in half without a lot of pressure. It was a move I'd seen Colin use before sometimes, and was a move that I didn't like and one I'd told him not to use when throwing someone out.

We threw the group out easily enough and I just wanted to get home. Colin said to me afterwards, had I seen the guy, the one I'd hit. I asked him what did he mean? Colin told me that the guy had a massive black eye, I shrugged and said I'd had only hit him once. I also knew that Colin was prone to exaggeration, so I thought no more of it.

The next evening I was standing on the door, when two detectives I knew from West End Central Police station came up to me, and told me that the guy I'd hit had made a formal complaint about me. They told me that they'd tried their best to get him to drop the complaint, but this kid wasn't moving. They'd managed to get him to agree to drop the complaint if I personally apologised to him. I told them that he could wait until hell froze over before that happened. They tried their best to make me change my mind, but I told them that he'd been in the wrong, not me. They told me they'd go back and try again to get him to drop the complaint and I thought no more of it.

A few days later, the two detectives returned, and said that the kid now wanted to press charges and that they had to arrest me for GBH (grievous bodily harm). That surprised me as that was a very serious offence. They then asked me to go to the station with them to be charged. They were really nervous because they knew if I said no they would need a lot of back up to take me if I didn't agree. I had too much respect for the law to cause them any trouble, much to their relief.

On the way to West End Police Station, they never stopped apologising to me, saying that this kid had insisted I be charged and because of the massive black eye I'd given him they hadn't had any choice in the matter.

If the situation hadn't been so serious I would have laughed at how they kept saying how sorry they were about having to arrest me. When we arrived at West End Central, they took me to the Desk Sergeant who was busy writing, to formally charge me.

When he looked up from his paper, he recognise me immediately and asked what I was doing there? The two detective told him I was being charged with GBH. The sergeant threw his pen down in disgust and bollocked the two detectives for not getting the kid to drop the charge. The sergeant then said to me, "I don't believe this, these two wankers should have made this go away!"

Until then, I hadn't realised how much respect I'd built up over the years on the door of *Crackers* and when I'd served in the specials at Bow Street. The police and CID in the West End of London, who didn't know me, had all heard of the doorman who wore glasses who'd stopped the IRA from getting inside to blow up the club.

The sergeant then told the two detectives who I was now beginning to feel sorry for, to process me through the system and get me out of the station on my own bail as quickly as possible. I was taken down to a room to have my fingerprints taken, and the officer doing that job also recognised me! He was shocked when told by the two detectives I'd been charged.

As he took my hands to roll them in the ink to take my fingerprints he kept shaking his head and apologising. By this time the two detectives had gone red with embarrassment. I was in and out of the station in less than thirty minutes, probably the fastest time anyone in West End Central's history had been released after being charged.

After a few days had passed, I got a message from Bob Wheatley, the owner of *Crackers*, that he'd pay for a barrister to defend my case. He didn't have to do this, but part of the reason was over the years when any of his doormen had been arrested and gone to court, they'd always lost the case. He was now determined not to lose this one, and so was I!

In the meantime, the two detectives came back to the club

and told me if I pleaded guilty they could guarantee a lower charge with a fine, and a suspended sentence. The GBH charge carried a maximum of five years in prison.

By now I was really angry with them and told them both to piss off and not to come back. It was a strange and uncomfortable sensation being on the wrong side of the law.

Up until then, even with all the seriously vicious fights I'd been involved in I'd managed against all the odds to keep a clean record, and had never once been in trouble with the police. I was determined to keep a clean sheet.

I made a few enquiries with some of my friends in the police and found a lawyer who then recommended a barrister to represent me in court. The date had been set at Marlborough County Court, in front of a stipendiary magistrate. This was indeed a serious business, and I was really nervous.

I arrived at the court in a smart dark suit, shirt and tie. I knew that first impressions were important and probably the judge might be expecting to see a doorman to arrive dressed casually with a broken nose and cauliflower ears. When the kid who I'd hit arrived in court, he was wearing jeans, an old jumper with a hole in the sleeve and looked like he needed a shave. Thank God by the time, he'd come to court there was no sign of the black eye I'd given him!

The prosecution opened the case against me, and during his speech, he accused me of putting my fingers into the kid's mouth and pulling his mouth open. I looked at the judge's expression on hearing this piece of evidence and could see by the way he looked at me that he wasn't very impressed.

I remembered when the kid was giving his evidence earlier he'd told the court that I'd hit him while someone from behind had put their fingers into his mouth. I was frantically trying to attract the attention of my barrister, to pick up this vital piece of evidence. But he looked like he was asleep! When my barrister got up to give his speech, he never mentioned this obvious, important point and I thought he was weak and quite useless.

I was so angry my freedom was in the hands of this wally. This called for drastic action on my part and I stood up and asked the judge whether I could conduct my own defence and sack my barrister. The judge warned me against this course of action, but I insisted that I wanted to take the chance.

I walked into the dock to give my evidence. I asked if I could cross exam the prosecutor, much to the surprise of the court.

I'd spent enough hours in courtrooms as a special, to know how they worked.

I then asked the prosecutor to repeat to the court what he'd said with regards to putting my fingers into the kid's mouth while I'd hit him? The prosecutor was reluctant to repeat his mistake, but when I insisted that he repeat his statement, the judge ordered him to repeat it. When he did repeat it I said to him, "I thought your client said that when I'd hit him, someone from behind had put their fingers in his mouth?" Before the prosecutor could reply, the judge looked at his notes in front of him and said "That's right he did say that".

So I'd successfully managed to make the prosecutor look

like he didn't know what he was talking about, making it obvious that I couldn't be in two places at once.

When the judge summed up the case, he said looking over to me "I think what we have here is a case of a very experienced, professional man, getting in his blow first and under law exposing his legal right of self-defence, so I therefore find the defendant NOT GUILTY! Case dismissed".

I cannot describe the relief I felt, as all my friends cheered. As I walked out of the court a free man, and importantly still with an unblemished record, the duty sergeant whispered in my ear "What did you hit him with?" I showed him my fist and said "Just this". He shook his head and said "In all my career I've never seen such a black eye!"

We all went back to *Crackers* and celebrated all night courtesy of Bob Wheatley who was well chuffed that we'd won the case. This was the first time a case against him had been successfully defended and won

.

SHORTLY AFTERWARDS I was standing on the door of *Crackers* with Colin on the night of Saturday June 4th 1977. Scotland were playing England in a friendly at Wembley and we were expecting a lot of drunks in the evening to be wandering around the West End. To make matters worse, we were two doormen short that night through illness.

Scotland beat England that day 2 -1 and in celebration the Scottish fans had invaded the hallowed ground of

Wembley, smashing up the goal posts and tearing up half the pitch.

The Scots had been wandering through the West End during the day before the match, drinking heavily. Come the evening, they were all well pissed. From when we opened the doors at 8pm, we could hear nothing but police sirens.

We guessed there's be trouble later. About fifty fans had gone into the pub next to *Crackers* and now at closing time had smashed the place up. The police had been called, but were too busy elsewhere to attend, and were stretched to breaking point with all of the trouble the Scottish fans were causing.

As these fifty odd Scottish fans spilled out onto Wardour Street, they'd formed a crowd around the door. There was only me and Colin standing there. Some of the fans then had the bright idea of going into *Crackers*. I politely but firmly told them that they couldn't come in.

Their spokesman (there's always one!) stepped forward, a big bastard who looked at me and Colin and said "Who's going to stop us?". I could have locked the door, but the fifty-strong crowd would have easily kicked the door in and have got inside, so I replied, "We will, if we have to". The big bastard then replied "You two can't stop all of us coming in." I replied, "No, you're right, but what I can guarantee is the first ten of you will go head first down the stairs behind me and finish in hospital and the police will be called and arrest the rest of you". He then says to me in his Scottish accent "You're cock-a-neys. aren't you?", to which I replied "Yes we are". He looks back at his mates and says "All cockneys are mad". I replied "You're right, we are mad you don't think anyone in their right mind is going to stand on the door talking to you lot do you?". He then says to his mates "Come on, let's go somewhere else, it's not worth the trouble".

As they staggered off, Colin with huge relief says "Les, I was shitting myself". I told him "What other choice did we have but to front them out and hope for the best?"

It was *déjà vu* when I'd stood in front of the Hell's Angels at Plumpton.

By now I'd worked for ten years on some of the toughest club doors in London. I'd been hit with iron bars, had glasses thrown at me, knives pulled on me, ammonia thrown in my face, and had been nearly blown up by the IRA. But in the main, I'd come through it pretty much unscathed. Some of it had been luck, but I like to think that most of the time it had been because of my own rules of not drinking alcohol while working, something which I always told new doormen I hired. *If you're up against a better man in a fight and he's been drinking, it can give you the edge, and always have someone watching your back.*

I was still only 28 years old. I'd managed to build the stalls into a better business and was working five days a week in Whitechapel Market in all weathers, but had made it worthwhile. Now was the time to hang up my bow tie and quit while I was ahead of the game.

TWENTY

THE FREEMASONS

Dick had now been promoted to Sergeant and, like many policemen, had joined the Freemasons.

He'd pestered me for ages to join his lodge in London, but I'd always been too busy.

I'd read so many different stories about this so called 'secret society' that I was intrigued to find out more about them. I agreed to be nominated, which involved two existing members of the lodge to put my name forward for the rest of the lodge to vote yes or no for me to become a member.

Dick was one, and his friend, a fellow police sergeant, nominated me. I then had to be interviewed by the master of the lodge and his committee to see if I was a suitable candidate. There then followed a secret vote by all the members of the lodge. They all had to choose a small white or black ball, which they placed into a ballot box. If only one of the members placed a black ball in the box, then you'd be refused membership, without even knowing which member had objected to your membership. Hence the saying of being 'black-balled'.

The lodge I joined was one of the oldest in England and was based inside Freemasons Hall on the corner of Great Queen Street in central London. This was the headquarters of the brotherhood, known as *The United Ground Lodge of England*. It was, I had to admit, a most impressive building inside.

A great deal has been written over the decades about Freemasonry. Some of it total myth, some true. To this day, there are a great number of conspiracy theories associated with the Freemasons. What I did discover during my time as a member was that there are thousands of lodges around the world and if you were ever to find yourself in need of help, you could go to one of these lodges, like the exclusive club it is, and they'd help you.

Some of these lodges include royalty, policemen of all ranks up to and including commissioner, lawyers, accountants, architects, Churchmen, all sorts of government officials as well as politicians and judges. Every American President from George Washington to present day has been a Freemason. It's also open to men only.

Freemasonry started from King Solomon's reign, where stonemasons building his temple wanted to protect the secrets of their trade and devised a number of secret rituals. Many of which are still used today in modern Freemasonry. Some of these involve secret passwords and handshakes to recognise a fellow Freemason.

Soon after the vote in the lodge I was told I'd been accepted as an Apprentice Mason. I'd already been told by Dick that if I regularly attended the fortnightly meetings for instruction then it would take me about eighteen months to become a Master Mason. Some Masons believed that once you reached and passed the third degree then you've made it, a bit like when you win your black belt in Judo, but Freemasonry has thirty three degrees, which only a privileged few ever reach. In Judo there are ten Dans, and only when you reach the first Dan the Masters tell you that's the beginning of your journey. In Freemasonry once you reach the third degree that's the beginning of a long road.

After attending a meeting in Grand Lodge, I was leaving the building with Dick and noticed a distinguished man with a beard. As I got closer, I immediately recognised him as Prince Michael of Kent. I asked Dick what he was doing there. Dick laughed and told me that he was the Grand Master in Freemasonry for England.

The Lodge I'd joined was 120 years old and they told me that I'd made history as their first Freemasonic greengrocer. Maybe the others had been too busy running their stalls? It did make me feel proud that I was now a member of this ancient organisation.

To pass the third degree and become a Master Mason involves learning what's called the Tracing Board, which explains some of the history and rituals of King Solomon's Temple.

When it came to my initiation ceremony for the third degree, I nearly blew it trying not to laugh. Anybody watching this very serious ceremony would have thought they'd just walked into a satanic black mass. There were candles placed around an opening in the floor in a darkened room.

The hole represents an open grave and you are led into this room blindfolded with your left breast exposed and your trouser leg rolled up above the knee. The reason for this is to show the members that you are not a woman trying to join the lodge.

A hangman's noose is placed around your neck. The other members then lower you into the hole. I knew because of my size that they were going to struggle at this point, and sure enough they nearly dropped me. That's when I had to try and compose myself not to laugh. Fortunately I managed to get through the ceremony without losing it.

My own personal view on my experiences of Freemasonry was that they raised a lot of money for various charities, and that I enjoyed the company and chance once a fortnight of unwinding, having a drink, and a meal.

Like all exclusive clubs, they of course favour their members. I personally never came across any dodgy deals being done amongst members, but that doesn't mean it never happened, I think that in certain lodges in some countries, like in any club, there has to be a certain amount of corruption. It's a case of one member helping out another.

If that lodge contains politicians, judges and other powerful members then there's always a chance for corruption. I personally think there are more dodgy deals done in golf clubs around the country, which have so many influential members.

Some years later when I started to travel the world extensively, I was amazed during my meetings with lawyers, accountants and architects and other businessmen how many were Freemasons. I can honestly say that yes, in some cases it helped me close a deal, but there were also many other meetings where it didn't.

On my travels I noticed signs on many buildings as far apart as Jamaica to Estonia that bore the symbols of Freemasonry.

I also am quite sure that Freemasonry got me arrested in Germany, where it is particularly strong.

TWENTY-ONE

JUDO

Now that I'd finished working at *Crackers*, it gave me more time to concentrate on my Judo.

It was mid-1978 and the Olympic Games were scheduled to be held in Moscow in eighteen months' time.

I was now practicing four to five times a week at my club in Vauxhall, the London Judo Society, or LJS as it was known. It was considered by many in the Judo world to be the second best club in London, with only the Budokwai in Kensington being number one. This was where the British Olympic Judo team practised.

The LJS was run by two men: George Chew, an ex-police sergeant, and Eric Dominie, who'd written books on the sport. Members of the British Olympic Judo team used to come to the LJS to practise their groundwork with one of the instructors there called Len Hunt.

Len was a small wiry man, who was considered a legend in the Judo world for his expertise in ground technique. I used to get on with him really well and he showed me more than one of his tricks. As big as I was, he could still beat me on occasion, and when asked by Chew and Dominie he confirmed to them that I was the strongest man he'd ever practised with. This was some compliment considering he'd got his first black belt in 1936!

When I'd first met Dick he'd used to take me to different clubs with him to practise and that's where I met Brian Jacks who I later became good friends with.

Brian was another living legend in the Judo scene; he'd gone to Japan at the age of fourteen to learn the martial art and had won an Olympic bronze medal in the 1964 Tokyo Olympics at the age of sixteen. He was a real character whose father was a black taxi driver from the East End. So both of us coming from the East End we had something in common, including a love of pie and mash.

At that time, the sport of Judo wasn't that well sponsored and to make ends meet Brian sometimes worked as a doorman in Soho.

One of the clubs was called *The Bird Cage*, and sometimes Dick and I would go and visit him. I always remember that he had a high-pitched voice that Dick used to take the piss out of, but never in front of him.

Whenever I practised with Brian, he always remarked how strong I was, and once when he was on the mat, he let me put my strangle on him, thinking he could break it and was very surprised when he couldn't.

I started frequenting the Budokwai to pick up some tips from the British Olympic team who practised there. One time I practised with Neil Adams, who later won a silver medal. He became more and more frustrated when he couldn't throw me, and even more so when I later strangled him on the mat.

My two instructors at the LJS told me that I now had a good chance of becoming a member of the British Olympic Judo squad for the 1980 Olympics. This news really excited me, and I was determined to go to Moscow to represent my Country.

It was all going well until a third Dan black belt came to the LJS for a practice. He singled me out to *randori* (freestyle practice) with him, no doubt expecting me as a first kui brown belt to be a pushover. He became angrier and angrier as he tried every move to throw me, without success. Then for one second I lost my concentration and he seized the chance to throw me. It wasn't a clean throw and I landed on the tip of my shoulder with him on top of me.

I had to go to hospital and the x-rays showed I'd chipped my shoulder bone. It was such a bad throw from an experienced man that Dominie and Chew barred him from ever practising in their club again. But it didn't help me, and I couldn't practise Judo for months, which lost me the chance of joining the British Team going to Moscow.

To MAKE up for it I had the wonderful experience of seeing my son born on May 15th 1979. I named him Leslie after my father and his father before him, carrying on a family tradition.

Every August Bank Holiday my old friend Harold Pendleton, the owner of the famous Marquee Club in Wardour Street, held the Reading Rock Festival. It was a three day event, which attracted crowds of over 30,000 people, with various bands playing.

The fans who'd attend the event used to camp over the three days. I'd worked for Harold at two previous festivals on security and had noticed a niche where I believed I could earn much more money in catering. So I asked Harold if at the next festival I could have exclusivity selling watermelons. He readily agreed, never forgetting the confrontation with the Hell's Angels at Plumpton. He gave me a handsome discount for the pitch and wished me good luck.

I hired a Luton box-van before the festival, drove to Spitalfields Market, and bought two hundred boxes of melons, containing five melons per box. I borrowed a trestle table and took a portable gas burner to make myself tea and breakfast and was set for the three days. As I drove to Reading I prayed that it didn't rain and was dry and warm.

My idea was to cut the melons into slices and sell each slice for 20 pence. Each melon would divide into eight slices, making £1.60, times five per box, making £8 per box, times two hundred boxes, which made £1,600, which at that time was a small fortune. This I knew would only happen if the weather was good, so it was a real gamble. I would sleep in the back of the van and hope for the best.

The weather stayed warm and dry, and business was booming. I couldn't cut the melons quickly enough to sell to the fans. On the Sunday Rod Stewart was top of the bill to perform in the evening. When he came on stage, within minutes I could hear there was a problem with the PA, the song he was singing sounded terrible it was off tune and the fans weren't happy. After only ten minutes the crowd had enough and started to throw hundreds of melon peels at the stage, and Rod Stewart and his band abandoned their gig.

Let me tell you, that if you get hit by a flying piece of melon rind it can be very painful. So, with hundreds being thrown at them I didn't blame them for running off the stage. I only hoped that I didn't get the blame and that he wouldn't remember me from the door of *Crackers* as the man who hadn't let him inside without buying a ticket.

It was such a success for me, I did it again the following year, but with the British weather being as unreliable as it is, I didn't do as well, as it rained heavily on two of the days. But I always have been a believer of nothing ventured, nothing gained.

TWENTY-TWO

ARM WRESTLING

I'D BUILT the stalls in Whitechapel into a decent business.

It was hard work, long hours, and standing out in all weathers. Whitechapel Market was full of real characters and I made lots of friends there. One of the more colourful characters was Frank Pittal, a Jewish man that sold ladies' shoes. He was a real life Del Boy, always on the lookout for a deal. There was also a mix of some Israelis who sold ladies' garments. What surprised me was that generally they didn't get on well with the other English Jews who worked there.

On March 6th, 1987, a car ferry, the *Herald of Free Enterprise*, capsized in calm waters outside the Belgian port of Zeebrugge and killing, 193 people, many of them families from Britain, returning from holiday. It was a disaster which shook the nation.

Many charity events up and down the country were organised to raise money for the relatives of those who'd died. I spoke to Frank about ways we could raise money for this sad cause. We decided that together we could organise a charity arm-wrestle in our local pub *The Star and Garter*.

One of the Israeli market traders was named Ami, who sold ladies' clothes. He was a stocky, tough ex-paratrooper, who would joke that he could beat me at arm wrestling. So Frank and I asked him if he would be prepared to arm-wrestle me for this good cause. He agreed immediately. We then approached our local pub who said we could hold the match there.

I came up with the idea of contacting Oliver Reed who was an infamous arm-wrestler, an ex-doorman, and now a very famous actor, to see if he would come to the event and arm-wrestle me. I knew that he had an affection for the East End of London and that anytime he got drunk he'd arm-wrestle in the pub he was drinking in.

He was living in Guernsey at the time and I discovered that his brother David acted as his agent. I found David's address after calling *The Sun* newspaper and telling them what we had planned. I sent David a letter, explaining what we were planning, inviting his brother Olly to arm wrestle me for charity.

Much to my surprise, a week later I received a letter back, saying that Oliver Reed was in London filming at the BBC on the day of the match and would love to come along and arm-wrestle me!

The Star and Garter was a small pub on Whitechapel Road opposite my stalls. I knew the landlord, Larry, well, who was a nice guy. He agreed that Frank and I could sell tickets to raise money for the Zeebrugge fund.

We soon sold over seventy tickets to stall holders who wanted to see me arm-wrestle Ami. There was a lot of side betting going on, which I didn't get involved with. There were quite a few Israelis there who wanted to see their man beat me. I got in contact with Dick to come and referee the match. Dick was a qualified Judo referee, as well as a second Dan black belt.

So, this was to be our first arm-wrestling show at *The Star and Garter*, on March 27th 1987.

On the night the pub was packed. Dick turned up in a bow tie and evening suit to referee, and looked the part. Frank was the night's Master of Ceremonies and was a natural at the job.

I was to arm wrestle Ami on a small pub table, sitting down. I won the first pin, with Ami winning the second. He had hands like shovels and was as strong as an ox. With his Israeli contingent cheering him on, he didn't want to lose face, so I put all my strength into the last arm-wrestle to win, as it was the best out of three pins. With all of my strength, I gradually pinned Ami's arm down on the table. He took it well and we had a drink afterwards.

Then the other traders, in exchange for a donation to the fund, arm wrestled each other. It was a huge success. I had completely forgotten about Oliver Reed coming, until a motorcycle courier walked in carrying a large brown envelope. He asked for Les Clayden and I signed for it, as I opened it up I found a large black and white photo of Oliver Reed when he was younger, which he had written on it 'Yes please, mines a pint!' and a personal cheque for £100 towards the fund.

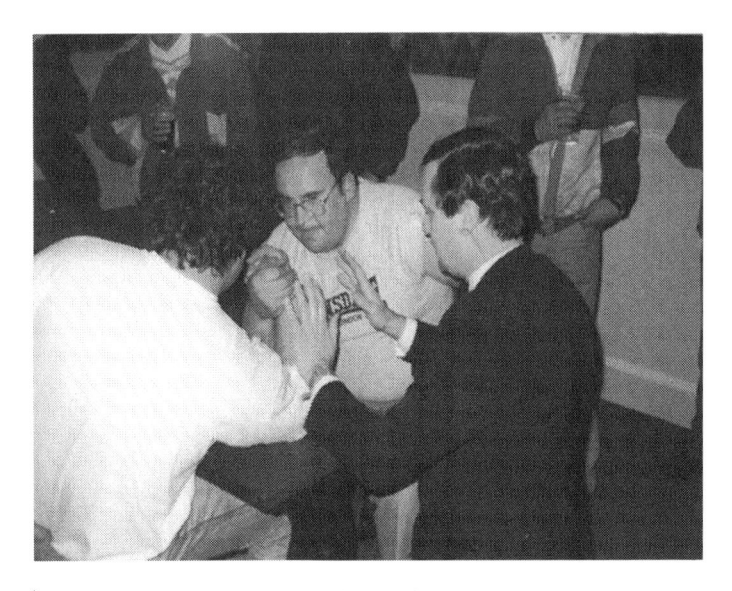

Me arm wrestling Ami, in the Star & Garter Pub, with Dick refereeing

There was also a note apologising that he couldn't attend because he'd been delayed filming. We auctioned the photo for another £50 but now I wished I'd kept it. I would have loved to have arm-wrestled this great man.

It was many years later, when I was in Malta on business, that I visited the pub where he'd died while in the middle of filming *Gladiator*. He'd been arm-wrestling visiting British sailors, which was just typical of the man!

Most actors' dream is to die on stage, but I am sure with Olly he would have been happy doing what he loved, drinking and arm-wrestling in a pub called 'The Pub'.

AFTER THE EVENT finished in the pub, Frank and I got

talking. Never one to miss a possible business opportunity, we saw a great potential in staging arm-wrestling shows.

Frank discovered that there were two arm-wrestling organisations in the UK, but there lay the problem with promoting the sport as they were both at loggerheads with each other. We also found out that there was an arm-wrestling table that could be dismantled. It was a stand-up table that came from America.

One of the arm-wrestling bodies was called the British Arm Wrestling Federation, and its main man was Clive Myers, an ex-professional TV wrestler, who was also now a professional arm-wrestler and a very good one at that. We were told that there were different weight categories and different hand grips and that it wasn't just about strength, but just like Judo technique played an important part in winning.

Frank and I decided that we could, with the right promotion, put this sport on the map and drag it out of just being a pub sport. Next, we decided to create an image for me to attract the press. We came up with the name "Gentleman Les", Frank got his dad's old bowler hat for me to wear, and with a smart suit the image of "Gentlemen Les" was born.

I began some special training with Clive, who was an ex-world arm-wrestling champion at his home and in the gym. I also started practising with a hand grip, which golfers use to strengthen their grip. I very quickly began to do sets of 200 with this grip, without stopping.

We wanted to bring the sport to the attention of the general public, and to be taken seriously and not just associated as a bit of fun on a pub table. We started to organise events in pubs and nightclubs. We took the stand-up arm wrestling table, which on its own generated immediate interest wherever it went.

We made friends with a very good arm-wrestler called Norman James, who refereed the matches. He would wear the American-style referee shirt, and we gave a demonstration to the crowd, then organised a competition. The nights were a huge success. Everywhere we went, people of all sizes and ages loved to arm-wrestle, especially after a few drinks.

Frank and I were a great team in generating press coverage. We built up a good relationship with the main local newspaper *The East London Advertiser*. The next step was local radio, it seemed everybody wanted to know about this new craze of arm-wrestling. Our biggest show so far was in a local wine bar where Frank and I would sell tickets and keep the door money, while the venue would have the takings from the bar. Frank would be the MC for the night and was brilliant on the microphone, while I would arm-wrestle some local hard men. We'd then organise a competition amongst the customers.

I'd been talking to the Marketing Director of the Romford Brewery, asking him to come to one of our shows, with a view of possibly getting some bookings from them. We'd build the atmosphere before the show, with a fanfare of music, similar to a world boxing championship fight. Then we'd give a demonstration of the rules and regulations, and organise a competition. The night was a great success, and unbeknown to me the Marketing Director and his assistant had been there all night observing.

They came up to me at the end of the evening to tell me that they hadn't expected such a good evening, and asked me to go to their office the following week to discuss some bookings.

Frank was brilliant on the mic, but surprisingly for a Jew was a poor businessman. So it was left to me to go on my own to the Romford Brewery to discuss a deal.

After my meeting with the Marketing Director, I came out with a signed contract for twenty road shows to take place in pubs and clubs that they supplied. They agreed to pay us £250 per show making the contract worth £2,500. When I told Frank about this, he thought I was winding him up and didn't believe me until I showed him the signed contract. He gave me a big hug and told me that he always knew I had a Jewish brain!

The first show for Romford Brewery was in West London. Frank was determined to make a good impression, so he went out and hired a white tuxedo to wear to present the show. We drove around West London, looking for this place, but it was dark and we were both unfamiliar with that part of London. I drove around a one-way system looking for the building, and kept coming back to the same place. It had a tower with a large illuminated cross on the outside. I turned to Frank and told him that this was definitely the place. His face turned whiter than the cross on the outside of the building and he told me not to wind him up. I told him again that this was the place.

A look of horror spread across his face when he suddenly realised it was a Roman Catholic Club. He then tells me, in all seriousness, that as a practising Jew he couldn't go inside. He said that if he was seen inside he would be expelled from the synagogue. I told him that if that was the case it was unlikely that there would be any other Jews inside and that if he didn't go inside with me he wouldn't be worshipping anywhere again!!!

So, very reluctantly, shaking his head, he went inside with me. As we walked into the place, the place was full of old-age Irish pensioners who'd never seen arm-wrestling before in their lives. So we go through the motions and soon they're queuing up to try their arm at the sport. They told us afterwards that it had been one of the best nights they'd had in years.

"Gentlemen Les" with my business partner Frank Pittal

That also made us realise that this sport crossed over all age brackets and I promised Frank that I wouldn't tell the Rabbi about him going into the Roman Catholic Club.

Frank and I now called ourselves L&F Promotions which stood for Les and Frank. The media started to take us seriously, and on one occasion before one of our shows, Capital Radio sent a chauffeur-driven limousine to pick me up from the stalls in Whitechapel to take me to their radio station in Euston to be interviewed about this new sport.

Never one to miss an opportunity to promote the sport, when Noel Edmonds came down to Whitechapel to film an episode of Noel's House party for the BBC, Frank and I grabbed him to take a photo of me and Noel arm wrestling, to appear in the next edition of *The East London Advertiser*.

As they were filming in an empty shop opposite my stalls, Noel Edmonds spoke to me during breaks. He told me that he'd started as a hospital DJ and, looking at the London Hospital which was across the road, told me about some of the wild nights he'd had with some of the nurses. I got the impression that with all of his fame and money he missed those days.

He asked me if I wanted to appear on the show which was watched by millions of people across the UK. I jumped at the offer, and was featured in one of the clips. I found him to be a genuinely nice man, whose fame and money hadn't gone to his head.

1989 Me, arm wrestling Noel Edmonds with Frank in Whitechapel Market

Our next new coup was to catch the arch prankster Jeremy Beadle, who was famous for playing pranks on people in his show *Beadles About*. Frank was involved in a charity auction for Great Ormond Street Hospital for Children and Jeremy Beadle had agreed to host it.

Our plan was simple, we disguised the arm-wrestling table on the stage with a blanket, and I hid in the wings wearing my trade-mark bowler hat. Frank called Jeremy onto the stage and then told the audience that he had a nice surprise for him. Frank then told Jeremy Beadle that for charity he'd like him to arm-wrestle the heavy weight Commonwealth champion. Frank then took the cover off the table and I walked out onto the stage. The look of horror on Jeremy Beadle's face was brilliant. We had successfully Beadled Beadle. He said "I'm not arm-wrestling him! ", and went to run off of the stage. Frank stopped him, and reminded him that it was for charity.

So very reluctantly he stood at the table, then whispered to me, could I arm-wrestle him left handed. Not many people knew that he had a deformed right hand, but we did so I told him not to worry. I let him win, and he was very happy. Jeremy Beadle had received some bad press over the years because of some of the pranks he'd played on people on his show. But I can honestly say he was one of the nicest men I've met. He spent the whole evening talking to everyone and was the perfect gentleman.

The night raised over £11,000 and a few weeks later I managed to get Peter Dean, one of the stars of *EastEnders*, to come and present the cheque to the hospital.

Me arm wrestling the late Jeremy Beadle at the charity night

Me and Peter Dean of East Enders arm wrestling at Great Ormond Street Children's Hospital where he presented a cheque for £11,000

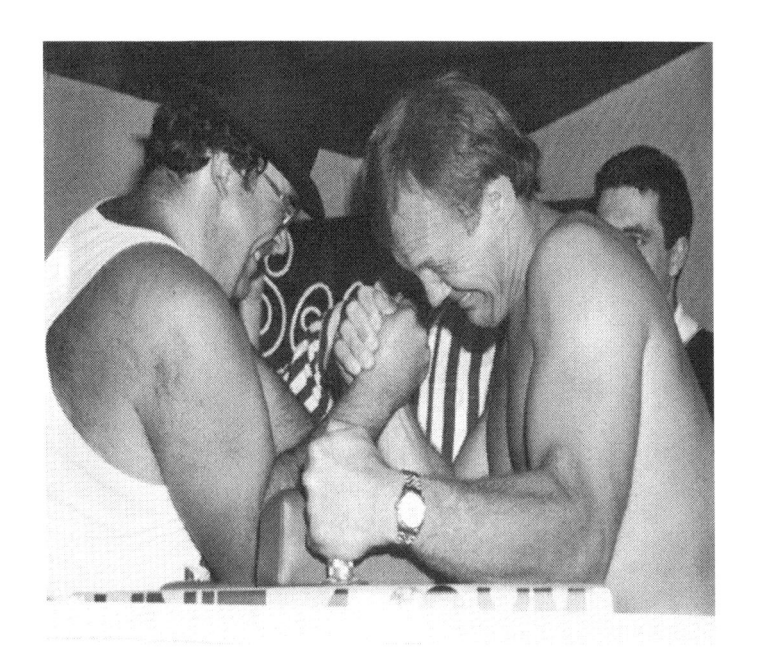

Me arm wrestling Brian Jacks at Sorralles night club in East London

For our next show we hired *Sorralles* on the Commercial Road, next to *The George* pub. I contacted my old friend Brian Jacks, and asked if he would be willing to arm wrestle me for charity. Brain was now a celebrity, making a big name for himself on the TV show 'Superstars', where he became famous for doing 60 arm dips in 1 minute! He won the TV series, and also later Euro-Superstars. After this achievement he later appeared on 'This is Your Life', with Eamonn Andrews. As a favour to me he agreed to come.

I was also very friendly with the Page Three model Suzanne Mizzi. I'd known her from the market since she'd been fourteen years-old where she'd worked as a Saturday girl for my friend Ginger. Even at that young age, we all used to say she should be a model when she got older, and that's exactly what she did. She was now one of *The Sun*'s favourite Page Three models, and received thousands of pounds in appearance fees. Whenever she was available, she'd come to one of our shows for free, never forgetting her time on the market. She was one of the most photogenic women modelling at that time.

Suzanne Mizzi and Brian Jacks in attendance we were guaranteed maximum publicity. It was a great night, even though Brian cheated me on the table by lifting both of his feet off of the ground which was against the rules so he could win the last pin. I didn't mind as it was for charity and not a serious competition.

From left to right, Brian Jacks, Gary Stretch (Middlewieght Boxer), and Suzanne Mizzi (Page Three Girl) with 'Gentlemen Les'

Frank and I, as L&F Promotions, were getting publicity wherever we went, in local newspapers and interviews on local radio stations. Now our goal was to get arm-wrestling on TV.

ITV had an evening show, called the *6 O'Clock Show* presented by Danny Baker, Chris Tarrant and my old friend Michael Aspel. It was a topical show covering interesting stories from around London. I thought it would be an ideal stage to launch arm-wrestling on television. I contacted the producers of the show, and sold them the idea to come and film one of our shows in the East End.

Frank and I booked a local nightclub to film in, and Frank found a local giant of a man from Wales to arm-wrestle, who he called Gordon the Welsh Dragon. Gordon ran a local gym, was 6'4 and weighed in at 23 stone! So no pressure for me!

The *6 O'clock Show* sent Danny Baker to film before the contest. I showed him on camera how I trained with the hand grip. I opened and closed it in my right hand fifty times, very quickly. He then tried it, and struggled to do one! He was genuinely impressed.

ITV filmed the final contest between me and Gordon which I managed to win. After the contest Danny Baker sat with Auntie Pam and her husband, talking and drinking all evening. He really is a very nice man and a true gentleman.

Me, with Danny Baker and friend Laurie at Sorralles night club after filming on LWT 6 O'Clock Show

From left to right, my Auntie Barbara, Danka, Danny Baker, far right Auntie Pamela. Taken in Sorralles night club

When the programme was broadcast, I was invited with Danka, Frank and his wife to watch the programme in the audience. After the clip was televised, Danny Baker wanted to talk about how successful the night had been and how exciting arm-wrestling was to watch, but Michael Aspel cut him short and stopped him talking about it.

After the show, we were invited for drinks with the three presenters. Danny Baker was very apologetic telling me about how he'd wanted to talk more about the arm-wrestling and how Michael had stopped him. I told him not to worry about it and that it was more important that he'd enjoyed the night.

I then walked over to Michael and asked if he remembered presenting *Come Dancing* from the *Lyceum*. He stuck his nose up in the air and replied "Oh that was a long time ago". I then reminded him about how he used to chase me around the ballroom to talk to. He went a bright red and I walked off, leaving him holding his glass of wine.

I have found over the years that some of the most famous people in the world can be the most down to earth, while some of the others think they are God's gift.

TWENTY-THREE

24 HOURS

I WAS ALWAYS LOOKING for ways to bring arm-wrestling to the attention of the general public and into the media.

I asked Frank one day whether anyone had ever arm wrestled non-stop for twenty-four hours. He looked at me as if I was mad and said he hadn't heard of such a thing. I told him as a publicity stunt I wanted to try,

Frank then got in touch with different arm-wrestling federations around the world to check if it had ever been attempted. The American and Russian Federations both told him it was impossible and that anyone who tried would break their arm in the attempt.

We then contacted *The Guinness Book of Records*, who confirmed that it had never been attempted. So we put L&F's publicity machine into gear. I decided that I would attempt this feat on a sit-down arm wrestling table, taking on different opponents over the full twenty-four hours. The idea was not to beat everyone I arm-wrestled, but to carry it out as a feat of endurance. *The Guinness Book of Records* told us what we needed to do for them to recognise the attempt. They told us we were allowed a two minute toilet break every hour, but it must be monitored by a recognised referee and independent adjudicators. *The Guinness Book of Records* agreed to send down one of their own adjudicators to monitor the attempt.

We contacted Dick, who got some of his police friends to witness the attempt as well as a qualified referee from the British Arm-Wrestling Federation. We planned the event at their headquarters which was in a gym called Unit 4 in West Norwood, London.

Frank sent out press releases and we received a very good response. I wanted to raise money for the children's ward in the London Hospital, Whitechapel.

The day before we were due to carry out the attempt LBC radio invited me to their station for a thirty minute interview to talk about it. That evening I received a call from *The Guinness Book of Records* that they couldn't recognise the attempt, because arm wrestling was not a recognised sport!

They suggested that I should cancel it. I told them to get lost, and how could a book that covered tiddlywinks and God knows what else, not recognise arm-wrestling. They apologised, but wouldn't budge. There was far too much at stake and I wouldn't cancel the attempt.

The next day at 7am on a Sunday morning I started my marathon arm-wrestle. We'd organised various arm-wrestlers and volunteers to arm-wrestle me over the twenty-four hours. The event was covered on numerous radio stations and *The Times* newspaper sent a photographer to cover the event. They thought it was perfect to have a photo of someone in a bowler hat, arm-wrestling for 24 hours in their newspaper. Other newspapers sent reporters and photographers down to the gym.

After several hours of arm wrestling and winning most of the pins, my arm began swelling, but I was determined not to give up. We had one of the adjudicators counting the pins on a counter. It wasn't difficult keeping awake as the adrenaline was doing its job. The problem was that my arm was getting really sore.

Towards the end of the twenty-four hours I was still winning some of the matches. When I got to the end, I can't even begin tell you the relief I felt. I'd completed 3001 arm wrestles over the full day, and was now the first man in the world ever to achieve this. I also raised over £1000 for the children's ward.

The marathon was covered the next day when I finished on the Monday morning, by every radio station in London, Kent and Essex. It also made news on ITV and BBC. We'd achieved what we'd wanted by getting arm-wrestling onto the television.

I then noticed that I had no skin left on my elbow from friction burns that I received from arm-wrestling on the table. I finished up going to the very hospital that I'd raised money for, to get it dressed.

I was very disappointed with *The Guinness Book of Records* and their views on arm-wrestling. I later took all of the press cuttings from the twenty-four hour marathon and with representatives from the British Arm Wrestling Federation, went to the London Headquarters of *The Guinness Book of Records*.

They told me that they'd place everything in their archives, and if, or when, they recognised arm wrestling as a sport, they'd include me as the first man in the world to achieve this feat.

I'm still waiting!

Me on my stalls in Whitechapel Market, holding the 24hr Marathon Arm wrestling Trophy

The next plan to generate money and publicity for L&F and arm-wrestling was to book The Pub, Club, and Leisure show at Olympia. This was a three-day event, where breweries and manufacturers connected with the trade promoted their wares from all over the UK. It attracted thousands of people over the three days, some just coming for the free samples of beer that they dished out. Frank and I thought that this would be a good way to promote arm-wrestling to the trade and hopefully get some bookings. We took Norman James to act as a referee, and together we gave demonstrations to the public, on the American style table with Frank MC'ing on the microphone.

We took along my TV set and video recorder to play the recent *6 O'Clock Show* clip, with a portable speaker and a mic for Frank. The exhibition organisers didn't take us seriously and put us upstairs opposite a large double stand which was giving away free Guinness by attractive models in swimsuits.

Frank was understandably nervous as the exhibition hall filled up with people. He asked me if we'd done the right thing with booking the stand. Looking at the stands around us, which had spent thousands of pounds on decorations and models to promote their brands, I could understand his concern, as we certainly looked like the poor boys of the exhibition.

I told Frank to just do what he was good at and that the rest was in God's hands.

Before midday the hall was already packed with people. Norman and I started to give arm-wrestling demonstrations on the table, with Frank explaining the rules. We then invited members of the public to arm-wrestle me, or Norman, or one of their friends for charity. We soon had crowds of people four rows deep around the stand with people of all ages wanting, especially after a few free samples of Guinness from the stand opposite, to have a go. I smiled to myself when I saw that the Guinness stand was virtually empty even with their free samples and we were absolutely packed! Unbelievable!

The L & F Stand at The Pub, Club, and Leisure Show, in the Olympia Exhibition Hall London

THE THREE-DAY EVENT proved a massive hit, and we got bookings from pubs who wanted us to organise competitions in their pubs and nightclubs. We also got a free all-expenses trip, plus fees from Marston's Brewery in Stoke-on-Trent, to organise and give demonstrations in their pubs. This time we took Clive Myers who was a brilliant showman on the table, and Norman James with us. Once again it proved to be a huge success.

We were now putting arm-wrestling on the map and even got a full page, in colour, in the *Sunday Times Magazine* in June 1989. I told Frank, now's the time we try national television to promote this sport. There was a BBC television show called *People* presented by the boxer Frank Bruno.

I said this is where we go next, and Frank's reply was "You're mad! They'll never show arm-wrestling". I told him not to bet on it!

The *People* show was a bit like the *6 O'Clock Show* but was shown on prime-time television with an audience of over ten million viewers.

I called the producer of the show and pitched the idea to him. He politely turned me down flat. Never one to give up easily, I called him back thirty minutes later and asked him what he was looking for. He then explained to me the type of things he wanted to cover. I listened carefully to what he was telling me, and then apologised for not explaining myself properly, and more less repeated back to him what he'd just told me. He then much to my surprise agreed to cover one of our shows for the programme.

I told the producer that this was a heavyweight commonwealth defence title. Larry, the governor of *The Star and Garter*, had opened a new nightclub in Bethnal Green Road, and readily agreed to let us hold it there. The BBC gave me very little time to organise the contest. So Frank asked Gordon, who I had beaten on the *6 O'Clock Show* if he'd like a rematch. He jumped at the chance to try and beat me on a second attempt.

I then told Frank we should try and get some sponsorship from the Romford Brewery. I went to the marketing manager and told him for £3,000 I would wear a shirt with the logo of one of their beers on it, and that they could place advertising material inside the nightclub. They told me that £3,000 was way above their budget but because it was being filmed by the BBC and going out at prime-time they'd do it.

Frank couldn't believe it when I told him how much I'd got from the Romford Brewery, and again he gave me a big hug and a kiss telling me for sure I had a Jewish brain.

All I had to do now was to beat Gordon, who'd been in serious training and was by far my most difficult opponent. I decided to do some special training with my old friend Clive Myers who was one of the best arm-wrestlers in the world. I went as often as I could before the match to train with Clive and pick up as many tips as I could.

The BBC decided that before the match took place that it would make good TV to get Frank Bruno to go down to Whitechapel Market to interview different stallholders to talk about the match. They also filmed me training with Clive and showed a clip of me relaxing afterwards in a Jacuzzi wearing my bowler hat and smoking a cigar while being interviewed by one of their presenters Jenny Barnet who was sitting next to me in the Jacuzzi!

One of the funniest clips was when she stood next to Gordon. Jenny was only just over 5 foot tall, and Gordon was at least 6'4 and over 23 stone. She only came up to his waist, as the camera slowly panned up, he really did look like a giant standing next to her. Gordon was also an ex-SAS soldier who'd served in Northern Ireland and was as tough as they come.

From what had started as a "No" from the producers of the programme, had now become the main story of the programme. We organised the event like a major world title boxing match. With fanfares and Gordon being led to the arm-wrestling table by a girl in a Welsh national costume carrying the Welsh flag.

Gordon the 'Welsh Dragon' before the arm-wrestling match

Ted the flower-seller from Whitechapel Market, a decorated old soldier proudly wearing his medals, walked in front of me carrying the Union Jack and I had two of Larry's busty barmaids wearing revealing leotards to carry my Commonwealth belt, which was as good as any world boxing belt. Before the match, there was a ceremony which unfortunately wasn't shown in the programme.

Michael Watson, the new middleweight boxing champion, presented me with the belt as the reigning heavyweight Commonwealth champion. He had just recently fought and beaten Nigel Benn for the middleweight championship. He kept looking at my belt and shaking his head said to me "Les, that's a really nice belt, and to think I got into the ring and risked my life to fight Nigel Benn and all I got was a poxy trophy!"

From left to right, Ted me and Colin before the arm-wrestling contest with Gordon

FRANK WAS as nervous as hell and wearing his white tuxedo. He was sweating like a pig under the camera lights but once we started filming, his nerves disappeared and he spoke into the microphone like a star.

The nightclub was packed to the rafters and the noise from my fans' shouting was deafening. The contest was to be the best of three pins. I won the first pin, and Gordon won the second. It all rested on the last pin. With all the strength I could muster, I gradually managed to push Gordon's arm down to win the match.

Colin from *Crackers* was there to cheer me on and the place erupted as it was announced that I was still the undefeated Commonwealth champion. It was one of the happiest days of my life.

Me arm wrestling Gordon (The Welsh Dragon) at Tantrum's Nightclub

If readers want to see this match, they can go on YouTube and type in Gentleman Les Arm Wrestling Champion or click this link for digital download readers

(https://www.youtube.com/watch?v=HqBrNV4ZowQ)

Michael Watson presenting me with the Commonwealth Belt

Me arm-wrestling Frank Bruno in the Bombay Grab Pub 1989

A FEW DAYS later after the contest, the BBC filmed me at another *pub The Bombay Grab*, in Stratford, giving Frank Bruno tips at the arm-wrestling table. It finished with both of us doing the Hokey Cokey, which some years later was screened, when Frank fought Oliver McCall at Wembley stadium, on the 2nd of September 1995 for the World Boxing Council (WBC) heavyweight championship, which he won on a unanimous points decision at the end of twelve rounds.

It reminded me on the day of filming his *People* show how he looked at my belt and kept saying with envy in his voice, what a nice belt it was. With all the money he had then, what he longed for most was a world championship belt.

Now he had one of his own to admire, and I was very happy for him.

After the *People* show was aired, I went shopping in my local Asda store and I couldn't believe how many people recognised me, with children even asking me for my autograph!

Shortly after the programme, I was invited to a charity event in Docklands at a conference centre. I was told Michael Watson would also be there and I was looking forward to seeing him again.

There were hundreds of schoolchildren there, and at the end of the event I was asked if I would sign autographs with Michael Watson. He stood on one side next to me, and it was announced to the kids to queue up if they wanted an autograph. Michael had just recently won the middleweight boxing championship, beating Nigel Benn that night against the odds. This was a real achievement. As the kids queued up for their autographs I saw Michael looking over to me as I had three times as many kids queuing for my autograph than he did. I've never felt so embarrassed.

Sometime later he defended his title against Chris Eubank and got knocked out. It was such a severe K.O, that he received brain damage and never fully recovered. It was a very sad end to a promising career. He was also one of the nicest men that I'd met, and I followed his long road to recovery closely.

Me and Michael Watson arm wrestling in the London Docklands Arena for a charity event

The next time we managed to get arm-wrestling on TV was a demonstration of the sport on Sky News. We took the table and Norman James to their studio and gave a demonstration with one of their presenters live on the news. I also got another £500 from the Romford Brewery to wear their t-shirt.

Frank and I were trying our best to get the sport recognised and entered into the 1992 Olympics. The main problem was there were two arm-wrestling organisations in the UK. One was the British Arm Wrestling Federation, which was run by David Shead and his girlfriend Marion Nesbitt. The other one was Pro-Grip, run by Clive Myers, and they hated each other! There was intense rivalry amongst them and it split the arm-wrestlers in the UK into two camps. It also made sponsorship for the sport incredibly difficult.

Hardly a week went by without me appearing in the *East London Advertiser* promoting arm-wrestling or raising money for charity. With this publicity came certain problems - it was a bit like being the fastest gun in town with young pretenders wanting the title. There was a writer for the *Market Trader*, which was a national trade paper, who had never met me but would regularly issue challenges to arm-wrestle me for his own publicity. There were young wannabes who would regularly come and see me on the stall asking me to arm wrestle them, but by now I was a professional arm wrestler, and I dismissed these amateurs with contempt.

One of the more serious challenges came from a local hard man called Lenny McLean, known as 'The Guv'nor', who was a bare knuckled fighter. His nephew knew Frank and came to me to say Lenny was tired of seeing me in the newspaper every week and wanted to arm-wrestle me. I sent a message back that I'd arm wrestle him for a bet of £3,000. I never got a reply.

Another local gangster who was an associate of the Kray Twins called Jack Spot used to come and speak to me on the stalls. By now he was far too old to arm wrestle, but liked to reminisce about the good old times with the Krays, cutting people up! I used to make excuses that I was too busy to talk to him. If he'd known that I was an ex-special police constable, I don't think he would have been so keen to talk to me!

It was now 1992, and the Japanese arm-wrestling federation had contacted Clive to ask if he could organise a British team to take part in a world championship taking place in Chiba City, Japan. They said that they'd provide accommodation for the three-day event.

Clive contacted some of the top arm wrestlers in the country to try and organise a team. He managed to get together, counting himself and me, a team of six.

To help cut costs we would fly there via Moscow. The first leg of the trip would be with the Russian airline Aeroflot, who were known as the flying coffins because of the number of crashes they were involved in. One of the reasons for the high level of accidents was down to poor maintenance of their planes. The reason Clive couldn't find more people to go was the cost. Even with accommodation being covered, it was still going to cost over £300 each. With no sponsorship to help, this was a lot of money to find, especially as most of the arm-wrestlers were tradesmen and not rich.

I was determined to go. Ever since starting Judo, Japan was a country I'd always dreamed of visiting. I asked Danka if she'd like to come with me and Clive agreed that she could be our mascot and carry the Union Jack flag for the team, even though she was from Yugoslavia!

So we prepared for this world championship with twenty-eight countries taking part, including the USA, Russia, Brazil, Japan and many more.

I was now forty-one years old, so I went into vigorous training for the event. Ever since the bad Judo accident that I'd suffered in my Judo club, I'd experienced recurring pain in my shoulder from arthritis. During my training with Clive I managed to pull a muscle in my arm and, together with my latest attack of arthritis, I was in a lot of pain and should have withdrawn from the competition. But it was too good an opportunity to miss and I hoped that I'd feel better by the time the event began.

At the last minute Clive found one other arm-wrestler to come with us, and I nicknamed our team 'The Magnificent Seven'. We were one of the smallest teams to enter the competition. The flight from London to Moscow was as bad as I was expecting. The food was so bad I didn't touch it. The flight from Moscow to Tokyo was with their new airline called Russian Airways. It was a brand new plane which was half empty which gave us plenty of room to stretch out and the food was as good as any in first class. We were served steak and caviar, and what was funny were the male stewards on board. On many airlines this job is filled by gay men, but these looked more like KGB bodybuilders. But they were friendly enough.

TWENTY-FOUR

CHIBA CITY

When we landed in Tokyo we took the train to Chiba city and checked into the hotel, which was a nice four-star.

From my Judo training I was used to bowing as a sign of respect. In Japan almost everywhere you go someone bows to you and I would always return the gesture.

Unfortunately the other members of the team, except Clive, weren't used to this, and didn't return the bow, which is taken as an insult. So I quickly informed them about the custom and there were no more repeats of what is regarded as disrespectful.

One of the other teams staying at our hotel was from Georgia, Russia. I couldn't believe the next day when we came down for breakfast that the Georgian team had set up a table in the foyer and were selling homemade vodka and souvenirs. The looks of bewilderment on the faces of the Japanese staff was a real scream (and I was worried about my teammates not bowing!)

On the first day of the competition we walked into the arena with Danka carrying the Union Jack and the rest of the team walking behind her, including me wearing my bowler hat. Immediately all of the press and TV swarmed around us and later that evening I watched footage of our entrance on the TV in our room.

Our small team had already set the place alight! We had two super heavyweights, myself and my good friend Trevor Lloyd who'd attended many contests with me. We also had two heavyweights, two middleweights, one of which was Clive, and a light heavyweight.

We all won our first rounds easily, but by now my shoulder and arm were killing me and I was seriously worried about my next round.

On my next bout I really struggled to win and knew it was going to be very difficult to win the next one. The rest of the team, were doing great and I was proud to be a member of this band of brothers.

On the last day of the competition I lost to a local Japanese arm-wrestler who looked more like a sumo wrestler. I was bitterly disappointed, but under the circumstances of the pain I was in, I couldn't have done any better. When the other competitors in my weight category had finished their bouts, it placed me third in the world.

Clive came second in his weight category and although he was now over 50 years old being the supreme athlete he was and great competitor, he too was very disappointed. He then entered into a higher weight category, which I thought was mad, and still managed to come second as well!

My friend Trevor Lloyd had also come second in the world, but had now entered left-handed. He got to the final and the atmosphere was electric. It was just like a scene from the Sylvester Stallone movie *Over the Top* which was based on arm-wrestling and where Clive had made a cameo appearance.

In Trevor's final match, I was standing at the front and was cheering him on, shouting tips until I was hoarse. Slowly he got the better of his opponent and won the match. He immediately ran off the stage and gave me a big bearhug telling me he couldn't have won it without me. Trevor Lloyd was now the left-handed super heavy weight of the world.

Me and Trevor Lloyd practising in Chiba City 1992

Altogether our small band of arm-wrestlers had won more trophies than any other team in the competition. The Japanese press were all over Trevor for pictures and one of their TV channels filmed him doing a stunt where they tied two lengths of rope onto his wrists and then attached them onto the back of two motorcycles which revved up, sending up clouds of smoke from their rear wheels, with Trevor holding the bikes back.

That evening after the competition, we all celebrated how well we'd done. I found myself in one of the Russian's rooms, where they were drinking their homemade vodka, which tasted as if it were 99% proof. One of their women arm-wrestlers took a shine to me, and sat on my lap and whispered in my ear things in Russian which I could only guess about. Also drinking in their room was an American John Brzenk, who was a world champion. After we both had drunk some of the vodka we arm-wrestled several times together and much to my surprise and everyone else in the room I beat him every time. I think the 99% proof vodka had numbed the pain in my shoulder and arm, enough to win.

WHEN THE COMPETITION had finished we all went to Tokyo for two days before flying back to the UK.

Tokyo was an amazing city. I went with Danka on the famous bullet train to Mount Fuji. About half way up this beautiful mountain with snow on its peak, I turned to Danka and asked her what was that terrible smell? We discovered it was sulphur from the mountain which smelt like rotten eggs which rather spoilt the beautiful scenery for me.

Back in Tokyo I saw what must be the world's biggest pedestrian crossing in the centre, where hundreds of people cross at any one time. We visited the Royal Palace, which had the biggest Koi fish I'd ever seen swimming in the moat surrounding it.

What also made me laugh was whenever we bought something in a large department store, even if it was a small item, there would follow a process of anything up to ten staff wrapping it up. The taxi drivers and lorry drivers all wore white gloves, something I don't think would ever happen along the Commercial Road in East London.

It was one of the greatest experiences of my life, which I shall never forget. On the Aeroflot flight back from Moscow to London, I warned the rest of the team not to eat the in-flight meal. They chose to ignore me, and I wasn't surprised the next day when they'd all gone down with food poisoning.

The competition had been one of the highlights of my career in arm wrestling. Frank and I had got the sport onto TV, radio and had managed to get extensive coverage over the years in newspapers. We'd managed to get local sponsorship, but never the one big deal with TV coverage, which would have helped secure major sponsorship.

The sport of arm-wrestling deserves to be in the Olympics, especially when there are in my opinion, some rather obscure sports which don't deserve to be there. Yet, to this day, it still waits to be included.

Frank and I had dedicated a great deal of time, effort and money, to put arm-wrestling on the map and to bring it out of its pub environment. We had at least successfully achieved that. Now was the time for me to move on.

After my grandmother had died, Charringtons Brewery asked my grandfather if he would like to move into a small flat. The house in Edwin Street was far too big for him to manage on his own so he agreed and they gave the house to Mother Teresa Sisters of Mercy.

They took over the house as a mission and helped the poor and sick in the East End. It was a bit like *déjà vu*, just like the time when Ghandi had visited the East End. I found out about this when two of the nuns came to my stalls asking for a donation of food for their mission. I couldn't believe it when they told me they' taken over my old house. They invited me to visit them and I told them that I would. At the end of my week I took a couple of sacks of food and drove to my old house in Edwin Street. They invited me inside and showed me around. I told them how my grandmother had used to love the garden and had grown roses there. The head Sister gave me a knowing look and explained that was why roses grew so well everywhere in the garden.

After that visit I often drove there giving them fruit and vegetables. They told me that whenever Mother Teresa came to visit London she'd go to visit them in the mission. Mother Teresa was by now a world famous figure who'd been photographed with Princess Diana and many famous world leaders. The nuns told me that they'd try to organise for me to meet her on her next trip to London. I said that I would like that and told them that my wife was from Yugoslavia where Mother Teresa had been born.

When I told Frank about my conversation with the Sisters, he immediately got excited and told me that we should try and get a photo of me and Mother Teresa arm-wrestling together. I told him to forget that idea. I never did get to meet her, or arm-wrestle her.

Many years later the Vatican beatified her making her a saint.

TWENTY-FIVE

CHANNEL 7

I'D WORKED in Whitechapel Market on the stalls for fourteen years, standing on the pavement in all the weathers this good country could throw at me.

I'd had enough, what with the long hours getting up at 4am and not getting home until 7 or 8pm - it had taken its toll on my body and mind. Also with the supermarkets getting competitive, it was now no longer worth the effort, as they had taken the cream of the profits.

So I sold the stalls to another stallholder and started to look for another job. I saw an advert in the *London Evening Standard*, from a company called Channel 7 (UK) advertising for telesales people. I thought from the name that it might be connected to television. I knew from the arm-wrestling that I was more than capable of talking on the phone so I went for an interview.

While I was waiting for several other candidates to be interviewed, I looked around the office and wasn't very impressed with what I saw. I was just about to get up and leave when they called my name to go in for the interview.

The manager who interviewed me asked me if I could drive, I wondered what that had to do with telesales, thinking it might be a trick question. He then told me that he thought I might earn more money as a closer than as a telesales operative. I'd never heard the term closer before and he explained that the job involved selling advertising to businesses. I agreed to try it as it seemed more attractive than sitting at a desk all day making telephone calls.

This was to be my introduction into the cut throat world of direct selling!

The manager told me there was no basic pay, only commission from the deals that were closed, which is the term used when you've sold a deal.

All of the appointments were made by the telesales office and they said I'd receive at least three a day but I needed my own car.

I went the next day to see my friend Ian Brown who was the manager of the Woolwich Building Society, opposite where my stalls had been. I asked him for a loan to buy a car, I already had my mortgage with them so that helped. I'd become friends with him when I'd organised a window display to help raise money for the British Olympic Judo team. By that time Brian Jacks had become a household name from his appearances on *Superstars* and Ian hadn't believed me that I could get Brian down for some publicity shots. So when Brian did come down, Ian was pleasantly surprised and we had become good friends.

I got a loan of £4,000 and bought a secondhand Rover Vanden Plas. It had low mileage and was a peach of a car.

I already owned a couple of suits for the 'Gentlemen Les' image. All I needed now was a briefcase and I was ready to go.

Channel 7 was owned by two Jewish men, Stewart Landau, who I later discovered had passed his Law exam but later told me he could earn more money and have more excitement with direct sales. His partner, Tony Fields, was a talented watch designer.

They'd both started in business by manufacturing their own brands of watches and selling them to the public. They'd place full page colour advertisements in upmarket magazines and newspapers showing a picture of one of their watches, which was advertised at hundreds of pounds. Then a team of their sales people would go onto the streets showing the ads and offering to sell the watch at a heavily discounted price. They had earnt enough money from this, to open up a company they called Channel 7 (UK). This involved them setting up a business information service, years before the internet was invented. Businesses would pay a subscription fee to be recommended on this service, which they promoted in the national press with full page advertisements. The ads invited the general public to call a free dial number if they were looking for anything from a plumber to a lawyer.

It wasn't until many years later that British Telecom's Talking Pages copied the idea.

It was a brilliant piece of marketing and would have been much more successful if only they'd invested more of the profits back into the company.

I'd never been on a sales course in my life. Channel 7's training involved me going out on the road with one of their top closers, Jerry, for three days to learn the pitch. After that, I was on my own, sink or swim.

On my first day out I got a small deal, on my second day I got a bigger deal, and on my third day I got two deals. I received 20% in commission of whatever the value of the deal was once the cheque had cleared!

In my first week, I'd earned more than I would have done working three weeks in Whitechapel Market. I'd taken to this job like a duck to water. All it involved was driving around, going into businesses and talking to the boss dressed in a nice suit. It was nothing like the hard work I was used to doing.

The Channel 7 service covered the whole of the UK. At first I covered appointments in London, but soon discovered that it was easier for the telesales to make appointments outside of London. I also learnt that some closers could only sell to the trades, others only to professionals.

I found I could sell to anyone. On any given day, I might pitch to a plumber working from home in the morning to a large law firm in the afternoon.

I would be lying if I said my Masonic handshake and cufflinks didn't help me on occasions, especially with the professionals I saw but as many of the Freemasons I met who signed deals with me there were just as many or more who didn't.

Very often I'd drive to a city and stay for two or three nights in a bed and breakfast. The telesales would then make appointments for me.

I quickly became one of the company's top closers and got a real buzz every time I closed a deal.

I would sometimes train new closers to learn the pitch. Some of them would be hardened sales people from double-glazing or other direct sales products. They'd sit in on my meetings and learn my pitch and how I closed a deal at the end of a meeting, walking out with a cheque. They'd often ask me what sales book had I read or what course had I'd been on. When I told them none, they'd just shake their heads and say, "I did everything against the book, yet still got the deal!". When I trained someone for the company, I would get a small override from their deals as well as my own commission. But if I didn't sell anything then I'd earn nothing. Fortunately, for me, those days were few and far between.

After working for Channel 7 for a year a new telesales person joined the company. He was older than the rest and spoke on the phone with a very posh accent. He called himself Martin St Clair and soon began working with me making my appointments. He was shit calling the trades, but brilliant at professionals, particularly lawyers, who I loved to pitch to.

We made a good team and earned some good money together. He was rather an odd character who spoke with what I would describe as a clipped Oxford accent. As I got to know him better, he told me his real name was Peter Everett. He said amongst the many jobs he'd worked at, one had been as an assistant pathologist at Southwark Mortuary, which was a coincidence as I'd been a special constable at Southwark Police Station.

He also told me that he'd worked at MI5, but Peter bless him was a bit of a fantasist in my opinion. I liked him and wondered how such an educated man had found himself working as a telesales operative. We had in the past taken on out of work actors, which I just put down to misfortune.

Channel 7 had now divided the best areas of the UK into franchise offices. Stewart and Tony would get a percentage of each office sales, without any investment and little work.

Peter came to me one day and proposed that we should ask Stewart for a franchise and work for ourselves. I was up for the idea, but the problem was where to go? All the best areas had now been taken.

The only territory left was Northern Ireland, because everyone was frightened to set up a business there, especially as this was the time of many problems with the IRA. Peter and I guessed that every local business in Northern Ireland were paying some sort of protection money to the IRA, or the UVF. If we went there as an English company then God alone knows what would happen?

Northern Ireland was at the height of what they called 'The Troubles', a time when bombs and rioting were commonplace.

So we came up with the idea that we'd open a small office in London to make the appointments and I would go to Belfast to recruit a team of closers.

That way we wouldn't' have a physical presence there and we'd have local people working for us.

We placed some ads in local newspapers in Belfast and when we had enough people to see, I flew to Belfast and stayed in the Europa Hotel. This hotel was in *The Guinness Book of Records* as the most bombed hotel in the world (and

I was still waiting to be included for my twenty-four hour arm-wrestling marathon). We formed a company called Eurovision Ltd. We thought because of Ireland's strong ties with the Eurovision Song contest, it might by name association help us?

Peter told me that because of the political problems in Northern Ireland between Protestant and Roman Catholics, we should try and recruit closers from both sides, so we wouldn't seen to be favouring anyone from a particular religion.

The Europa hotel was a five-star and I had booked my stay in a suite. During the interviews I had a mixed bag of people to see. One I immediately liked was called John. He told me he was a protestant and had been selling double-glazing. I immediately hired him and made him my manager. He knew Belfast well and would help me to avoid the main trouble areas.

I hired a small team of closers with a mixture of Catholics and Protestants. John told me that as an Englishman, I'd find it difficult to sell in Belfast and to let him do the talking. I told him to 'wait and see", and I'd take him out on appointments to teach him the pitch.

After a few pints of Guinness that evening, I went to bed. The next morning John and I went out on the leads Peter's office had made for us.

John drove me in his car and for the first time I saw up close the problems of Northern Ireland. There were British Army patrols and armoured cars on street corners. There were clear dividing lines between the Protestant and Catholic housing estates, a far cry from me selling on the mainland.

On the side of buildings inhabited by Protestants there were paintings of the Union Jack flag and pictures of hooded men carrying guns who were the Ulster Volunteer Force. This was the paramilitary group formed by the Protestants to fight the IRA.

As I looked around at all of this, the thought occurred to me, *How the bloody hell am I going to make money here?*

On my first appointment, which was with a small accounting firm, I closed the deal for £600. John thought I'd been lucky, but after that day closing two more deals, his tone changed.

He told me he'd never seen anyone, especially from England, doing this amount of business. I'd taken £2000 by the end of the first day. A great start,.

We celebrated back at *The Europa*, John drinking his beloved Guinness (which I hated but never told him), and me on double Bacardi and cokes.

Within a short space of time, I had a small efficient team of closers operating in the province as it was known to the locals. I would fly over on Mondays, staying until Saturday morning, doing good business. Soon I was flying club with BA and always stayed in one of the best suites at the *Europa Hotel* - business was that good.

After a few months, I went out with my guys on a Friday night to our favourite bar, The Crown, where the bar staff were dressed in long white aprons. It had stained glass windows, with individual booths one side and a large bar opposite.

One of my team noticed Brian Keenan who'd been taken hostage in Beirut with Terry Waite. drinking with his two sisters. After the hostage crisis he'd become somewhat of a local celebrity so my friend sent him over some drinks while we stayed at the bar. When he'd finished the drinks, he offered to buy us a round. He turned to me and said, "What are you drinking, Guinness". I replied a little bit too loud, "I wouldn't drink that poison if you paid me". The reply I gave him in an English accent didn't go down too well. As the noisy bar went very quiet, Brian replied to me "That's an insulting thing to say" and true enough, it was, thinking about it later. So I replied "not really. My poison is Bacardi and coke". With that he just laughed, slapped me on the back and bought me a double. With that everyone in the bar returned to their conversations. It reminded me of a scene from a western.

John asked me afterwards "Why did you say that?" I replied, "Because it's true". He told me I was mad. I replied, "You don't think a sane person would work here do you?" Then we both got drunk.

There were certain areas in Belfast John wouldn't let me sell in as they were too dangerous, which was only common sense.

Belfast was a small city, and it limited us to where we could do business. So after six months we started to run out of leads. Peter and I had the idea of trying Dublin in the Republic of Ireland. When I told John what I was going to do, he said that against all the odds I'd successfully sold in Northern Ireland but in the South he said it would be another matter.

He told me it was impossible to get a decision at the end of a meeting and that they were so slow, it would take them a week just to make their minds up. Our business model worked on selling on the day, not a week later when half the things you told them would have been forgotten. I told John we had no choice but to try.

Again we placed ads for closers in the main local Dublin paper. I booked a suite for the interviews in the *Gresham Hotel* next to the Ha' Penny Bridge. The suite had a great view of the river, and the bridge. In the living room of the suite there was an oak bar, fully stocked. I looked around this impressive room and thought *This is the other side of life*.

The men who came for the interviews were nowhere near as lively as the people I'd recruited in Belfast. I was beginning to wonder if John had been right about this place. There was only one way to find out and that was for me to see if I could get a cheque at the end of the meeting.

There was no doubt that life in the South was lived at a much slower pace than the North, and the mentality there was quite different as well. The first day out selling, I took one of my new guys out with me, who kept telling me, "Leslie the people here won't give you a cheque at the end of a meeting, especially to an Englishman". This was *déja vu* from Belfast and I was determined to prove him wrong.

The first two leads I went on wouldn't give me a decision at the end of the meeting but on the third appointment, I closed the deal for £1,000 much to the surprise of my new guy.

I now had to change the mentality of the new closers in Dublin to get a decision at the end of a meeting. The ones who wouldn't try hard enough I sacked and replaced with more hungry open-minded people.

Yes it was harder to do business here, but not impossible. I now had two teams working for me, one in the north and one in the South.

We were selling all over Ireland very successfully. Of the two places my heart remained firmly in the North. Having said that, what really impressed me was the genuine warmth of the Irish. They were great people to go out and enjoy a *craic* with.

ONCE JOHN and I were in a pub in Belfast and the actor/comedian, Derek Nimmo walked in with his driver. He started saying in his loud posh voice "Oh what a lovely place". John and I burst out laughing. I then asked Derek, mimicking in his own voice, if he'd like a drink with us. John asked him if he could do that thing with his toes but no surprise he declined. We had a great laugh with him anyway.

When I went to the bar in *The Europa*, I noticed a very attractive woman smiling at me. She asked me would I buy her a drink. I replied "Sure why not". We spent an hour by the bar where she asked me a lot of questions about what I was doing in Belfast. This made me suspicious, she then offered to go back with me to my suite but I told her I was too tired. I knew she wasn't a prostitute because she didn't ask for any money. There was something not quite right about her

The following week I was in my office in London booking my trip to Belfast when the phone rang and someone with an Irish accent asked to speak to me.

I took the call and this guy told me that he'd never know an Englishman to come across the water and take so much money from businesses in Belfast before and that took balls. He asked could we meet to discuss doing some business together and he was also prepared to come to London to meet me. The way that he spoke, I guessed he was a member of the IRA.

When I declined the offer he said "Maybe we could meet for a drink when you next come over to the *Europa*". He then told me the date of my flight and when I was arriving in Belfast which only Peter and I knew!

Peter told me that it was a known fact that the IRA had informers working inside the *Europa Hotel*. When I then told him about the strange meeting with the woman in the bar he was convinced she'd been working for the IRA.

By now in the last nine months we'd taken over half a million pounds from sales in Ireland so it wasn't a surprise that we'd come to the attention of that evil organisation.

Peter wouldn't let me go to Belfast and for the next few weeks I stayed in London and let the boys sell in Dublin and Belfast. Peter and I decided that maybe now was the time to move on and not push our luck. I agreed with him, having had already two lucky escapes with the IRA. I didn't want to chance a third!

TWENTY-SIX

EUROVISION INTERNATIONAL

Peter and I asked for a meeting with Stuart Landau, the owner of Channel 7.

We told him that we'd exhausted Ireland as a territory. He wanted us to carry on flogging a dead horse. We told him that as a business, Ireland had come to an end. Stuart had been very lucky in business finding good people to run his franchises for him, he had been *very* lucky but wasn't in my opinion a great businessman.

We asked Stuart about taking Channel 7 into Europe. He was very sceptical about getting deals and money on the day. We said that we wanted to try Holland as there was a high level of English spoken there and they were friendly towards the English.

He reluctantly agreed to give Peter and me a franchise in Holland and I believe he thought it would fail. We placed a couple of ads in local newspapers in Amsterdam for closers and I flew out to interview them. I booked a suite in the

Golden Tulip hotel for the interviews. We'd received enough response from the newspaper ads to at least give it a try.

Peter and I then opened a new account with one of the oldest banks in Holland for credibility, so we could pay cheques in Dutch guilders into the account, (This was before The Netherlands had joined the Euro.)

I then went out with the new Dutch closers on appointments to teach them the pitch. Everyone spoke English so language wasn't a problem. The two main Dutch closers were called Jan and Klaus. They were experienced closers and I knew they'd do well in Europe. I sold for the first time in Europe and found it easier than in England!

Like in Ireland I'd stay in the hotel from Monday until Friday or until Saturday morning. The suite with extras was costing us over £1,000 per week but we were earning the money. Gradually I built up a team of salespeople covering all of Holland.

We went on to become the most successful franchise in Channel 7. As always with sales, there were big eyes from other franchises in the UK and Stuart, being greedy, started to give countries away like sweets now that he knew Channel 7 could be successfully sold in Europe.

Peter had never liked Stuart and this caused even more friction between them. The other problem was Peter was too soft with the telesales people in the office, who saw him as a bit of a pushover.

It all came to a head one day and Stuart bought out Peter from the franchise, to leave me alone with Stuart as a partner. Socially I got on very well with him but in business he was a real bastard!

One Friday evening I was in the *Golden Tulip* with one of the Dutch closers, Jan. He'd parked his car at the back of the hotel. Jan lived in Belgium and his car had Belgian number plates on it. When he went to drive home, he found that someone had slashed all the tyres on his car. At that time there was a lot of animosity between the Dutch and the Belgians. Now he was stuck until the next day until he'd got his car fixed. He asked me if he could sleep on the couch which I told him wasn't a problem

I went to bed and was just about to go to sleep when I heard a loud bang, which sounded like a bomb going off. I jumped out of bed, ran into the lounge but there was no sign of Jan, only a trail of blood leading to the bathroom. I ran into the bathroom to find Jan sitting in the bath, with blood pouring out between his legs.

I could see the colour draining from his face so I quickly grabbed a towel and rammed it as hard as I could between his legs to stem the flow of blood. There was another closer in the room who called reception and told them to call an ambulance. In the meantime with all the strength I could muster, I kept the towel rammed between his legs.

The paramedics took at least twenty minutes to arrive by which time Jan's face had gone grey and he was slipping in and out of consciousness.

The two paramedics immediately hooked up a saline drip to Jan and told me not to take the pressure off the towel I was holding. I told them I couldn't keep the pressure on much longer as I had been holding it for over twenty minutes. They then told me that if I let go he would die. Jan was a big man and they struggled to get him out of the bath and into the ambulance.

After they'd taken him to hospital, I discovered what had happened. Jan had got undressed to sleep on the couch and had sat on top of a glass coffee table. Being a large man, the glass top had collapsed and shattered with Jan falling though the table, cutting himself badly, close to his scrotum.

He had to have over seventy stitches in hospital and they told him had the cut been a few millimetres closer to his scrotum he would have died. They also told him if I hadn't been as strong as I was to keep the pressure on the wound, he definitely would have died.

Jan had been lucky, but because of his injury he couldn't work for many months. One year later he was still limping from his wound.

We were doing great business in Holland and quickly covered that small country.

STUART SUGGESTED that we move into Belgium. So we booked a hotel in Antwerp and went through the usual motions of interviewing closers. They just didn't' understand the concept of closing on the day except for one or two - they were a dead loss. We had to send our Dutch closers to cover the leads in Belgium.

After a particularly long day in the hotel in Antwerp interviewing and training, Stuart suggested I go with him to a local football match. It was only the promise of a good meal afterwards and drinks in a nightclub that made me capitulate. He was football mad and ever since I'd known him he'd been a big supporter of Queens Park Rangers. He followed them up and down the country and was very knowledgeable about football. I on the other hand wasn't the least bit interested. He told me the local club Boom were playing Standard Liège and it should be a good game. So somewhat reluctantly, I agreed to join him.

As we arrived at the stadium, the game had just started. He went to run and buy the tickets from the box office, when I noticed a side door into the ground that was open. I told him not to buy the tickets as we could go in that way. I remembered the days when I used to bunk in at the local cinema in the East End. As we started to walk into the ground, a ticket collector appeared, asking us for our tickets.

His English was poor and all he kept saying was, "ticket, ticket". Holding out his hand. I replied to him saying, "No, no! Stuart from QPR!" and pointed to the emblem on Stuart's jumper which was embossed with QPR. With that he showed us into the ground, to VIP seats.

About ten minutes later, I could see the ticket collector talking to another man in a suit pointing at us. I thought we may have been rumbled and told Stuart to look busy and make some notes. So he put on his glasses, took out a pen from his jacket and began scribbling on a piece of paper, as if he was making notes on the game and players. Half way through the first half of the game, I noticed a TV camera point at us. I told Stuart to smile as we were on Candid Camera! He became nervous and said "I hope we don't get into trouble! I replied "Don't worry, the worst they can do is throw us out".

At half time against all the odds, Boom were winning 2-1. The man in the suit reappeared and waved for us to join him. I said to Stuart "Now we've been rumbled". We walked over to the man in the suit who spoke good English and he invited us into the VIP lounge. He remarked that he'd seen us on television during the first half. Stuart's face was a picture and I had to stop myself from bursting out laughing.

He said he'd been told that Stuart was a scout for Queens Park Rangers. Stuart had no other choice than to say yes. We were then given free drinks and food.

During the second half, Standard Liège equalised, making the score 2-2. Then Boom came back and won the match 4-2. The game was better than I'd been expecting and with the free food and drink I was enjoying myself.

At full time the man in the suit reappeared and waved for us to join him again. He took us back to the VIP lounge and introduced us to the chairman of the club whose birthday it was. Everyone was ecstatic at the win, especially on the chairman's birthday. The drinks flowed and Stuart began to relax and get into the swing of things.

Stuart knew his football and was in deep conversation with the chairman of Boom's football club, about possible transfers of players to go and play at QPR! He even agreed on a provisional price for one of Boom's star players! He told the chairman QPR would fax over the offer later in the week!

We were then invited as the chairman's guests to a very nice restaurant, with some of the players and directors of the club to celebrate the win and the chairman's birthday.

We had a great time and I ended up arm-wrestling some of the players as well as the local hard man who was a nasty piece of work. He told everyone he'd never been beaten at arm-wrestling, well that was before he'd met 'Gentlemen Les'. I beat him easily and he didn't take the defeat well and wanted to fight me after. I told him if he wanted to fight with me, he would finish up in hospital. With that some of the players threw him out. It didn't spoil a great night and all because Stuart was wearing a QPR Jumper!

Now that Stuart had a taste of the easy money he could take from Europe, he set up a franchise with an ex-closer I had trained on Channel 7 called Sam Imber. I liked Sam and we'd got on well. Stuart gave him the franchise for South Africa and Hong Kong.

As Channel 7 expanded with more franchises, Stuart lost control over their selling techniques, which with some of them were dubious to say the least. Also in some countries such as South Africa and Scandinavia, the police handled the complaints much more seriously than complaints received in the UK. They didn't take well to a foreign company selling and asking for money at the end of a meeting. I heard of one poor woman closer in South Africa being arrested and treated very badly when questioned by the police there.

Another closer in Sweden was held in prison for several weeks and Channel 7, back in the UK, was featured twice on Esther Rantzen's *That's Life* and was even mentioned on BBC Breakfast News. The reason for all of this was the heavy selling techniques employed by some of the closers and the false promises they made.

By this time, I'd finished my franchise with Stuart. Although we'd made good money, it just wasn't worth the agro. The overheads were also very high so I decided to go back on the road selling, which I was best at.

I started working in Germany. I found the Germans nice

people to do business with and for the most part honourable, unlike in Holland where it was common for them to sign a contract then change their minds and not pay.

I travelled all over Germany, even doing business in the old East Germany in cities like Leipzig, Halle and Dresden. Once again, I became the top closer in the company.

On one occasion, I was doing business with a very rich lawyer in Bad Homburg, just outside of Frankfurt. He was working from his home which was easily worth a million plus. During our conversation he remarked on the Masonic cufflinks I was wearing. He then revealed that he was a 33rd degree Freemason. I knew that there were only a handful of them in Europe and this was indeed a very powerful man.

I didn't want to take his money, in case he wasn't satisfied with the results. I started to make excuses to him saying maybe this product wasn't right for him. That only made him more hungrier to buy it. The reverse sale had boomeranged back on me. The smallest deal I could go down to was £1,000. Normally it would have been at least £3,000 or £5,000 for one year's service. This was pocket money for him and he couldn't sign the contract quick enough!

We shook hands at the end of the deal, he then showed me pictures of himself in full masonic regalia with some very powerful people who I immediately recognised. There were presidents and prime ministers from Germany and other countries around the world.

It was some months later when I was on business in Cologne that I believe that this deal caught up with me.

I was working in a town just outside of Cologne. Business was unusually bad. After a couple of days I had a strange feeling I was being followed. I noticed two men in a car a few times over the week waiting outside where I was working. On the last day Friday, I had a meeting with a small law firm. During the meeting the lawyer asked me a few times if I'd ever worked in Turkey. I told him no never and thought it was a strange question to ask.

He then said he thought he'd seen me before which was impossible, as I'd never been to that town before. During the meeting, two men walked into the office, showed me their badges and asked me to go to the police station with them. When I asked them what was it about they replied, just to answer a few questions.

I got into their car and they drove me to the local police station. Inside they took me into a small office, where a plain clothes inspector and sergeant, were seated. They started to accuse me of fraud which was ridiculous as whatever business that signed with Channel 7 always received the service they paid for, if not always the business they expected!

After about an hour, they said I'd had broken German law with the contract I was asking business to sign. I then pointed out that one of the main terms and conditions on the contract stated it fell under English law. (Stuart being legally trained had always made sure that all of the contracts were watertight). They didn't have an answer to that. I then told them that we sold all over the world without any problems.

They told me they were still arresting me and took my fingerprints and photographed me. They then took me back to their office where they showed me a statement in

German which they wanted me to sign. I had no doubt in my mind that this was a confession of guilt that they wanted me to sign. I told them I wanted a translator and kept asking for my international right to make a phone call, which was refused. They finally produced a translator who had obviously been drinking and whose English was not as good as one of the policemen who'd been questioning me! He told me I had to sign the statement without him even translating it. This was an obvious set up and I was beginning to panic.

I refused to sign the statement and told them they were breaking international law by not allowing me one phone call. After another hour passed, they gave into me and asked who I wanted to call. I told them the British Embassy.

After another thirty minutes passed, they handed the phone to me and to my great relief an educated voice on the other end of the line told me they were calling from the British Embassy.

I explained everything that had happened, who I was and what I was doing in Germany. The man from the embassy told me to keep talking on the phone to him while he got a colleague to call the police on the other line.

As I was talking to him, he told me under no circumstances to hang up, as he'd known people to disappear for days while in police custody. This was before the UK joined the EU. I had visions of digging a tunnel like in *The Great Escape* if they took me away. While I was talking to him, a phone rang in the office and after a few minutes one of the policemen handed the phone over to the inspector. There was a short conversation in German and the inspector now not looking as cocky as he was before handed over the phone to me.

The man from the Embassy told me that I was being released without any charge. After what had just happened, I couldn't believe it and asked him if he was sure. He told me yes and I thanked him for all of his help. I still don't know what to this day he'd said to the police but it had obviously worked.

The inspector who'd now had the wind taken out of his sails reluctantly let me go. He told me that they'd ordered a taxi for me and I wasn't to leave the station until it had arrived. He repeated this again which made me suspicious. I had visions of waiting downstairs and then being rearrested after he'd spoken to his superiors.

So when no one was looking I walked out of the station to the main road, stopped the first taxi I saw and told them to take me back to my hotel and wait for me. When I went to my room, it was a real mess and had obviously been searched by the police. As I paid my bill at the reception, I asked if the police had produced a search warrant to look in my room. The receptionist looked shocked and replied, "No of course not, they're the police,"

And here I was thinking that the Gestapo were dead and buried!

The taxi took me straight to the airport and I flew home swearing, I would never return.

When I got back I told Stuart what had happened and he hired a top international lawyer who was the lawyer for the footballer Jurgen Klinsmann, to investigate what had happened.

This lawyer was German and knew their legal system very well. After several weeks and after he'd spoken to the local prosecutor, as well as friends in different departments in the German Legal system, he came back and said he couldn't understand it

In all the years he'd been a lawyer he'd never known a case like it. In his own words he said, I must have upset someone very important and powerful.

I guessed immediately who he was talking about. It could only have been the 33rd Mason I'd done business with. After that incident, it was a long time before I was to ever to return to Germany.

TWENTY-SEVEN

BBC WORLD TELETEXT

By this time I'd had enough of Channel 7.

It was getting more difficult to sell it wherever we went so I was relieved and surprised when Stuart told me he had a contract to sell CNN teletext.

Teletext was used extensively at that time in the UK and I'd booked several great holidays on it in the past. He'd secured a contract to create a business guide on one of its pages, country by country, city by city.

I began seeing it in countries across Europe. Once again Stuart quickly started up franchises to sell it as well. He liked the idea of other people doing all the work and investing their money into opening offices, recruiting staff, and then paying him a percentage of their sales.

This idea is okay as long as you have full control of the operation to ensure quality control. What he did was to make contracts with the franchisees so they created their own limited companies and the clients were making the contract with that company and not his. So if there were any comebacks, it wouldn't be down to him and he wasn't in the frame. It didn't take too long before CNN pulled the plug because of the complaints they were receiving from businesses that weren't getting the business they were expecting.

During this time, I told him to try and get a contract with BBC World Text. He laughed at me saying, "Everyone knows you can't advertise on the BBC". I explained that BBC World was the commercial arm of the BBC and they did have some advertising and sponsorship.

It didn't take him too long to secure a contract with BBC World Text to sell advertising on their pages. What made me laugh was the fact that Stuart had been featured twice on BBC Television's *That's Life* and I found it amazing that such an organisation hadn't done the necessary due diligence on him and his company.

I decided to try and sell this new product in Prague, Czechoslovakia. The reason behind my thinking was I knew that the BBC was highly respected in Czechoslovakia from its radio broadcasts during the Second World War and then thereafter when Russia took control of the country. It was one of the very few free radio broadcasts that could be received.

I flew to Prague which was my first visit to this country and one of my first appointments was with the Hilton Hotel. I pitched the General Manager and marketing director who asked me to give them a discount. So I negotiated the next seven nights for me to stay in one of their best suites with breakfast, as a barter, with them also paying £1,000 for good measure! I said it would have to include a meal in their fabulous skyscraper restaurant that overlooked the city.

That evening I moved into the Hilton Hotel for free. In the evening I walked across the street and found a nice-looking restaurant. I ate their local speciality which was duck with red cabbage. After a few beers and a bottle of wine, as well as a superb meal, I asked to speak to the owner.

He came over to my table with a giant of a man who spoke better English than he did. I told them what a great meal I had and it was even better than the Hilton where I was staying. His friend's name was Igor and the owner's name was Milan.

Stuart had previously printed up some certificates for a good food eating guide to sell to restaurants. I told them I worked for the BBC and gave them a Good Food Certificate to put on the wall of their restaurant. Igor translated everything to Milan who was so happy that he not only gave me a double brandy, but also wouldn't let me pay for the dinner. At the end of the evening, after he closed the restaurant, he insisted I join them for a drink.

We went outside and got into his brand new Jaguar. He drove us out of the city for about thirty minutes, I started to wonder exactly where they were taking me.

We eventually arrived at a bar which from the outside looked closed. We went inside, where these two men were obviously well known. It was a Lapdance Club! We had more drinks and Milan asked me through Igor to pick any girl I wanted and go upstairs with her. Not knowing these two and not knowing what would happen next, I politely declined and they drove me back to the Hilton.

The next evening I took the Good Food Certificate to them as promised. Again, I was given more free drinks and food.

As we got talking, I told Igor about my arm-wrestling. He looked at me and laughed, telling me that he'd never been beaten. Looking at the size of him, I could believe it.

He then cleared the table and challenged me to arm-wrestle him. If I'd been arm-wrestling him on an approved table, I would have been more confident about beating him, but sometimes, It could be more difficult on a normal pub table where your elbow can slip.

We agreed on the best of three pins and he was genuinely shocked when I won the first pin. He was as strong as an ox but with the skill I had, he never stood a chance and for a second time, I beat him. All of the locals were watching this including the owner Milan.

Igor took the loss well and insisted I drunk Russian vodka with him all night. He told me he was Milan's bodyguard. I thought it was a bit strange for a restaurant owner to have a bodyguard. After a few more trips to Prague, I found out why.

On my third trip to Prague, I went back to Milan's restaurant. They would always make me welcome and it was nice to have some people to talk to. That evening they again insisted on taking me back to the lapdancing club which I found out doubled as a brothel!

Igor told me that the next day was his wife's birthday and invited me to the birthday party.

I bought a nice gift and was looking forward to spending the evening with them. They'd set up a long table which was full of drinks including champagne and caviar. Sitting around the table were about fifteen men. They were all wearing black suits, dark shirts and ties. They looked dressed more for a funeral than a birthday party.

Igor introduced me to them as his good friend from the BBC. As he took me around the table he told me they were friends and good business partners from Italy, Russia and the Czech Republic. As I looked at this group of men, it reminded me of a scene from the *Godfather* and I was convinced that they were members of the Mafia.

As I shook hands with them at least two gave me a Masonic handshake. The evening was surreal with one of the Russians climbing on the table drunk then in quite good English, reciting Shakespeare. He then looked at me and asked if the man from the BBC approved. I replied, I would try and get him a job with the Royal Shakespeare Company.

After many bottles of champagne and vodka, the party finished in the early hours. The next time I went back to the restaurant, a Dutchman who I'd made friends with who worked at the Dutch embassy in Prague asked me if I knew who the people were that I'd been drinking with at the birthday party. I replied that they were friends of Igor's. He told me that he couldn't be seen drinking with them as they were dangerous and that he'd never seen them before accept someone as they'd accepted me into their circle. I replied that I wasn't interested in their business and enjoyed their company and having a drink with them.

On another trip to Prague, I stayed in a hotel on the famous Wenceslas Square. I walked across the square one evening for a quiet drink in a small bar that was playing music. I sat at the bar alone having a beer. Two women started talking to me asking me if I wanted them to come back to their room for a massage. They were the local prostitutes. I told them no thanks. Then later, another woman asked me if she could sit next to me. I told her yes if she wanted to. She started telling me how she was trying to support her daughter in Hungary and showed me a picture of a small girl. I bought a drink to be sociable and when the bar closed she asked me if I would like to go with her to another bar. When I said no, I was tired, she offered to come back to my room for a drink.

I made an excuse and said sorry I was too tired. She then put her arms around my waist and pulled me towards her. I pulled away, wishing her goodnight and walked back across the square to the hotel. When I got back to my room and started to get ready for bed, I discovered that my pocket had been picked and I'd lost over £150. I quickly got dressed and ran back to the bar to look for this woman who I was sure had picked my pocket when she'd put her arms around me.

When I got back to the bar, it was already closed. I walked to the nearest police station to report the theft. The police weren't interested and told me that they could arrest me if I'd taken her back to my room. I explained to them that I'd refused her offer and I believed she'd picked my pocket.

The next evening, I went back to the bar looking for this woman. She wasn't there, so I asked the barman if he'd seen her. The night before his English was okay. Now conveniently, he had forgotten all of his English. I suspected that he was working with her pointing out potential victims.

Over the next few nights, I returned to the bar looking for this woman but she never turned up. I then phoned my friend Igor. He'd always told me that if I needed any help to call him. I explained everything that had happened to me and he said he'd look into it and try and get my money back.

A couple of weeks later, when I returned to the same hotel. I noticed that the bar opposite where my money had been stolen was now boarded up and closed. I thought that this was unusual as it was in a good position, especially for tourists.

I asked the doorman of the hotel if he knew why the bar was closed. He told me that it was a mystery and they were all shocked when it had suddenly shut up shop.

I smiled to myself and thought of Igor and his friends.

TWENTY-EIGHT

SWIMMING WITH STINGRAYS

A FEW MONTHS later Stuart informed me that he'd made Sam Imber, the closer I'd trained on Channel 7, his new partner in BBC World Text.

He'd already gone into partnership with Sam on CNN Text. One of the main reasons was Sam, like Stuart, was also Jewish and, like Freemasons and Roman Catholics, Jews prefer to do business with other Jews.

Stuart gave everyone the impression that it had been his idea to get the BBC World Text contract. I never even got a thank you from him for giving him the original idea, but that's typical of the cutthroat world of sales.

Sam and Stuart asked me if I'd like to go to the Cayman Islands to try and sell BBC Text. This wasn't as some reward, but they knew if I couldn't make it work then nobody else would.

I booked a trip to go to the Cayman Islands for ten days. It was, and still is an offshore jurisdiction for money laundering, international banking, and simply a good place to hide money. It was a tax haven known amongst millionaires and billionaires around the world. That meant there was an abundance of law-firms, banks and accountants there to pitch to.

There was no problem for the office in London to make the leads for me, especially as everybody spoke English. Going there on the back of a brand like the BBC, I was expecting to do good business.

On my first day, I had four appointments, with a mixture of lawyers and accountants. On the first day I hit a brick wall when everyone told me the same thing,- that all of their TVs came from America or were supplied from there where Teletext didn't exist! So unless they were expats they'd never seen it before. Sam and Stuart had sent me to this place without checking this important fact.

The second and third day, I got the same response from the businesses that I tried selling to. I had now gone on leads for three days without selling a thing, something that had never happened to me before.

I was getting desperate, even in the meeting with expats they still couldn't see the service I was trying to sell them and even worse, if it was an American company, they didn't even know what I was talking about!

Because of the nature of the business that was conducted in the Cayman Islands, there were many scams carried out there which also didn't help me.

The Cayman Islands also being a very wealthy place, made it bloody expensive for me, everything from accommodation to food and especially alcohol was very expensive.

I was feeling down and miserable which was very unusual for me. I went to a local beach bar to drown my sorrows which made me even more miserable when I found out how much they charged for a local beer! I got talking to a local who told me he owned a small boat and was organising a trip the next day with some American tourists to go for the day to Stingray City.

I asked him what Stingray City was. He explained to me that there was a reef barrier some miles offshore where boats would go with tourists to feed the stingrays. He told me hundreds of stingrays would go there at a certain time of the day to be fed. He said that you could swim with them. I asked wasn't that dangerous. He laughed and told me that you can only get stung by a stingray if you stepped on their tail while they were resting on the seabed.

It sounded the stuff of dreams and I said I'd come the next day. I asked him how much did it cost. Again he laughed and told me just to bring some beers and he would bring smoked salmon bagels. He thought I was Jewish!

So the next day, I met him on the beach with two packs of beer and true to his word he brought with him some smoked salmon bagels. There were four others, two American couples and we set out in his small boat to Stingray City.

The Cayman Islands are not just another major offshore financial centre, but also one of the largest producers of bananas in the Caribbean. There are plantations all over the island.

Errol, the boat captain, started talking to me on the way to Stingray City about different fish recipes and barbeques he liked to cook. I then asked him if he'd ever tried barbequed banana. He looked at me as if I was mad and said he'd never heard of it. I told him that it was my own recipe and that I'd invented it to supplement a good barbeque. I told him I was surprised with all of the bananas they grew there, they'd never heard of it.

I explained to him my simple recipe of barbequed banana. He was so impressed, he called his mum on his mobile while steering the boat one handed and told her "ma! I got this crazy Englishman on the boat, he tell me about barbeque banana!" He then explained his recipe over the phone to his mum. It was so funny and I kept winding him up saying I couldn't believe that he didn't know about it with all the bananas grown there.

It took about forty-five minutes to reach the barrier reef and as he stopped the boat and lowered the anchor, I noticed about a dozen smaller boats in the vicinity. Errol had bought some fish with him, which he threw overboard. There was an immediate ripple beneath the waves as if the sea was boiling.

Then I saw dozens of stingrays around his boat as they ate the fish that he'd thrown overboard.

The other boats nearby also started to throwing fish over the side of their boats. Soon there were hundreds of stingrays swimming in the area where we'd all anchored. They were all different sizes from baby ones to some with a ten-foot wingspan.

Errol then gave us all some chopped fish, and told us the stingrays would eat the fish from our hands. We then jumped overboard into the calm sea, to be surrounded by them. It was a surreal experience to be in their natural habitat and feel them eating fish from my hand. There were so many of them, I felt them touching my body as they swam around to be fed.

It's one thing to watch these magnificent fish in the aquarium but truly a magical experience to swim with them and feed them.

Errol told me after, that some women had told him that they'd experienced an orgasm from the stingrays flapping around their bodies and their fins touching them. All I knew was even if I didn't do any business here, it had been worth coming for such an amazing experience.

When I got back to my hotel, I felt completely relaxed and the swim with the stingrays had put everything into perspective for me. I began thinking of another angle for my pitch to overcome the problem of no teletext on the island. I had five more days to try and turn the trip around and not lose a lot of money.

I went out the next day on leads, I knew the money we were asking the businesses for was small change to them, but they still had to be convinced that they'd receive some sort of return for their investment. I tried my revised pitch and got the contract signed on the first meeting, it worked! I got one more contract that day and three the next.

The experience I'd had at Stingray City had cleared my mind and body to focus on the problem of no teletext, and I had now cracked it.

By the end of the trip I'd taken over £30,000 in sales. I now had developed a successful pitch and began covering all of the islands in the Caribbean, none of which had teletext!

I went back to the Cayman Islands several times on business but I always made sure I found time to go to my favourite place with my friend Errol.

TWENTY-NINE

THE BRITISH NATIONAL THEATRE SCHOOLS

Peter Everett, my old partner from Eurovision, contacted me with a business idea to start a drama school.

He had theatrical experience, and the way he dressed wearing a silk cravat smoking a pipe with his Oxford accent, he could easily be mistaken for Noël Coward

His idea was to open a part-time stage school teaching dance, acting and singing. Peter had some great ideas, but like Frank was short on business acumen. We had to find somewhere to hold the classes and the right teachers.

My son Leslie was attending Bishop Challoner School in Bromley, Kent. It was a private Roman Catholic school. Although Leslie and I weren't Roman Catholics, it also took pupils from other religious denominations. Dick's son also attended the school and he knew the headmaster. So it became our first obvious choice.

Peter and I came up with the idea to call the stage school. The British National Theatre Schools which we both agreed was a great name. We spoke to the headmaster of Bishop Challoner, who agreed for three hours on a Saturday we could hold the classes in the school for an agreed fee. He also agreed that we could use the school hall for the registration. We placed some local ads for the registration day, and waited to see who would come along.

Peter and I were there to register students and explain the syllabus, while Danka and Leslie would help to register new students. We'd run two terms a year, and hold a show in a local theatre at the end of the second term.

On the day of the registration we had more people turn up than we were expecting. By the end of the day, we had enrolled fifty-odd new students, which we divided into two classes.

Peter agreed to handle the administration of the stage school and devise the syllabus while I still flew around Europe Monday to Friday on business, coming back to help out on Saturdays.

We found some very good teachers from *The Stage* and placed an ad for a music teacher. Peter could read and write music as well as play the piano. He certainly was a talented man who'd been wasted making leads as a telesales operative.

Peter told me he could take the music class, but that would not give him enough time to direct the show at the end of the second term. We had a few applicants for the job of music teacher. One of them was from Bosnia, who I immediately liked. He'd come to the UK as a war refugee, from the terrible war that had taken place in Yugoslavia.

When I introduced myself to him and spoke some Serbo-Croatian, he nearly fainted with shock! I'd learnt from

Danka some basic sentences, he just wasn't expecting to hear it from an Englishman. Peter didn't want to give him the job, saying that he was worried that the guy wouldn't understand the type of music we needed in the school and for the show.

I said we should give him a chance as he had excellent references. His name was Zlatan Fazlić. True, his English wasn't perfect but I always believed music speaks all languages.

Zlatan was a master of the keyboard and he'd won second place in a national piano contest in the old Yugoslavia. He'd also been awarded the gold badge by his university in Sarajevo as best student of the year. Far more important to me was that the kids loved him!

By the end of the second term, we'd grown to three classes as word had spread amongst the parents on how much the children were enjoying themselves.

We booked the Churchill Theatre in Bromley for our show, which was a bit ambitious considering it held over 1,000 people. We decided to have a nice programme printed for the show and I set about selling adverting space in it to help raise money towards the cost of the costumes.

Peter always managed to surprise me every time I thought he was telling me a cock and bull story. He would sometimes deliver the goods. It turned out he knew the private secretary to Prince Edward, a lieutenant colonel named Sean O'Dwyer, who much to my surprise and delight got us a letter from Prince Edward supporting the schools and sending his best wishes, which we published inside the programme.

As Peter quite rightly said in his posh Oxford accent "This gives us great kudos!"

A personal message from H.R.H. The Prince Edward

BUCKINGHAM PALACE

16th September, 1993

Dear Mr Everett,

I was most interested to learn of the work of The British National Theatre Schools and I regret that prior commitments prevent my attending the Gala night at the Churchill Theatre.

I am delighted to support the efforts of your children in their pursuit of skill and knowledge in the Performing Arts. Great Britain has a long tradition of excellence in the Theatre and this venture, which encourages talent in children of all walks of life, can only help to sustain these high standards in the future.

I send my best wishes to all the children for a most successful evening.

Yours sincerely,

Edward

On the night of the show there was the usual drama backstage with nerves but the show was an unqualified success with over 900 people in the audience. Now with the success of the show and Prince Edwards letter, we could expand the operation. It was 1993.

The next school we opened was Blackheath Girls' School in Blackheath.

During the registration I noticed one man who looked familiar to me dressed in motorbike leathers waiting to register his daughter. He took his daughter over to my son to register her and while Leslie was filling the paperwork out I realised who it was. It was Jools Holland, the famous musician who had his own show on television. His daughter was a pupil at Blackheath and wanted to join. Afterwards Peter introduced me to him as the chairman of the schools (at least we now had two!) He was very charming and later I got to know his wife, Christabel McEwen who'd previously been married to a Lord. She was very down to earth, and a really nice person.

We then went on to open a third smaller school in Purley, Surrey. We booked the Ashcroft Theatre in Croydon for our next show which was to be a "Salute to the West End" from 1932 to present day 1994. Once again I sold advertising space in the programme to companies like KPMG and other local businesses.

I introduced Judo into the curriculum which Dick and I taught. It proved to be very popular with both parents and students.

It also taught the students how to fall on stage without hurting themselves. Dick was now a Police Sergeant but while he'd been in the Police force, he'd taken and passed history and law degrees - which was pretty amazing, considering he'd left school at sixteen with no qualifications.

We introduced LAMDA (London Academy of Music & Dramatic Art) in poetry which Richard was very good at teaching the students. We achieved on average over a 95% pass rate in the LAMDA exams.

I also included fencing in the curriculum, and we became the first part-time stage school in the UK to not only teach fencing but also hold exams in the sport. I would often be asked by parents, what did fencing have to do with drama? I would politely point to some of Shakespeare's plays where sword-fencing took an important part or role as well as many feature films where fencing appeared. We had a wonderful fencing teacher called Manola who was also an examiner for the British Fencing Association.

In the programme for the Ashcroft show, we received letters of support from Sir Andrew Lloyd Webber, Lord Del Fonte and Phillip Schofield. We put in pictures of our growing band of teachers and I found an old picture of Dick when he was much younger and used to model and placed it in the programme without telling him. It was hilarious when on the day of the show when I gave him a copy of the programme, and watched as the blood drained from his face.

Up until now, Peter had organised and directed the shows. Although I had no acting degree or experience, I asked if I could direct two pieces in the variety show. Peter reluctantly agreed. I decided one of the pieces would be a song from the *Blues Brothers* and the other piece I devised was a scene from *Cyrano De Bergerac*, which was one of my favourite films with Gérard Depardieu. With the *Blues Brothers*, I cast my son and another student to play the two Elwood brothers from the film and choreographed the dancing, while Zlatan taught them the song. With the other piece, I wrote and directed the scene, with Manola choreographing the fencing.

On the night of the performance we had over 1200 people in the audience, and for the first time I felt really nervous as to whether the audience would like what I'd directed in the show.

I didn't need to worry, because as soon as the opening bars began to play 'Everybody Needs Somebody To Love' the audience spontaneously started to clap in time and at the end of the song Leslie and his friend Simon got a big round of applause.

Later in the second act, when the piece I'd devised for *Cyrano De Bergerac* finished, it received a huge round of applause. To Peter's credit he came up to me after and said he'd thought the two pieces would flop but they turned out to be the best received in the whole show!

The next day, Jools Holland's wife Christabel came up to me in the Blackheath school and asked me who'd directed the *Blues Brothers* and *Cyrano De Bergerac* pieces in the show? I told her it was me and she replied that they'd been her two most favourite pieces in the show!

I was chuffed that I'd pulled it off, never having the chance to go to university and leaving school with just a few 'O' Levels, I felt that I'd had achieved something special.

After the success of the Ashcroft show, we opened our fourth school in Sevenoaks, Kent.

We booked our next show at the Lewisham Theatre. It was to be a musical written by Peter and Zlatan called, *Children of The Crystal*. This time I got the show sponsored by the National Westminster Bank. Peter and I formed a production company which we called Drury Lane Productions Ltd and had the idea to use it as a casting agency.

Peter thought *Children of the Crystal* would be his big break into the theatre world. Unfortunately, it never happened and like so many other musicals in the West End, it flopped. The show was a success, but no one was interested in investing money, or taking it further.

Sir Andrew Lloyd Webber wishes the show every success.

Phillip Schofield

I wish you every success with this production.

Lord Delfont

We staged a small show at Walthamstow Hall, Sevenoaks, and without any warning on the evening of the show Mohamed Al Fayed, owner of Harrods, arrived with his wife. We weren't even aware that one of his daughters was a student of ours and in the show! They'd kept her identity a secret for security reasons.

My daughter Natasha found herself during the interval serving him and his wife tea from plastic beacons, which she was really embarrassed about. At the end of the show, he thanked Peter and I saying how much his daughter enjoyed coming to our stage school. He was a charming man.

One of our less experienced teachers there was a lovely lady called Lauren Booth, who was the daughter of the actor Tony Booth, who'd starred in the TV series *Till death do us part*. She was the half-sister of Cheri Blair. The younger children, who Lauren taught, loved her and she was a really nice person to work with.

We opened two more schools, One in Ewell Castle, which was Oliver Reed's old school, and another in Surbiton, Surrey.

The next flagship school was to be Roedean, in Brighton. This was one of the most exclusive girls' schools in the UK.

For the two schools in Surrey we booked the Harry Secombe Theatre to put the show on. I was still flying all over Europe selling BBC text, returning home for weekends to teach and help run the schools.

We now had six stage schools with over 300 students. I felt immensely proud of what we were achieving. We gave scholarships in all of the schools to some students whose parents couldn't afford the fees, who we felt were talented and deserved a chance. Our exam results in LAMDA exams were high and we introduced fencing, Judo, mime, audition technique and pieces to camera into the curriculum, as well as drama, singing and dance.

I even made a TV commercial with Ruby Wax for Brent Cross Shopping Centre just to show the students that anything was possible!

PETER EVERETT *(Writer/Director)*

Peter Everett is the founder and Artistic Director of the British National Theatre Schools, and initiated its policy of offering children from all walks of life, the equal opportunity of studying the Performing Arts.

Peter trained at the Oxford Academy of Speech and Drama under Ken Parkin, and completed classical studies at Kirby College.

His professional career started at Lincoln Repertory Company in 1963, where he trained under Victor Spinnetti and Kay Gardner. Since his 'halcyon' days, Peter has worked in many demanding roles throughout Europe.

In 1978 he became established as a Director, and ended that year as Technical Director to the royal performance of 'Iolanthe', when he was presented to H.M. The Queen Mother.

Television credits include, 'Northeast Roundabout', 'The six o'clock show', 'The Dream Factory', and a one hour documentary on his life for B.B.C. radio. Film credits include 'Rotten to the core' for the Boulting brothers, which was filmed in Eire. He has directed B.N.T.S. shows at the Churchill and Ashcroft Theatres.

He is currently Managing Director of Drury Lane Productions, and is in the early planning stage of directing a film based on the life of Marc Bolan and 'T Rex', with a working title of, 'To Ride a White Swan'. Peter is married and lives with his wife and son in the village of Dulwich.

ZLATAN FAZLIC *(Composer)*

Zlatan trained at the Academy of Music in the University of Sarajevo, and at the High School of Music in Tuzla.

He specialises in keyboard, Harmony and notation. Zlatan has a natural feel for the Blues, and he worked as a pianist in residence to the famous 'Cotton Club' in Nicosia. He has played all over Europe, and won second place in the Yugoslav national Piano contest. He was awarded the Golden badge by his University as the best student of the year.

Zlatan is currently studying at the London Guildhall of music, and has recently been appointed as Musical Director of the prize winning 'Spectrum Choir'.

He is unmarried and lives in Surrey.

LESLIE CLAYDEN *(Producer)*

Leslie Clayden is the Executive Producer of 'Children of the Crystal', and is also the Chairman of the British National Theatre Schools.

He began his career at the Lyceum in the Strand, and, at the age of 19, was appointed the youngest Manager of Mecca. Whilst with Mecca he was involved with major productions such as, 'Miss World', 'Come Dancing', and the 'Carl Alan Awards'. He went on to Stage manage the 'Rolling Stones', 'Led Zeppelin', 'T Rex' and many of the world's top pop groups.

In recent years Leslie has moved into the sporting arena, where, as Commonwealth Arm Wrestling Champion he frequently appears on Television. Recent coverage has included, Frank Bruno (B.B.C.), Sky News, L.W.T., and co-Producer of a one hour network documentary for Television South West. Other work has included productions for the London Docklands Arena and the Hackney Arts Festival.

Leslie is also a judo Black belt (1st Dan), and, as an Arm Wrestler, flew to Tokyo where he came fourth in the World Arm Wrestling championships (Super Heavyweight category). Throughout his long career, Les has raised thousands of pounds for charity. He lives in Bexley Heath with his wife and two children.

BNTS students learning fencing at our school In Roedean, Brighton

BNTS students at our school In Blackheath 1995

THIRTY

OLGA

I was still flying all over Europe selling BBC World Teletext.

I flew to Warsaw, Poland to see if I could sell it there. Poland had yet to join the EU. The zloty was low against the pound which made everything cheap for me. I was staying in a four star hotel in the centre and had only been there a day when I decided after I'd finished work to go out for a drink

I walked across the street to a small outdoor bar. It was autumn and still not too cold to sit outside. I sat at a table and the only other people there were two girls opposite me, drinking beer. I ordered a beer and lit up a cigar. There was a slight breeze and the smoke from my cigar blew across to their table.

They weren't smoking which was unusual for Poles who tended to be, like most Eastern Europeans, heavy smokers. They were both pretty and one kept staring at me every time my smoked drifted across their table.

For devilment, I blew more clouds their way, which seemed to annoy one of them even more. I walked over mainly from boredom and offered to buy them a drink.

The one that had been staring at me replied in good English, "No thank you. We don't have the money to buy you one back". I thought that was an honest answer and replied, "I don't want you to buy me one back, I'm offering to buy you both a drink." They said, "Okay," and invited me to join them.

Selling around the world sounds a glamorous job to many but it can be incredibly lonely so it was nice to have someone to talk to. I was really enjoying their company, one was called Inga and the other one told me her name was Olga.

As it started getting colder they asked me if I wanted to go with them to a restaurant. I said why not and they took me to a nice basement bar serving local food and drink.

As the night progressed and the drink flowed, Olga asked me if I'd seen the Old Town of Warsaw. I replied that all I'd seen was the airport and the hotel. She laughed and asked me if I wanted her to show me around the old town the next evening. I told her that would be nice, and she asked me what hotel I was staying in and I gave her my room number and name of the hotel. She said she would call me at six o'clock the next evening after I'd finished my work.

I had a great evening with these two local girls and walked them to the tram station.

Olga told me that she lived with her parents and had to get the last train home. The next day when I was covering appointments, I kept thinking of Olga and what a great night I'd spent with her and her friend Inga.

I returned to my hotel, not expecting to hear from her again. So I was pleasantly surprised when the phone in my room rang. It was Olga asking if I still wanted a tour of the Old Town. I told her yes I would, and we met half an hour later. We took a taxi to the old town of Warsaw which had been completely rebuilt after being destroyed during the Second World War.

It was a beautiful place with restaurants, bars and shops. We found a nice little restaurant and ate a typical Polish meal together. She told me she was the only daughter of two teachers. Her father was a professor at one of the universities teaching engineering and her mother had also been a teacher, but was now retired due to health issues.

During our meal, Olga told me that she'd never been married and didn't have a regular boyfriend. She was a beautiful woman who told me she was 29 years old. I was 49.

She asked me if I was married and I lied and told her I was divorced. The truth was Danka and I had drifted apart over the years. All of the travelling I'd done, as well as working every weekend at the stage schools hadn't helped. I had lied to Olga because this woman fascinated me and I didn't want to lose her by telling her I was married. Even with all of the extensive travelling I'd done, I had never once cheated on Danka even though I'd had plenty of chances.

Now I was going through a mid-life crisis and couldn't stop thinking how my dad had died at the age of 51. I kept on thinking that at 49, I only maybe had a couple of years left and was now determined to have a fling before I kicked the bucket.

We dined out a couple of more times that week and I was really sorry to say goodbye to Olga.

I promised to call her when I got back home.

On the flight back home, I couldn't' stop thinking about the pretty Polish woman with the charismatic personality. A few days after I got home, I called Olga, and could tell by her voice that she was pleased to hear from me. We spoke for about forty-five minutes and agreed to meet up the next time I came back to Warsaw.

With the job I did for Stuart, I could decide when and where I worked because I paid for all of my own expenses. I decided to go back to Warsaw even though the business there wasn't great. I booked to go back ten days later and called Olga who was surprised and happy that I was coming back. I told her I'd call her when I had arrived in Warsaw.

I arrived in Warsaw on an early flight and checked into my hotel. My first appointment was with an accountant in the city centre. I went into his office to make my presentation and noticed in the corner of the room a TV which was switched on with the sound turned off. This was pretty unusual compared to other meetings I'd covered.

He was a nice man and I began to explain the benefits of joining BBC World Teletext. Even though, like the Caribbean, almost no one in Poland had the Teletext service on their TVs but like Czechoslovakia the BBC was very well respected in Poland and remembered for their overseas service during the war and after, with the Russian occupation.

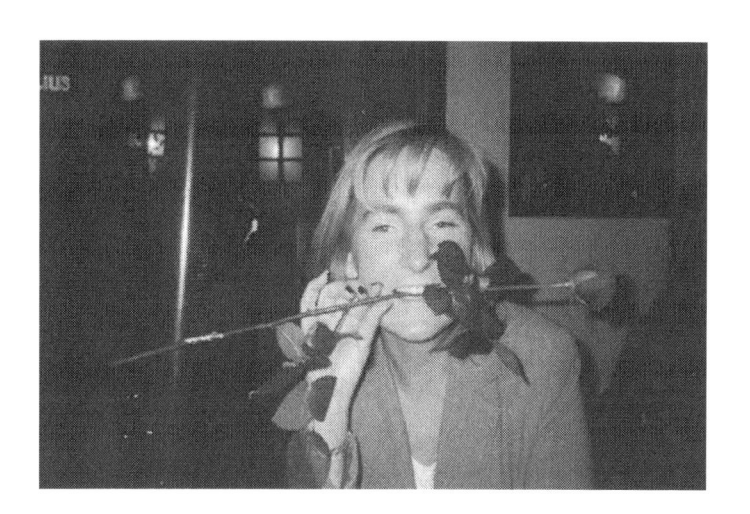

Olga in a restaurant, in Warsaw Old Town 2001

I kept noticing on the TV film of a plane crashing into a skyscraper. What was strange was the film clip kept repeating itself. I just put it down to a trailer for a new movie. As I carried on making my presentation, I noticed a news stream going across the bottom of the TV screen. It was saying a plane had crashed into a skyscraper in New York. I asked the accountant if he could turn up the volume, which he did and we both sat mesmerised as we listened to the news report. There was now footage of a second plane crashing into the Twin Towers.

A horrified look came over the accountant's face and he told me his daughter worked and lived in New York. He immediately tried calling her several times on her mobile but there was no signal.

I had flown to Warsaw on the morning of September 11 2001.

It seemed to me that the world had gone mad. I couldn't'

wait to speak to Olga to discuss what had happened. That day, and the next I kept trying Olga's mobile but there was no answer. I couldn't understand what had happened to her.

I started to worry if she'd been in an accident? For the whole week I was in Warsaw, I didn't manage to speak to her. What with the news of the Twin Towers plus the thought of flying back to London that weekend really depressed me.

A few days after I got home, Olga finally answered her phone. She told me that her father had taken her to her aunt's chicken farm which was about 100kms outside of Warsaw, where there was no service for her phone.

I told her how disappointed I was about not seeing her as well as being depressed about the Twin Towers being attacked. She was very apologetic and asked when I was coming back to Warsaw.

In all honestly the two trips to Warsaw had been tough from a business point of view and in reality I had no real reason to go back. But I was fascinated by this woman and I wanted to see her one more time at least.

I booked my usual hotel which wasn't *The Ritz*, but was at least central. I called Olga on my arrival and she said she'd meet me at the hotel after I finished work that day.

We agreed to go out that evening and to meet at 7pm. By 8pm there was still no sign of her and I began to think that this had all been a waste of time and what the hell was I doing there.

I'd bought some wine and had already drunk half a bottle in frustration when I heard a soft knock on the door. I opened the door expecting to see someone from room service, instead it was Olga. All of my frustrations and anger disappeared when I saw the big smile on her face.

She came into the room and I asked her why she was so late. She told me she'd had difficulty getting away from her father who was very controlling and would never have let her leave if he'd known she was coming to see me.

I asked where she wanted to go to eat. She said she'd rather stay in the hotel and order something from room service. I replied I didn't mind as it was so cold outside. She then asked me if she could take a shower and I replied of course she could. Whilst she was taking the shower, she asked me could I come and wash her hair. I couldn't believe my luck and quickly got undressed and went into the shower.

Olga had beautiful long dark red hair which I loved. She also had an incredibly sexy body. She told me later that she was a natural 38DD and had been a semi-professional rock dancer.

As I washed her hair, she turned around and kissed me full on the lips. It felt like I'd been electrocuted.

Later that day, I called her to arrange to go to the Old Town. That evening she began to tell me about her father. I could tell that every time she mentioned him she became nervous, which I just put down to him being a control freak. She told me that sometimes she'd drink too much to try and forget him which I thought sounded a bit strange, but never pressed her more on the subject.

The rest of the week was like a dream. I didn't realise at the time but I was falling in love with this woman.

I flew back home and felt like I was walking on air but, on the other hand, bloody guilty for what I'd done.

Olga had now become like a drug to me and I couldn't stop thinking about her. I knew I had to see her again. It was her personality, and we seemed to have so much in common. I was like a teenager when I was with her. We'd laugh and play jokes on each other and it was all the things that was missing in my marriage. It was now November 2001 and Olga's thirtieth birthday was approaching.

I couldn't go back to Warsaw on business as it was so bad so I thought I'd try Krakow and meet Olga there for her birthday.

She agreed to come down by train for the week I was there and spend her birthday with me. I booked a nice hotel just off the main square and waited for her. She said she'd arrive the day before her birthday and I would meet her at the main train station in Krakow.

As I waited on the platform, I kept looking up at the clock and thought of the scene from the film *Brief Encounter* with Trevor Howard, when he was standing underneath the clock on Waterloo Station waiting to meet Celia Johnson.

When Olga got off the train, her smile made my heart jump and she ran to me, threw her arms around me, and kissed me passionately on the lips.

We went back to the hotel and didn't leave the room until breakfast

The next day was Olga's birthday and I arranged for a large bouquet of flowers to be delivered to the room. She'd already told me that she wanted to cut her hair, which I was dead against as I loved her long red hair so much.

I gave into her in the end and took her to a hairdresser. She chose a style she liked from a magazine and then told me she wanted it dyed blonde!

Olga in Krakow 2001

I waited in a nearby coffee shop while her hair was being cut. When she walked out of the hairdresser's, her hair was now shoulder length and blonde which made her look even younger!

I then took her to a boutique to choose a dress to wear for the evening. I'd already booked the best French restaurant in town to celebrate her birthday. When we went out that evening and I looked at her, I thought I was the luckiest man on the planet to have such a gorgeous girlfriend.

We went to the restaurant and as a starter, Olga ordered frog's legs in garlic. Even with all the travelling I'd done, I had never tried or fancied frog's legs. When the dish arrived, she insisted I tried one. I told her no way, but she wouldn't take no for an answer and pushed one into my mouth. I had to admit it wasn't as bad as I'd been expecting.

This was one of the reasons why I loved her so much. She would make me try new things and I would reciprocate. After the meal, we decided to walk across the square. It was early in the evening and as we were wondering where we should go next, I noticed some smartly dressed people walking into a club.

I said to Olga, let's go and check this place out. When we got to the door, there were couples waiting to go inside. I could hear music being played and thought to myself we could have one drink just to see what it was like? There were two doormen standing there who just nodded to us as we walked inside.

The place was quite large and very busy with lots of smartly-dressed couples. So with Olga's new hairstyle and dress, we certainly didn't look out of place. I saw a queue of people waiting to get drinks and told Olga to wait while I would fetch some drinks. As I waited in the queue, I noticed the people in front of me taking their drinks and not paying for them. So when it was my turn, not speaking any Polish I just pointed to what I wanted and the barman gave me two drinks which I then walked off without paying.

When I told Olga what had just happened she didn't believe me and thought I was joking. I told her that I was being serious and at that moment, a waiter came around with a tray of appetisers. As I looked around, I noticed that everyone was talking in small groups. I thought I'd try my luck again and see if I could get another drink free. I wasn't asked to pay and when I got back to Olga I told her "I like this place".

I noticed some of the people there were staring at us, but with Olga's figure that wasn't unusual. I guessed that we'd walked into some company's Christmas party so I started to wave to people upstairs as if I knew them. There were at least two hundred people inside so I was hoping not everyone knew each other.

After more free drinks and food I danced with Olga. That drew us even more attention, but luckily for us no one came over to speak to us. I could see, however, the expression on some of their faces wondering who we were.

By now, I couldn't care less and was having a thoroughly good time, especially as I wasn't paying for anything.

About halfway through the night, a photographer came over to us and took our picture for what I presumed was for their company magazine.

I would have loved to have seen the expressions on their faces when it was printed and they wondered who we were. We were one of the last to leave at 1am.

The next evening at the hotel, Olga started telling me about her father. She told me that when she'd been a teenager, he used to take her on holiday to the mountains without her mother. She said that sometimes he'd touch her in places which he shouldn't have. I got so angry I wanted to go straight to Warsaw and kill him. She told me that because of what he did to her, she sometimes drank too much to forget because she felt guilty. I told her it wasn't her fault, she then told me that her mother had twice attempted suicide. After all of what had happened that week in Krakow as well as the shocking truth that Olga had told me about her father, it made it even more difficult to say goodbye. Now it made even more sense to me why her father hadn't wanted her to go to Krakow.

When Olga got back to Warsaw and I returned home, she told me on the telephone that she wanted to go into an institution to help her deal with her demons.

This place was a long way outside of Warsaw and she told me she'd be there for at least a month. I imagined it as a pretty bleak place but respected her wishes to get better. She told me that if we were to have any chance of being together she needed to get better. She told me that she could keep her mobile with her and I could call her every day. I knew this wasn't going to be easy for either of us.

After she'd arrived at the institution, she told me on the telephone it was a cold, miserable place. She said there was a mixture of people there receiving treatment for many different problems. It made me even more depressed to know she was in such a place alone.

I called her at least six times a day to give her as much support as possible. A few of the times I called, she told me she was near to checking herself out but stopped herself at the last moment thinking of our future together.

While Olga was in the institution, I went to Zurich on business for a week. One afternoon as I was walking thought the centre, I could hear some street musicians playing jazz.

Jazz is one of the very few styles of music that I truly hate, but Olga loved it. So I walked over to them and asked them to play something when I was ready. I then called Olga and told her to listen, holding my mobile to their instruments asking them to play some jazz. After five minutes of playing, I asked her whether she'd liked what she'd heard? She was lost for words and I could hear her sobbing quietly to herself.

On another occasion, while she was still in hospital, I was on business in the Isle of Man. Olga used to tell me that living in Warsaw she was a long way from the sea and how much she missed it.

As I was walking along the beach at midnight, looking at a full moon while thinking of her, waves crashed onto the shore. I called her on her mobile and told her to listen. I then held the phone towards the waves while walking along the shore and after about five minutes, asked her what she could hear. She told me in an excited voice that it sounded like the sea. I then explained where I was and what I was doing.

During this time, we'd text each other thirty times a day or more. I would always start my text with 'PP' which was an abbreviation of Polish Princess and she would text me back with 'Crazy E' for 'Crazy Englishman'. We were like two teenagers in love.

While she was still in hospital, I went to one of my stage schools, where we had a particularly good choir. I told the class I wanted them to sing to someone special as an audition. I then called Olga and told her to listen. The class did me proud, I think they thought Andrew Lloyd Webber was on the other end of the line listening. Afterwards, Olga cried at what she'd heard.

I do believe it was during this time whilst she was receiving treatment in hospital that I really fell in love with her. She told me afterwards that she'd felt the same and it was only my phone calls that had kept her going. Now I knew it was time to tell Danka.

Danka had always been a great mother, always putting Leslie and Natasha first. This meant that I always came second. It's not easy to divide time between two children and a husband and it didn't help with the different jobs I did, which always involved long hours or weeks away from home.

I'd worked hard all of my life to try and provide everything my family needed, even sending Leslie and Natasha to private schools for a while. Danka had always kept the home nice and I now had a three bedroom semi-detached house in Kent with a large garden and the mortgage paid for. The problem was I simply wasn't happy.

Olga had made me feel alive again, for the first time in years. I truly believed that this was my last chance to be really happy again before I died. I knew it would be hard especially on Leslie and Natasha. It was therefore a real shock to me when I told Danka about Olga. I wasn't expecting her to react the way she did, considering how often we'd argued when I was at home.

She took it very badly, even though I'd told her she could keep the house as Leslie and Natasha was still living there. I think that it's part of the Serbian mentality that even though they may not like something, they don't like giving it away which is why I believe the Yugoslav war was so bad when Croatia and Bosnia wanted to break away.

Danka never found out about my affair with Olga. I'd told her about it and had done what I thought was the honourable thing which was to give her the house with no mortgage. We'd had lived a lie for the past ten years for the sake of the kids which, I knew, had been a mistake.

I think most women would be angry if their husbands leave them but what makes it much worse is when the other woman is younger. Now, for the first time in my life I rented a flat for Olga and I to live in while I got my life back together.

While I was making arrangements to move out of my house, Stuart Landau told me that he'd been trying to get a contract to sell advertising on Ryanair. This was the cheap flight Irish airline. He'd been negotiating with them for months but wasn't getting anywhere. He told me I could try if I wanted mainly because he thought I wouldn't' get anywhere with them.

He said if I got the contract he'd go into partnership with me. I thought this could be just what I needed to make a new life for Olga and me as well as supporting my family.

I called the marketing manager of Ryanair and at first he was very offish, but slowly I talked him around. After several calls he admitted to me that he didn't like Stuart. When I asked him why, he told me because he came across as the Del Boy character from *Only Fools and Horses*. I laughed and began some serious negotiations with him

After a couple of weeks, he finally agreed to give us a contract to sell advertising on their website at a reasonable rate. We fixed a date to fly to their head office in Dublin. When I told Stuart, he couldn't believe it and I think he was a bit jealous that he hadn't managed to negotiate it himself.

Stuart and I flew to Dublin and arrived at the appointed time at Ryanair's Head Office. We waited forty-five minutes before the marketing manager showed, which considering how far we'd come was rather rude I thought. But after waiting forty-five minutes, I was just glad he did show up and hadn't changed his mind!

We came away with the contract and celebrated with a few pints of Guinness.

I rented a nice one-bedroom flat opposite Beckenham Park for me and Olga. I was so excited to see her and hoped she'd like it. I picked her up from the airport and drove straight to our new home. She loved it and I was relieved. Towards the end of the first week her mood changed, which I put down to moving to a new country. Unfortunately it was much more serious than that. When I returned one evening after a meeting with Stuart about our new business, I found Olga drunk in the flat. She'd gone out and bought a bottle of vodka which she'd almost finished. I'd never seen her like this before and I was shocked.

I made the mistake of asking her why she was drinking when she was already drunk. She stared to shout at me and I should have known better than to talk to someone who was drunk. When she tried to leave the flat to buy more alcohol, I had to physically block the door and she then became violent and attacked me. I managed to stop her from leaving the flat and eventually she went into a deep sleep.

The next day she felt terrible and I tried again to ask her what was wrong? She told me that sometimes she thought of her dad and to forget what had happened she would drink. She had no memory of the night before and of attacking me.

I told her now she was in England, we could get help for her. I didn't realise how difficult that proved to be.

Olga told me not to worry and that she'd be all right and didn't need any help. I believed her and that was my next mistake. I was worried but hoped it had been a one-off episode.

I HAD to set up a new office for the Ryanair contract which involved a lot of time and work. We rented a suitable office in Old Street, which was a mixture of offices and flats. When I went to look at the office the room opposite had a Brazilian Flag hanging as a curtain. When I asked the estate agent what that was all about, he told me that Ronnie Biggs' son lived there! I couldn't believe it when he told me and smiled. I wonder what Ronnie's son would think if he'd known his neighbour had nearly gone to Brazil to kidnap his dad.

We took the office and I began interviewing closers and telesales operatives for the Ryanair contract.

I got Olga to help. She'd told me that in Warsaw, she'd been a PA to the head of Coca Cola and Sony so she knew what she was doing.

What I couldn't understand was that some mornings Olga would run twenty laps around the park yet on other occasions sleep all day. What I didn't know then was that she was still drinking some days when I was in the office.

Eventually it got so bad I took her to see a doctor. It was a woman doctor that told me that Olga was a 'binge drinker' and not an alcoholic. That made me feel better.

Christmas was coming and we decided to go for a break in Poland. Olga told me of a place near Krakow called Zakopane in the mountains. She said we should also visit Wieliczka Salt Mine. I told her that I thought all the salt mines were in Siberia and that's where Russia sent its political prisoners to. She laughed and said I was in for a surprise.

She wasn't joking. It was the most amazing place I'd ever seen. It was 327 metres deep and as we travelled down the shaft in a rickety old lift, which I wasn't too sure about, I saw life-sized statues made out of rock salt. They reminded me of Madame Tussauds. As we got deeper down the mine, it seemed to get bigger. When we reached the bottom there was a large space, where they would hold concerts and there were also shops and a restaurant where we drank tea. It was truly an unbelievable place that I'll never forget.

Me and Olga in Zakopane in 2002 New Year's Eve

Olga in Tatra National Park 2002

WE THEN TRAVELLED to Zakopane the place just took my breath away. It was covered in snow with wooden restaurants, deep in the mountains with a nature park at the bottom. It was breath taking. We stayed in a luxury five-star hotel which cost less money than one night in a four-star in London.

Olga had been there before and knew where to go on New Year's Eve. The restaurant was fully booked but because they knew her, they squeezed us in. Hanging from the celling were hundreds of women's bra's of all different sizes and colours! When I asked Olga, what was that all about, she told me, that the owners would go behind the women's backs when they were drunk and slip of their bra's as a joke. I told her for their sake, they didn't try that on her. We ate and danced all night and I knew I wanted to spend the rest of my days with this beautiful woman. We talked about buying a house there once we'd saved enough money and open it as a bed and breakfast

When we returned to London, Olga started to drink

heavily again. It got so bad this time that I decided to try and find her a counsellor. I made enquiries and she agreed to go to Mind to get help.

She told me that she wasn't an alcoholic but needed help to get over her father. She went twice a week and at first it seemed to help. What was confusing for me was that sometimes she'd not had a drink for several weeks then, for no particular reason, would get so drunk that she couldn't get out of bed. This seemed to me to be much more of a problem than just binge drinking.

It came to a head one day when I couldn't wake her up and I was so desperate for help that I called an ambulance. They took her to hospital where the doctors examining her decided she was drunk and immediately lost all interest. They told me not to waste their time and take her home.

When Olga got drunk she'd shout and scream at me. It got so bad that we had to move out of the flat due to complaints from the neighbours.

I found a smaller place which we moved into. I told her to give us a chance together; that she had to get help to stop drinking.

She agreed to go to a voluntary organisation in Beckenham where we lived which specialised in helping people with alcohol related problems.

Once again they gave me mixed messages about how serious her problem was. One counsellor told me that Olga wasn't an alcoholic but had problems with memories of her father. On hearing this Olga would give me a big smile and tell me outside, "See I told you, I'm not an alcoholic"

Another doctor would say the same, or yes she was a binge drinker. I was lost as what to do next.

Our local doctor, who was Chinese, was the only one who really wanted to help and tried his best to get Olga treatment. He told me he might have to section her if she got any worse. That would involve getting two doctors to agree that she might harm herself when drinking.

Shortly after in our new flat, Olga got drunk again and attacked me as I tried to stop her from drinking. She was so loud that a neighbour called the police. When they arrived Olga shouted at them and they arrested her even though I pleaded for them not to.

I called Dick who said he'd try and help. The next morning I went to Bromley Police station, to ask if they'd release her with a caution. I was worried that if it went to court, she might get deported, as we weren't married.

I pleaded my case to them and with Dick's help they agreed to release her with just a caution. I told Olga she must go back to our doctor to try and get help. She agreed, provided I bought her a can of beer before she went!!

When we arrived at the surgery, the doctor took a sample of blood from Olga and prescribed some medication to calm her down. When the results of the blood test came back he told her that he'd never seen before such a high level of alcohol in a blood sample. I asked him if he could arrange a detox. He told me that it wasn't that simple as there was a long waiting list.

After less than a year, my business with Ryanair had gone rapidly downhill. I just couldn't concentrate on running it and find the time to look after Olga. I had to close down the office. The rest of the staff had seen Olga get drunk on occasion as well as me coming to work sometimes with scratches on my face, where Olga had attacked me.

I told Olga we needed to go back to Warsaw to get her a detox. I contacted her parents and told them she'd agreed to this and they found a hospital in Warsaw where Olga could be detoxed.

The hospital told us the detox would take at least three to four days. It was a grim-looking place and I was afraid of the outcome. Her parents booked me into an apartment near the hospital and I waited. On the second night at around 1am in the morning, the hospital called me to come and collect Olga as she was very upset.

I got a taxi there and in broken English they told me that she'd discharged herself and they couldn't keep her there against her will.

I took her back to her parents' and in the taxi she seemed perfectly normal, until she started talking Polish to an imaginary friend who she thought was sitting next to her.

She was hallucinating. When I got her to her parents' house. She carried on talking to her imaginary friend until she fell asleep. She slept for the next two days and when she woke up she had no memory of what had happened.

We flew back to London a few days later. I found a new counsellor for her, who was willing to talk to her even if she'd been drinking which none of the others would do. They'd all tell me that they couldn't counsel someone who was still drinking but only when they'd stopped. I just didn't understand how someone with a drinking problem was supposed to stop without help?

Again we had to move because of complaints about Olga's

drinking. I'd lost a lot of money from the Ryanair operation, not being able to run it the way I would have liked. In all honesty though, they were really difficult people to deal with. I had no choice but to go back on the road again to sell and try and make a living.

By this time I'd got my son Leslie a job in Stuart's office making leads for me which he was very good at.

I decided to go to Malta to sell BBC World Teletext. I dared not leave Olga alone at home, so I had some business cards printed for her saying she was my PA. I also hoped that this would keep her mind off of drinking.

The business in Malta was very good and Olga enjoyed coming to meetings with me during the day. On our second trip there she persuaded me one evening to sing karaoke in the hotel. I told her I couldn't' sing. She told me I could. This was one of the things that I loved about her where she'd convince me to try and do things I would never have dreamed of doing before. I'd never sung karaoke in my life.

My father had been a very good singer but I was convinced I was tone deaf! What made matters worse for me was there was at least 200 people in the audience of the hotel where we were staying.

After Olga had driven me mad for about an hour to get up and sing, I gave in to her. I got on stage, introduced myself to the audience and told them I was going to sing one of Oliver's Reed's favourite songs '*Wild Thing*'. I then went on to explain how he'd died in a pub in Malta drinking and arm wrestling.

Me and Olga in Malta 2003

I then started to sing the song and Olga jumped up on stage and began dancing. At the end of the song, I got a standing ovation. I'm not sure if they were cheering me for my singing or for Olga's dancing?

The next morning in reception, strangers were coming up to me and shouting '*Wild Thing.*' Once again, Olga had proved to be right and that's why I loved her so much.

The next day, as I was getting ready to go to a meeting, Olga was sitting on the bed and suddenly went white as a sheet and began shaking. She wasn't moving and had stopped breathing. I panicked, thinking she'd died. I shook her, her eyes rolled back into her head and she went very still. I called reception telling them we needed an ambulance urgently.

The ambulance arrived and took Olga to the local hospital. They carried out an MRI and other tests. They told me that she'd suffered an epileptic fit. I told them about her problems and they suggested carrying out a detox which I was pleased to agree to. Unfortunately, they didn't understand the extent of Olga's problems and it wasn't successful. After the second day in hospital, she started to hallucinate. I knew that the hospital hadn't given her the right medications. They called me in the middle of the night to go and see them. When I arrived, Olga was in a terrible state and very confused. She began to shout and I tried calming her down. The hospital called the local police, who on arrival and seeing Olga's state, told me that they wanted to put her into a mental hospital, which I flatly refused.

As Olga became violent, I grabbed her to stop her from attacking the policeman. She then grabbed my arm and began biting me. The policeman who was about 6"4 and bigger than me said, "She's biting your arm!" I replied "Its better her biting me than him. I told him I'd been a policeman in London and he felt sorry for me and agreed with the hospital to let her go. I was now at my wit's end and wanted to take her back home to the UK. Thankfully by the next day she'd calmed down enough to take the next flight home.

After a few weeks of Olga not drinking, and me mistakenly thinking that she was getting better I took her to Cyprus on business. It was a nice hotel on the beach and I thought that the sunshine and a week in Cyprus would help her relax.

All was going well until the end of the week. I came back from work one afternoon to find her drunk. She'd gone to a local shop and had bought a bottle of vodka. We were due to fly home that evening. She hadn't packed our clothes and was lying semi-conscious on the bed. I panicked, thinking that we'd miss our flight.

I managed to take her into the shower to try and wake her up. After a struggle to get her dressed, I packed our cases and took a taxi to the airport.

When we arrived at the airport, it was packed with tourists. I checked our luggage in then turned round to speak to Olga, she had disappeared, and there were so many people. I couldn't see her anywhere. The panic was just beginning when I noticed her sitting on the floor in the middle of the airport! I went over to her and gently asked her to stand up, I didn't want her to make a scene just before we got on board the plane. She refused to stand up and as I was quietly trying to persuade her to stand up an airline worker came over to us to ask what was wrong. There were already dozens of people looking at her, so I told the worker that my wife was suffering with low blood pressure and was feeling dizzy. They kindly found a wheelchair for Olga and I pushed her to the plane. We managed to fly back without any further dramas.

When we got home, she stopped drinking and agreed to go back to counselling. All was well for a few weeks until she had another relapse and was taken to the local hospital.

This time in A&E she'd suffered three or four elliptic fits before I managed to convince them to admit her. The hospital then carried out a detox and this time it seemed to work. When we returned home she told me she wanted to stop drinking and I managed to get her into the Priory. For the first time she finally admitted to me and more importantly to herself that she was an alcoholic. She told me that she was too young to die.

I'd been trying for months to get Olga into the famous Priory Clinic through a local charity. The Priory had a good reputation and was well known for treating stars with alcohol and drug problem. They charged thousands of pounds for the retreatment. I found a local charity that worked with the clinic and had put Olga forward as an urgent case. Needless to say there was a very long waiting list. So when I received a call from them telling me Olga had been accepted and could start treatment the following week. I felt like crying with joy. I knew this was her last real chance of beating her addiction. I told her about this place and she was keen to give it a try.

It was a two week daytime course and after her first week of treatment, she seemed to be much better. She was doing homework of an evening and for the first time ever agreed to go with me to an AA meeting in Bromley.

We went to the meeting together and sat there for two hours listening to some really depressing, harrowing stories. About half way through she asked if she could leave. Outside I asked her what she'd thought of the meeting and stories that she'd heard. She gave a big sigh and said, "I need a drink after listening to that". I didn't know if she was joking or not but secretly felt the same, so we went home and I made a pot of tea.

Olga seemed to have been enjoying the course and I believed that she would finally stop drinking. About half way thought the course, I went to a local shop to buy some things for dinner. She told me she wanted to make me a Polish soup. When I returned, I immediately recognised the signs that she'd been drinking while I'd gone to the shop.

The despair I felt at her not even being able to finish the two week course was unimaginable. We finished shouting at each other, which I knew wouldn't help matters. She went upstairs to her bedroom, and as I sat in the lounge wondering what the hell do I do next? As I'd run out of options, I believed the Priory was our last chance. As I was thinking about what to do next, I heard a loud bang. I jumped up, ran to the hallway to find Olga lying unconscious at the bottom of the stairs. She'd fallen from the top of the stairs to the bottom. She didn't appear to be badly hurt but I saw this as a chance to get her back into hospital and maybe stop her from drinking. I called an ambulance to take her to A&E to the same hospital that had recently given her the detox.

She was now conscious, as we waited to be seen. A young woman doctor who I thought would be sympathetic to our problems, came to examine Olga. Sadly this wasn't to be the case. This young woman doctor who insisted to me that she was in charge merely told me that Olga had been drinking and I should take her home. I explained that she'd fallen down the stairs and insisted that they took an x-ray.

This doctor who I believe that, because of her religious beliefs, thought women shouldn't drink alcohol told me. "You know your wife is an alcoholic. What do you want me to do about it?" I replied that she had a duty of care and she should at least admit Olga for observation hoping that after twenty-four hours in hospital, Olga would have sobered up enough to come to her senses and go back to the Priory to finish her treatment.

This doctor was having none of it and told me to take

Olga home. I replied that now she was in hospital, she was their responsibility and I was leaving her there. The doctor threatened to call the police and I replied "Fine! Do that!" And I walked out leaving Olga in the examining cubicle.

By now it was 1am in the morning and I got into my car and started driving around the Hospital grounds wondering what to do next.

After twenty minutes, I saw someone in the distance walking in the middle of the road. I couldn't believe it when I saw it was Olga!

I stopped the car and asked her what had happened. She shrugged her shoulders and told me that the doctors had told her to leave and left her alone in the cubicle.

She said that she'd just got up and walked out of the cubicle. I couldn't believe they'd treated a vulnerable woman in such a way. I drove back to the A&E and told the woman doctor what I thought of her then left.

I took Olga home and called a local doctor the next day. He told me that I shouldn't stop Olga from drinking as it was dangerous, but that I should try and give her small amounts of alcohol. I didn't understand this thinking which seamed crazy to me but I tried it anyway. I called The Priory clinic and explained that Olga had relapsed and asked them what they could do to help. They told me that they couldn't see her until she was sober. This was always the catch 22 situation I often found myself in. How do you get help to stop someone drinking, when the professionals won't help while the person is drinking?

The only counsellor who'd see Olga when she'd been drinking was away on a course.

Over the next ten days, Olga refused to eat. I couldn't even get her to drink soup. I called the doctor back who examined her and he told me not to worry and that she was getting enough vitamins from the small amounts of alcohol she was drinking

After eleven days, she started being sick and I noticed there was some blood in her bile. I called an ambulance and lied, telling them she was unconscious. The ambulance arrived and agreed to take her to Lewisham hospital.

I was so relived on the way to the hospital thinking at last she'd get some help. When we arrived in A&E, Olga was semi-conscious. They took her into an examining room while I waited outside. I was hoping that this time they'd give her another detox, so I could then get her back into The Priory.

After about an hour, a doctor came out to speak to me. I told them about the recent detox Olga had received at the Queen Elizabeth Hospital. I followed him into the examining room to see Olga surrounded by doctors and nurses. This looked serious to me, and I was told to wait outside.

Thirty minutes later, a doctor came and told me they were taking Olga into intensive care, but he didn't think she'd survive. I thought I was going to collapse at this news and told him that she'd been talking in the ambulance and was just drunk. He shook his head and said they weren't sure what was wrong with her and had called King's College Hospital for advice. I asked if she could be transferred to that hospital. I knew it was a teaching hospital and that there were good doctors there. He replied that Olga was too sick to move and he honestly didn't expect her to live for the next couple of hours.

They moved her into the intensive care room. I then called Stuart, who'd always had a soft spot for Olga and her problems. He came quickly to the hospital and we both spoke to the doctor in charge, who was a German woman. We told her that money was no object and who or where could we send Olga for help. Once again she told us that it was too dangerous to move her.

The hospital allowed me to stay with Olga and I sat next to her bed holding her hand and praying to God to give her one more chance. I kept whispering in her ear that when she recovered we would marry and start a family which was something I know Olga had always wanted.

I believe when someone is unconscious, they can hear you if you talk to them. I kept telling her to fight and that she'd be okay.

The nurses in intensive care came and told me that only the life-support machine was keeping her alive and asked did I want a priest to come and say the last rites as she was a Roman Catholic.

Olga had never been religious but had told me that she did believe in God so I agreed. A young priest shortly arrived and said the last rites. I asked him why God was taking someone so young, with all her life in front of her to live. I'd told him about Olga's problems and he told me that maybe God was taking her to stop her suffering anymore. He tried to console me but I was in shock and devastated.

They switched off the life-support machine and pronounced Olga dead. She'd been in intensive care fighting for her life for eighteen hours, after the consultant told me that she'd last a maximum of two. I truly believe that she fought as hard as she could to survive but had finally lost her battle with alcoholism. It was one month before her thirty-second birthday.

I went back to the flat and called her father in Warsaw, who spoke some English. Her mother couldn't speak a word. When I told him what had happened, he didn't sound so surprised, and I told him I'd call him back over the next few days.

The hospital told me that because of her age and because they weren't totally sure of the cause of death there would have to be an autopsy.

When I called her father back he told me to save money just to bring her ashes back to Poland. I told him that Olga had expressed her wishes to be buried with her grandmother near her favourite aunt's farm. I told him I would bring Olga's body back to Warsaw.

He then asked me if there was any insurance and I explained that no insurance company would cover her with the problems she had with drinking,

He then said her mother would come to London to accompany her back. He sent Olga's mother on a bus from Warsaw to London knowing she didn't speak a word of English.

I managed to find a Polish friend of Danka's to help with translations. After Olga's mother had arrived, I took her to the chapel where they were keeping my beloved. We went in and I nearly fainted with shock when I saw her in the open coffin. I hardly recognised my beautiful soulmate who looked at least sixty years-old. I asked afterwards why she'd looked so old and they told me it was because of the effects of the autopsy. I made arrangements with the funeral directors to fly Olga back to Warsaw on the same flight as her mother and me. On the flight back to Warsaw I was thinking of how many times we'd flown to Poland together and how happy we'd been? I'd never thought that one day I'd fly back with Olga in a coffin in the hold of a plane

When we got to Warsaw, her father told me about the funeral arrangements he'd made for Olga. She was to be buried where she'd wanted in a small village, 100 kilometres from Warsaw, close to her favourite aunt's chicken farm next to her grandmother.

When we arrived at the church, there was already about fifty people waiting there which surprised me. Shortly after, two buses full of people arrived from Warsaw. They were colleagues and friends of Olga's.

For a small village, the church was quite large but now with over 200 people attending the service it couldn't accommodate everyone with seats and many had to stand. I knew Olga had been popular but was surprised and pleased that so many people had come to pay their respects.

She'd always been the life and soul of the party and had had a smile that would light up the darkest room. Now she'd light up heaven, I knew. After the church service, I gave a speech that was translated into Polish to the mourners. I told them about the countries we'd travelled to (Olga loved to travel). I spoke about our deep love for each other and how I'd lost a soul mate.

When the service had finished, I asked some of Olga's friends who spoke English had they known she was an alcoholic. About half said they hadn't known and the other half said that she'd been an alcoholic ten years before she'd met me.

When I asked her father why he hadn't told me before she came to England about her drinking he replied that she'd asked him not to. I don't know whether it would have made any difference had I known?

A few days later I flew back home. I kept going over in my mind all of the events leading up to Olga's death. I couldn't stop thinking about how the woman doctor had refused to admit her and if she had, would it have made any difference?

The hospital told me that the autopsy had shown Olga had died from hardening of the arteries in her lungs which had burst. Effectively she'd drowned in her own blood, which had been caused from years of alcohol abuse.

I contacted my local newspaper, *The Newshopper*, to complain about the doctor who'd let Olga walk out of A&E drunk. They sent a reporter and photographer to my home. A week later they printed a half page in their paper under the headline "Drink Kills" with a beautiful photo of Olga.

I next spoke to James O'Brien on LBC Radio about what had happened. He was extremely sympathetic and asked a question on air "how could this happen"?

I was determined that this doctor should be severely disciplined. I made a formal complaint to the hospital and to the General Medical Council. What happened next over the following months was something I'd seen many times in the past with such organisations such as the police, where colleagues closed ranks around one of their own and lie to protect themselves.

They went through all the motions of an enquiry but after eighteen months nothing was done. One of Olga's counsellors who I spoke to told me that he thought she was a young woman at war with herself. He told me that if she hadn't met me then she would have probably died eighteen months earlier.

I called The Priory to tell them what had happened to Olga and they never even sent me a sympathy card.

Many years later, I try to be positive and think of all the great times and laughs we had together. I do believe Olga is finally at peace and one of God's angels

Many books finish with *The End...*

**BUT
THIS IS ONLY THE BEGINNING!**

ABOUT THE AUTHOR

Leslie Clayden was born in the East End of London and went on to work as a Special Constable, a bouncer, security for Miss World, become an arm wrestler and took over the family business as a third generation stallholder on a pitch in Whitechapel Market!

He has encountered celebrities and criminals alike, appeared on television and donated money to charity from his arm wrestling bouts, a sport he dedicated many years towards making more mainstream.

A true raconteur, lover of life and gentleman, 'Swimming with Stingrays' is Les's first book and took more than twenty years to reach publication.

He has two children and lives in Kent.